WINNING

THE INNER GAME

Mastering the Inner Game
For Peak Performance

L. Michael Hall, Ph.D.

Winning the Inner Game: Mastering the Inner Game for Peak Performance

ISBN Number: 1-890001-31-7

A Second Edition of *Frame Games* (2000); published originally as *Frame Games*: ISBN Number: 1-890001-19-8.

Registered with the United States Copyright Office in Washington DC: TXu 929-819 (January, 2000)

Published by:

Neuro-Semantic Publications®
P.O. Box 8
Clifton, CO. 81520 USA
(970) 523-7877

Printed By:

Action Printing — *Jerry Kucera*
516 Fruitvale.Court, Unit C
Grand Junction, CO. 81504
Cover designed and created by *Candi Clark.*
(970) 434-7701
Actionpres@aol.com

Web Sites:

www.neurosemantics.com or www.runyourownbrain.com
www.self-actualizing.org
www.meta-coaching.org

WINNING THE INNER GAME

PREFACE

Winning the inner game
makes success in the outer game a cinch.

In life, there are two games. It doesn't always seem that way though. It seems that there is only one game—*the outer game*, the game of what we do, our achievements, our performances, our actions, whether we hit a home run and celebrate with the winning team, or limp off the field in defeat. Actually, above and beyond the outer game is *the inner game* where the real action takes place. It is a game that this book is all about.

This book is about finding the inner game, understanding how it operates, and learning to successfully play that game. Do that, and you'll have the outer game in the palm of your hand. Fail to do that and you'll keep buying more self-development books trying to understand *the Game of Life* and how to succeed in all of its dimensions, yet missing the actual leverage point.

Discovering the inner game opens up a whole new dimension of life, it opens up all of multiple layers of frames that make up our belief *systems* and reveals the Matrix. The Matrix? Ah, yes, the Matrix of our mental and emotional frames that defines and forms the inner world that we live in and come from. It is there that we construct the inner game with its rules.

Reading this book is like taking the Red Pill and escaping your current Matrix of inner games. Then with training, you re-enter the Matrix of your frames to change it from the inside. This is the danger of change, the danger of creating a revolution in life that upsets the world we know and adventuring into the unknown. So be warned: *Winning the Inner Game* will forever change the way you look at yourself, others, work, the world, and your future.

If you're ready for a revolutionary transformation of your frames of mind, your inner game, all that's required is the willingness to take the Red Pill and to go on an adventure, the adventure of taking charge of your life, your frames, the inner games that you play in your mind. Our *inner* and the *outer* games are games constructed by our frames. To win at these *frame games* we will need to discover the games, learn to change the games, alter the rules, and become a winner at the games that you want to play.

Exploring the ideas and processes within this book will lead you to discover the very levers of change and the secrets of transformation. What will you discover? You will discover that life is all about frames and framing. Ultimately, it all comes down to that. What frames of mind have you created? What Matrix of frames do you live within? How much flexibility do you have with frames? This is the ultimate source of your "reality."

The design here is to equip and coach you to become a *frame master*, able to read the code of experience all around you so you can replicate excellence in ways you never thought possible. The design is to wake up to the Matrix that now has you and like Neo in the movie, *The Matrix,* to exit the Matrix and receive the training to re-enter it with the power to shape it as you will.

This book comes from one of the newest and most exciting fields in the twenty-first century, *Neuro-Semantics*. If you're fascinated by your power to create meaning and meaningfulness, Neuro-Semantics is about how you *construct* meaning in the first place and then *embody* that meaning in your posture, walk, muscles, face, and eyes. Neuro-Semantics explores how we *perform our meanings* in our actions, behaviors, skills, competencies, emotions, and health (or lack of health) to create our own outer games. As a whole mind-body psychology, Neuro-Semantics focuses on modeling the best and highest performances of human possibility and working with the inner game of our frames to set up the most robust and empowering Matrix.

Life is all about frames and framing.

As Morpheus said to Neo in the movie, "I am only offering you the truth," so with this exploration. This is not truth with a capital T, but the *truth* of your life, of your reality, and of your experiences. Such truth is a function of our frames and framing. "What is reality?" Our experience of reality is a function of our mapping. And when you know that you actually live in frames within frames within frames, a matrix of frames, then you know that your experience, reality, skills, emotions, and sense of self is in your hands to a much greater extent that you have ever dared imagined before now.

Winning the inner game makes success in the outer game a cinch.

If you are ready, then as Cipher said in the *Matrix* movie, "Buckle up, Dorothy, because Kansas is going bye-bye."

Chapter 1

GAME EYES

The champion's true edge lies in the mind.
When you win the inner game,
it's only a matter of time before you win the outer game.

"The greatest discovery of my generation
is that human beings can alter their lives
by altering their states of mind."
William James

I would like to hand you a very special pair of glasses. I would like to put into your hands glasses with lens that enable you to view your life, health, fitness, career, work, relationships, finances, hobbies, etc. through the lens of *life as* a *game.* Putting these glasses on enables you suddenly to see not only *what* happens in the real world of actions, but also the *rules* of the game—the invisible structures that give meaning and form to our actions.

If I had such glasses to give you, and if you put them on, you would immediately discover that there are *two games* that you play every day of your life. There is the *inner game* of your mental frames and there is the *outer game* of your actions, skills, and performances. These games go on simultaneously, each influencing the other.

The first game, the *inner game*, makes up *the things in your mind*—your ideas, understandings, visions, values, plans, strategies, beliefs, rules, concepts, premises, etc. about what you are doing. This inner game of your frames makes up what you have learned and invented for yourself and what defines, for you, the meaning of things. This first game is the most crucial game. As we play this *game* in our heads we set forth the rules of the game, who can play, how to score, what a win means, how to play with others, when to stop the game, etc.

> What if you were to see all of life as a game— how would that change things?

The second game, the *outer game*, makes up all about *your actual behavior in the external world,* how you get along with others or don't, what you do or can't do, the performances you engage in to achieve your goals. This outer game on which you mostly focus fills the content of your conscious awareness. It is the outer game that people see and experience. It is the outer game that people use to appraise your skills and competence as they make evaluations about who you are as a person. It is the outer game that people see and respond to.

Yet the two games go together like a hand and glove since the *inner game* of our frames determine and govern the *outer game* of our performances. When we put these two games together, we have frame games. A *frame game* is the synthesis of all of the facets of our mental-emotional-and-behavioral system which then makes up the structure of our internal and external experiences.

If you could *see* frame games with those special glasses, you would be able to peak into the structural framework of the games. Then you would know not only the rules of the games, but also how and why they work as they do, and what to do to change, improve, or transform them. Of all the ideas in this book, this is the over-arching idea. If you had new eyes to see all of life as a game, yourself as a player of those games—

- What would you then realize?
- What would you then be able to do?
- How would you take charge of your inner and outer games?
- What old games would you let go off?
- What new games would you create?
- How much more exciting and passionate would you be about life?
- What games would you like to play and win?

About the Term "Game"

The term *game* may at first seem an unbecoming metaphor inasmuch as it is sometimes used in an exclusively negative way as when we describe someone as a "game player." In the dating scene, this describes someone who is not authentic or honest, someone who has hidden agendas and is just "playing games." In the context of business, the "game player" is the person who may be running a scam or politicking to make points to create an unfair advantage.

The term *game* also got a bad rap in the field of psychotherapy, when Eric Berne described the *Games People Play.* In that model (T.A., Transactional Analysis) all of the games that Eric Berne described were negative and destructive as indicated by the colloquial names he came up with: "Ain't It Awful?" "If It Weren't For You!" "Let's You and Him Fight." "Now I've Got You, You S.O.B."[1]

Every mood, attitude, skills, behavior, role, ritual, etc. that we experience is *a game.*

Yet a *game* doesn't necessarily have to be negative or even positive for that matter, it is just a description of the actions that we play out in our behaviors that make up the *performances* of our life—at work, in our career, in creating wealth and financial independence, in relationships, love, with friends, in our hobbies and sports, in our search for meaning and spirituality, in a word—in everything.

In this, a *game* simply refers to the behaviors, actions, performances, roles, rituals, even feelings that we experience in everyday life. As we engage in a set of patterned responses to another person, to our job, to food, to ideas, etc., we are playing a "game"—a structured set of interactions that has rules and meanings. The *external* games that we play can be seen, heard, and felt by simply watching the actual things we do and say. The *internal* games are harder to catch, yet they are just as real. We play *mind games* in our heads—these show up as the patterned ways we think, perceive, interpret things, believe, value, etc.

Of course, with these definitions, you can now see that we cannot *not* play games. We have to. In this sense, every mood, attitude, skills, behavior, role, ritual, etc. that we experience is *a game.* And if we can look upon them as games, then we can ask questions that play with this metaphor to open up new perspectives, understandings, and choices:

- What games are you playing?
- Are you winning at the games you play?
- Are you playing games that enhance your life and empower you as a person?
- Have you had enough of any particular inner or outer game?
- Do you feel in control of your games?
- Are any of the games playing *you* instead of serving you?
- What will you win when you win that game?
- Did you come up with that game or did you just inherit it or somehow fell into playing it, but it doesn't really serve you well?
- Would you like to change some rules of that game?
- Do you know how to transform the game or to even quit a game?
- What games do you play with your health?
- Are they the games that healthy people play?
- What games do you playing with food; do they make you slim and fit?
- What are the games that you play at work?
- Are they the games that business experts play?
- Are the games you're playing fun, enjoyable, and make your life worth living? Do they invigorate and empower you?
- Would you recommend them to your friends or children?

Mapping Life using the *Game* Metaphor

Viewing our behavior as *games*, assumes that all of our games make sense, are meaningful, and that we are seeking to achieve something. This is actually true of even the most negative and hurtful of our games. From the inside even the *blame game*, the *de-stressing by eating* game, the *do to others before they do to you* game, etc. make sense.

Frame games starts with this assumption rather than by demonizing such games. We do this in order to understand *how* they get set up and *what value* they provide us as a secondary gain. This allows us to accept games for what they are—just behaviors without judging or condemning them. This then gives us some space to explore the positive intentions behind them. It also allows us to separate the *players* of those games so that we can see one of the deep truths of *frame games*—the problem is never the person, it is always the frame or the resultant game. And we are more than our frames and games.

> ***The frame is the problem.***
> ***The problem is the frame.***
> ***The person is never the problem.***

Do you see the value in this approach? We can now explore and run a frame analysis without communicating that there's something wrong with a person. People are always gloriously fallible human beings who think by framing and if something goes wrong in a person's mind, emotions, body, career, skills, relationships, etc., the problem is almost always *the frames that drive limiting or sabotaging games*. And when you know that— you are at choice point. You can choose to keep or refuse a frame. You can choose to release or refine a frame and play an entirely new and more empowering game.

The *Game* Metaphor

Having suggested the lens that could give you new eyes—eyes for our inner and outer games, the *game* metaphor enables us to think like a master player. There are a number of *game-like qualities* that we can easily apply to our everyday actions and experiences. Play along with this metaphor and notice all of the relevant factors that it brings into play. As you put on your *game* glasses you will notice such things as the following.

1) Games imply an identifiable structure.

Games make sense because they manifest a structure. We can't play a game if we don't know its form, the moves we can make, how to set the game up, etc. The game *structure* allows us to recognize and see parts and facets of the game. As all card games involve dealing, distributing, and maneuvering with cards, we can classify games, "Oh, a card game." Sport games differ from parlor games. Now we need to go outside and step up a different arena.

- What is the structure of your game?
- How does the game work?

2) Games have both explicit and implicit rules.
When we're introduced to a literal game, we inevitably begin by asking, "What are the rules of the game?" "How do you play this game?" "Who begins?" "What are the boundaries, the components, what's allowed, what's not, how many players can we have, how does the game end, etc.?" Some rules are explicitly written out, some are not. Yet the rules govern the structure of the game.

- What are the rules of the game?
- Are there any hidden rules covertly hide away from sight?

3) Games involve agendas, intentions, purposes, and payoffs.
All games are motivated. There are intentions above and behind every game. Some are healthy and valuable, others are toxic, ego-centric, and destructive.

- What is the purpose of this game?
- Why should I play?
- What do we get out of it?
- How do we make a point?
- What counts in the game?

4) Games contain degrees of rigidity and flexibility.
Games differ in terms of flexibility. With any game we can explore how much room there is for adaptation and adjustment.

- How rigid are the rules, how much room is there for bending the rules, incorporating new elements?
- Does, or can, the game evolve, etc.?

5) Games involve ways of keeping score.
In every game we can score or loose points and do so until we have enough to win the game, forfeit, or lose the game.

- How do we keep score?
- How do you make points?
- Can you lose points? How?
- What do the points add up to?
- What do you get then?

6) Games have numerous variables that make up the whole.
There are a lot of variables which affect how we play games and how any given player will play. These include: the payoffs, the size of the payoffs, the way other players play (their style), the ability of players to communicate, the level or degree of cooperation and/or exploitation, the level of confusion and/or desperation, one's insights and skills in the game (ability to think and play strategically), beginning assumptions of each player, and the "personality" of the players.

- What are the variables in the games that I play?
- What variables are critical? Which are peripheral?

7) Games provide an opportunity to develop competence and mastery.
In the process of developing high level expertise and even mastery in a game, we usually develop guidelines, heuristics, and secrets about the game. This allows us to develop trade secrets and insider's knowledge, things that one can rarely find in the rule books. With such expertise we develop our intuitions about the game and how to play. This *know-how* knowledge supports mastery.

- What insights, tricks, understandings, etc. does a pro know that a beginner or amateur does not know regarding a game?
- How does one learn to play like a master?

When a Frame or Game Goes Bad
Now while frame games are *game neutral*, there's no question that a game can go bad. From kids arguing about monopoly, scramble, or football to hockey players getting into fist fights, games can go bad. Some games are manipulative scams from the start. So, if the person is not the problem, but problems arise from problematic frames, then the ability to be mindfully aware of frames, of our personal frames and of the frames of others, the frames of organizations, groups, cultures, etc. is critical. Game awareness enhances our personal power as it puts us at choice point.

This means that to understand a problem or an excellence, we need to discover the frames and the frames-within-frames that govern the game. How can we tell when a *frame* has truly become a *problem?* What are the clues to this? What are some of the indicators that we are caught in a closed-loop frame matrix and the game is now playing us? What follows here are some warning signals.

1) The inability to act on the knowledge that you have.
Here's a game, you know lots of things, but you find yourself *not* acting on your knowledge. You fail to translate your knowledge and skills into action. You procrastinate, make excuses, or just can't get yourself to come through. This is the "I just need to know a little bit more" game.

- Do you know more than you do?
- Do you know lots of ways to improve the quality of your life and yet, for all that intelligence and wisdom, you still can't pull it off?

2) The continuance of the same problem year after year.
The game *has* you when you keep experiencing the same problem year after year. No matter what you do, what solutions you think you have achieved, the problem keeps reappearing like a broken record or a virus in your computer.

- Are you deluged with lots of good advice for solving a difficulty and yet the same problem continues to recur?
- Do you have a sense of *deje vu* regarding a re-occurring problem?

Game awareness enhances our personal power and puts us at choice point.

3) The feeling of being controlled.
The frame, as a matrix of frames, seems to have you imprisoned in a set of perceptions, understandings, and feelings so that while you know that others live in other realities that are more empowering, you feel locked in.

- Do you feel played by some unknown game that keeps putting you through the same pattern over and over?
- Does it seem that no matter what you do, the "system" seems to be plotting against you (whether the system is your work, family, body, etc.)?

4) The attempted solution makes the problem worse.
The very solutions that seem like they should work actually make things worse. When this happened, we are generally in a downward spiraling of the problem since our attempted solutions feed the problem.

- Does a way of thinking, feeling, or acting that "logically" should solve things only make them worse?
- Do you find that the more you fight the problem, it gets stronger?
- Does the problem seem to feed on your attempted solution?

5) The sense of going round in circles.
When a meaning frame really locks us into experiencing some toxic games, we often feel that we are going in circles with everything we do. It feels like a game with no exit.

- Do you feel that you're just going round in circles trying to find better solutions for developing better habits in eating, exercising, relating, succeeding, etc.?
- Do you feel stuck in a pattern?
- Do you feel like a powerless victim unable to change things?

6) The discovery of diminishing returns.
Sometimes a frame and its subsequent game once worked, and even worked very well for years, but somehow, you now get fewer and fewer benefits from it as it produces less and less value for you.

- Are you finding that the longer you use a pattern, the less and less useful or effective it becomes?
- Are you feeling increasingly frustrated and dissatisfied with the diminishing returns from your efforts?

Traditionally we have located many of our so-called "problems" at the symptom level. We target our immediate emotions, habits, thoughts, actions, and responses that we don't like and define them as the problem.

I have a problem with my anger.
She has a problem with her sharp tongue.

He has a real problem with always putting others down.

Yet these behaviors are only *symptoms* of a higher or more real problem. That's why you can "fix" (or think you have fixed) these problems, only to then have them pop back.

What does it mean when this happens? It means you're only dealing with the *symptom,* not the real problem. The actual problem operates as a particular frame-of-reference, perhaps even as frames embedded within frames, and operational frames create self-organizing systems. This explains how a frame can endow a problem, habit, perception, emotion, etc. so it has a life of its own. *At that point, the game is playing us.* This explains why all of the things we do at the symptom level only puts a bandaid on the problem. It only deals with symptoms. Turning up the radio so we don't hear the grinding and sputtering of the car's engine does not solve the problem of low oil pressure in the engine. To get to the real problem we have to identify and change the frame which is the focus of this book.

All of our outer games of performance are determined by our inner game of our mental and emotional frames.

Game Eyes for the Inner and Outer Games

Looking at our performances as our *outer* games and the meaning and mapping frames in our heads as our *inner* games provides a revolutionary way to understand ourselves, others, as well as what's going on in the world. Seeing ourselves and others with these new eyes is revolutionarily simply, and yet profound.

Now *frame games* is not a panacea nor is it even a new facet of psychology. It is simply a model that enables us to quickly recognize the structure of the processes we experience in every aspect of life. While *frame games* is not designed to explore the subtleties of psychological experiences, it is designed to enable us to get to the heart of things with amazing speed as we'll demonstrate in the coming chapters.

Game eyes enable you to look at any behavior, any pattern, habit, ongoing activity, ritual, etc. and to ask, *If this is a game, how does it play and what are the rules?* And from there, you can begin to explore who made up those rules, do they work, do they make life healthier and more inviting, do they infuse you with more energy and vitality, do they enrich your life?

These new eyes for games enable us to recognize the difference between a game having meaning versus whether it creates the results you want and is meaningful in a rich and rewarding way. This difference arises because games can take on a life of their own long after they have lost their purpose or usefulness. We can keep playing them even when they may no longer be productive to anyone.

Game eyes enable us to recognize that behind or above every *outer* game is an *inner* game that contains the rules, descriptions, definitions, and meanings.

> *All of our outer games of performance are determined by our inner game of our mental and emotional frames.*

So while there is indeed rhyme and reason to our games, there may not be healthy or useful reasons. Every game comes from and expresses some higher meaning frame in our head and these frames are made out of ordinary stuff— the ideas, thoughts, beliefs, understandings, decisions, values, models, paradigms, definitions, learnings, etc. To play any game, a *frame of mind* is required. In this, it is our frame of mind that actually governs and controls the games that we play.

The Game Context

If you do not know *the frame games* at work in your life, or how to play them mindfully, then you can count on one chilling alternative, namely, ***the games will play you.***

Where do we play our inner and outer games? In none other than in the field of *our mind-body-emotion system.* That's why our inner games lead to actions, emotions, skills, performances, and habits. Together, the games that our frames initiate direct *our mind-body states* which is our thinking, emoting, behaving, relating, etc. Our frame games are critically important precisely because they govern and determine *the very quality* of our experiences and life. Our frame games exercise an influence over us about the meaning of life and the way we play that meaning in our actions.

Later I'll describe how our very brain and neurology wires us all up with a frame brain. In this we actually have no choice but to create, set, and accept various *frames* and then to play out those frames in our daily games. Before doing that there's something else to consider, something that may scare the hell out of you. Namely, **if** you do not know *the frame games* at work in your life, or how to play them mindfully, then you can count on one chilling alternative, namely, ***the games will play you.***

The games will *play* you by running what and how you perceive, the emotions you experience, and your very style of life. In fact, you will become a puppet to the games and to the forces that actually control your life. Like Neo Anderson in the movie, *The Matrix*, you will be a slave of the frame games that your culture and family set for you and that others invite you to play all day long. They will play you.

When you first *awaken* to this, you might feel out-of-control and resentful of being so "played." Yet if you awaken a bit more to the reality of *frames*, you'll begin to realize that *you can choose* which games to play, which to refuse, and which to refine. When that happens, everything changes. Then you are on your way to becoming a *frame game master.* Then, from that state of mastery, you will be able to choose the matrix of frames that you live within and play out. What does all of this mean? It means that—

All of life is a game—played inside of frames within frames of frames.

If your very nervous system and brain works to create *frames* and you and I then live out of those frames in the *games* that we play with ourselves and others, then all of life is a game. We play out the frame games that we've learned and have been culturalized into inside of the governing frames. If you're ready to put on those *game glasses* and develop the eyes and mind to see life as a game, then let's begin the exploration. Come then, I can't tell you what the Matrix *is,* I can only show you the door and invite you to enter. You have to learn about the Matrix yourself.

Summary

- *It's all about frames.* We think by framing and we create our life experiences by our framing. This makes the style and quality of our mental-and-emotional framing all important.
- If all behavior, experience, and performance is a *game,* we can now back up to the frames that set the rules for the games that we play and make more empowering decisions about the quality and nature of the games that we are playing. As a game master, you'll be in charge of your own Matrix of frames and able to quality control our life.
- The ultimate goal is to take charge of the inner games that we play in our mind so we can then take control of the quality of our external performances and move more mindfully and elegantly to the peak performances that allow us to achieve our dreams.

End Notes:

1. Eric Berne's book, *Games People Play* (1964) launched Transactional Analysis or T.A., a popularization of psychoanalytic psychotherapy.

Chapter 2

FRAMES ALL THE WAY UP

"When a person has learned a symbolic system well enough to use it, she has established a portable self-contained world within the mind."
Mihaly Csikszentmihalyi
(1990, *Flow,* 127)

*"I have good news and bad news for you.
The bad news is that yes, you indeed have a serious problem.
The good news is that it's entirely in your head."*

The movie *The Matrix* begins with a scene of Neo having fallen asleep at his computer. About midnight he began to stir from that uncomfortable position. That's when he noticed some words appearing on the computer screen, *"Wake up, Neo, the Matrix has you."*

Similarly, when you opened your eyes this morning and began stirring around in anticipation of the day, your mind did what *minds* always do when we "boot up" our thinking programs of beliefs, understandings, and expectations and become conscious again, you accessed a *frame-of-reference.* That's because you, like all of us, think *in* frames and think *from* frames. That's also because you live your life and operate from a Matrix of frames. So similarly, *a Matrix also has you.*

Yet there are differences. In Neo's case, a new species of artificial intelligence (A.I.) had created a 1999 Sydney Australia Matrix and fed it into human brains and nervous systems to keep them imprisoned and blinded from the real world. In our case, we are the ones who create, invent, and absorb our personal Matrix of frames. That's because when it comes to human experiences and mind, *we think by framing* which then makes us the framers, and so it is *frames all the way*

up.
While we play two games, the inner and outer games, the *inner game* of our *meaning frames* which make up all of the things we do in our heads is the most critical game. It is the game that governs and controls the *outer* game.

Of course, the dynamic structure of experience is systemic so that what we do on the outside enters back into the inside as feedback. What happens in the activities, events, successes and failures, etc. as we play the *outer* game, we bring back in to notice, represent, and use to draw conclusions from. This information then enters into the play of the *inner* game. It is a circle—a loop of information in and out, and information about information.

"Thinking" itself is *framing* and only occurs inside of *frames*. So does feeling. In thinking and feeling, we *refer to* something, someone, or some concept. And with that, the adventure begins, the adventure of information processing by which we create meaning—the meaning of life, the meaning of any particular thing. Here's how it works.

The Framing Adventure
The framing adventure begins with an event occurring "out there" in the world. This event may take the form of some action, speech, behavior, or experience. On the first level, this is the outside *referent event* that initiates everything.

As we notice it, see, hear, feel, smell, or taste the event or experience, we *represent* it in our mind as pictures, sounds, sensations, smells, tastes. We record it as a snapshot or movie in our mind, something that we can play on the theater of our mind. In this way we create an internal representation of the world. This takes us to the first inside level, the primary level of thinking.[1]

Later, when we think again about that event or when we think about a similar situation, we use our representation (literally, *re-presentation*) as part of our library of references. The representation becomes our frame of reference—what we refer to in order to make sense of things. This moves us up yet another level, up from the mere *representation* of the referent, so that we now have *a frame of reference*—what we use to make sense of our thoughts and experiences.

As an example, suppose someone says or does something that hurts your feelings. Perhaps a friend abruptly contradicts an idea or event and talks over you correcting you in public on just about everything you say. As a result, you feel discounted, embarrassed, and "run over." How you play that movie in your mind is the first set of representations that you create.

From there, you then sulk about it and on it, replaying it again and again like a B-rated movie you didn't like the first time. As you do, you begin to load it up semantically as you give it more and more meaning and significance. For you, it becomes an insult, a put-down, a violation of courtesy, a wound to the relationship, etc. For you, it becomes what the other person is capable of and perhaps who that person *is* at his or her core.

Eventually that movie and memory becomes your frame of reference for that person. As it becomes the filter through which you see your friend, you develop eyes for anticipating hurt. It may even become your filter for thinking about all people.

The fact is, using the same frame of reference repeatedly eventually habituates it so that we jump yet another level and set it as our *meaning frame* or our frame of mind. This now becomes the way we see things, our perspective, our belief system. It operates as our perceptual filter or meta-program as it reflects multiple layers of frames (multiple meta-states). [These terms will be explained as we go, so no need to play the *Phobic Reactions to New Words* game, at least not yet.]

With even more habituation and repetition, and more jumping levels, the frame of mind grows up to become the very frameworks that governs how we think and feel, our inner mapping about what's real, how we express ourselves, and so the framework of our personality.

Now we are ready to turn this layering of levels that creates our matrix of frames into a model so that we can begin to imagine and *see* it, even if only in diagram form at first. This gives us *Figure 2:1.*

The Framing Adventure

1) Referent Event
2) Represented Reference
3) Edited Reference
4) Frame of Reference
  a) Linguistic meaning
  b) Emotional associations
5) Frame of Meaning and/or Mind
  a) Evaluative meaning
  b) Multiple frames of meaning
6) Intentional meaning frames
7) Metaphorical frames and meanings
8) Overall Matrix of frames

Figure 2:1

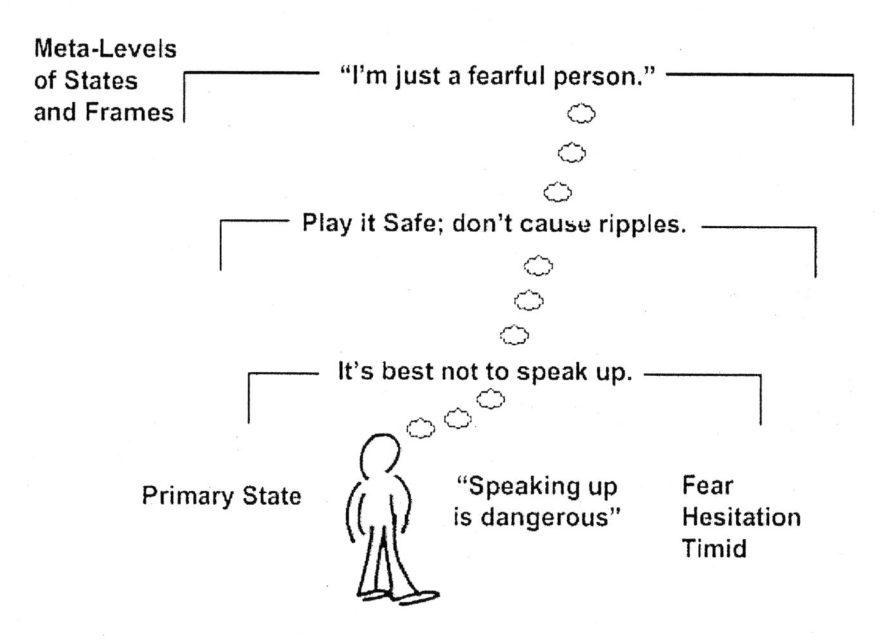

The Mystery and Magic of Framing
The many ways our nervous system and brain processes information and constructs the inner maps of the world which we then use to navigate meaning and action is a truly creative and magical process, and one that is still mysterious. Even today the neuro-sciences is only beginning to understand many of the systemic mechanisms involved. Fortunately for us, we do not need thorough understanding to be able to use the system.

As meaning makers, we construct meaning at multiple levels. First we use our *senses* to represent the world "out there" in sensory see, hear, feel terms on the theater of our mind. This allows us to create a facsimile map of the world and to use it as we "think" about an event when it is not present to our senses. Yet our representational thoughts and meanings is just the first step.

Once we have a set of representations we can begin to edit the movie, altering and changing how we represent an experience. It is as if we have control knobs so that we can make adjustments in the picture and image, the sound track, even the smell and taste track, and then we can step in or out of the movie, identifying with a character or stepping back to be the director of the movie. This *cinematic framing* is one of the most powerful facets of our mind as we construct meaning and herein lies much of the magic of NLP—the alteration of our movies [3].

If, for example you step back to examine how you represent a memory of a criticism, how do you encode it? What sights and sounds play out in your inner movie? What tone of voice does the critic use? What volume, pitch, and accent?

How big is the critic in your movie compared to you? When you think about the event, are you *inside* the movie so that you are re-experiencing it?

At the next level we begin *defining* and *labeling* things. Since we use words in doing this, we begin creating *linguistic meaning.* This answers many of our questions: What is this? What do we call this thing? How do we classify it? [4a]. Do we label it an "insult" or a "put-down?" Do we call it a "betrayal of friendship?" How do we classify it? Is it "my friend being out-of-sorts?" Whatever words we use endows it with a linguistic reality that then classifies it so that thereafter we think about it in those terms.

At this level also we attach emotions to our references. These associations create our *meta-associative meanings*. What feelings or emotions do we associate with our representations and words? The fact of the matter is that we can associate any emotion to any representation. And whatever feeling we associate with it, links up that feeling thereby endowing it with that affect. [4b]

Then there is the level of *evaluative meaning.* How do we evaluate the meanings we construct? Do we evaluate it as good or bad, useful or limiting, valuable or worthless, practical or impractical? There are hundreds if not thousands of criteria that we can invent to use in evaluating the meanings that we have created. [5a]. Do we evaluate it in terms of our person, dignity, or the relationship? Or do we evaluate it in terms of the other's state of stress and feeling unresourceful? Is it a common human fallibility or mis-speaking or is it a sign of unethical corruption?

At this level we frame meaning in a broad range of ways to create our *frame of mind.* How do we frame the meanings? Do we frame them as beliefs, values, identity, decisions, intentions, memories, imaginations, possibilities, impossibilities, etc.? The list of twenty-six meta-questions provides more than two dozen frames for many of the conceptual mental categories or phenomena. Nor is it the case that each of these are different things, they are not. They are only different descriptions of the same thing—different facets of the same diamond of awareness. [5b]

In other words, what do you *believe* about "interrupting," "talking over," "connecting," "public exposure," etc.? What do you value or dis-value about these ideas? What memories or expectations play into them?

One of these frames is that of intention, which takes us to the level of *intentional meaning.* Why do we frame or evaluate it this way? What's our intention or agenda? What are we seeking to do in viewing things this way? What is our motivation or long-term objective? Intention differs from attention in that it describes the level of meaning "in the back of the mind' that makes up all of our reasons for *why* we are doing and thinking as we are. [6]. What intentions do you immediately imagine in another when a friend disagrees with you and says so in an animated way? What intention do you immediately access and assume?

Yet another one of these frames is that of metaphor, which enables us to create *metaphorical meaning.* What is it like? If we were to compare it to an animal, what animal would it be? If it were a color, what color? [7]

In all of these facets of meaning-making, *we set frames.* From representational frames, cinematic frames, linguistic frames, evaluative, associative, belief, value, intentional, and metaphorical frames—all we do in our heads as we play the *inner game* of setting frames that create what we "hold in mind" (which is what *meaning* means). In other words, in human experience it is frames all the way up. That's why we are the framers, the designers of our individual Matrixes. [8]

Because we have a frame brain, we are the framers who set frames that define and invent the meanings that we live in and search for. Framing is what brains do. As we refer to things, represent references, think in terms of a reference as our frame of reference, repeat so those references become our frame of mind and eventually the framework of our personality, we have created our inner world, our Matrix of meaning frames. All of it is our creation. [8][2]

Exploring the Thread of Thought

What is the value and power of unifying all of the stuff that goes on in our head and bodies with one process such as *framing* and *referencing* which can then take so many different forms and expressions? The value is that it gives us *a simple* and *single thread* from which we can weave the entire fabric of our consciousness and experiences. What's truly revolutionary about this is that now we can begin exploring the fabric of consciousness at any point. We do not have to find the original thread, or even understand all of the weaving patterns that a person uses to construct his or her matrix of reality. We only need to pick up the thread wherever we are and go from there.

> In human experience it is frames all the way up. That's why we are the framers, the designers of our individual Matrixes.

Does that sound fascinating? It is far, far more fascinating than what I can describe here. With this approach I can now begin with any line of thought or emotion that any person offers, a statement, question, metaphor, accusation, celebration, or whatever and enter into the Matrix of that person's world. I can follow that thread to see where it goes and how it makes up that person's mapping and meaning structures. And it's simple in that I only need to ask about the person's frames and references.

- Help me out, I'm not fully clear about what you're saying. What are you referring to? (Level 1)
- And how do you represent that? If I were to peak into the theater of your mind and see what you see inside, what would I see? (Level 2)
- Is that image in color? And is there a sound track with what you are

seeing? And are you inside that movie or outside? (Level 3)

- What do you call that? And what does that term mean to you? (Level 4)
- What do you feel about that? Let's say all this is true, absolutely true, so what? What would that mean to you? What other ramifications would that have for you? (Level 5)
- So your evaluation about that is what? How have you come to make that evaluation? Do you like that or not? Do you have to evaluate it that way? (Level 5)
- What do you believe about that? What's your expectations? (Level 5)
- What's your intention in doing that? And when you achieve that, what does that give you? And what's your intention behind that? Is there any higher intention driving that? (Level 6)
- What's all of this like for you? What would you compare it to? What else? (Level 7)

While I've written as if this were a linear process, it is obviously not linear. This, of course, is one of the problems with a two-dimensional medium like paper which doesn't allow for writing simultaneously about multiple dimensions of meaning. (But then again, if I could write in such loops, who could read it?) I write about each as if they were separate, yet in reality they are intermixed and occur simultaneously and are systemically interconnected. We spiral and simultaneously use feedback and feed forward loops which is what makes following anyone's line of thought challenging.

We create frames of meaning as we frame meaning up the levels of our mind by layering thoughts-and-feelings upon thoughts and feelings to create ever more complex and sometimes convoluted meanings. These create our inner frame games and become the Matrix that we operate from.

Exploring Your Reading Frames

To make this practical, let's apply this to reading a book. So what frames did you begin with as you began reading this book? What are the initial *inner games* that you have been playing in your mind?

- Did you wonder what wild and wonderful things you'll get to learn, discover, and experience by means of this book? If so, perhaps you have been playing the *Exploration Game* or possibly t*he Possibility Game.*
- Have you been distracted in your reading, reading a bit here and there, taking care of other things, getting lost, wondering where you are, wondering if you are even understanding the line of thought? Perhaps you began reading, but then started thinking about some urgent things on your "to do" list and keep finding your mind floating away to other images. Then perhaps you are playing the *Distracted* game, or the *I Can't Concentrate* game, or the fearful *Maybe I have ADD* game.

Figure 2:2

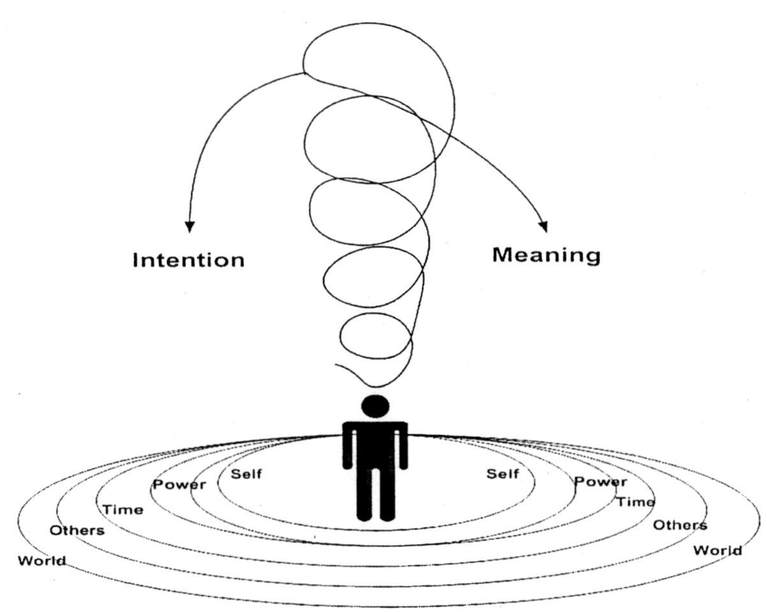

- Perhaps you have been applying everything you read to someone else, someone you dearly love or someone that you're in conflict about. Then maybe your inner game is that of *John Ought to be Reading This Stuff.*

Whatever inner game you've been playing, it is just that—a game that expresses meanings that you have invented to date. It is the inner game that you know well about the experience of reading. None of these games are right or wrong, they are rather un-useful, useful, or powerfully useful. Of course, as goes your *inner* game, so goes your *outer* game. Our inner game inevitably leads to actions, behaviors, and performance that we know as our outer game. It leads to what you can or cannot do, what you can or cannot achieve, and what we can or cannot experience.

> As goes your *inner* game, so goes your *outer* game.

The conclusions that we draw as we frame up the levels of meaning create for us what we think things "are," what we consider them for, and then the *games* that we play. From our framing some people learn to play all kinds of games. For example:

- *It's a Dangerous World* game. "Don't trust anyone." "People can't be trusted; they only hurt you."
- *It's a Beautiful World full of Wonderful Things to Explore* game.
- *I'm Stupid, Inadequate and Won't Amount to Anything* game.

- *I'm Loved and Valued Just for Me.*
- *To Feel Better, Put Others Down.*
- *He Who Has the Most Toys in the End, Wins.*

With any idea we can *set* a frame that creates a meaning matrix with all the details of the inner game. Once we do that, we will then think, feel, act, and respond from *within* those frames. We no longer just "think" in the sense of representing information. "Thinking" becomes more complex as we frame our representations in multiple layers of frames.

This model explains why we often use our first *references* or experiences to evaluate later experiences and how that can create a very limiting framework. This partially explains our tendency to over-value first experiences and first impressions. This may also explain why we have a tendency to over-believe and trust an actual experience as we assume that it is the experience that creates our reality. It is not. It is our *framing* of the experience that creates our reality. By itself, *experience means nothing.* Meaning is never in the event, but is always in the mind of the meaning-maker.

It is framing all the way up. Yet once set, the *frames* operate as a self-organizing system. The frames we set at the highest levels in our matrix of meaning will have the most influential role as to what gets replicated and reproduced in our feelings and behaviors. As a result, our frames will *attract* the very experiences, people, and situations that will confirm its orientation, structure, beliefs, etc.

By itself, *experience means nothing.* Meaning is never in the event, but is always in the mind of the meaning-maker.

As references and reference points, our frames *attract* experiences, events, situations, and people that accord to them. Like a self-replicating DNA "code," they begin to take on "a life of their own" and pursue their own survival.

It is framing all the way up. Yet once set, the *frames* operate as a self-organizing system. The frames we set at the highest levels in our matrix of meaning will have the most influential role as to what gets replicated and reproduced in our feelings and behaviors.

These reasons demand that we become *aware* of frames, even our own frames. After all, our frames are the *code* that organize our thinking, feeling, perceiving, acting, etc. so that our mind-body system creates more of the same. In this way our frames draw and attract confirming experiences. As the experience becomes more and more familiar to us, it attracts other experiences that support that sense of familiarity. It becomes the fabric of our reality. We commonly refer to this process as "a self-fulfilling prophecy." With ugly, hurtful, and toxic frames, this becomes a big problem. With beautiful, healthful, and enhancing frames, this becomes a tremendous boon for resourcefulness and effectiveness.

Figure 2:3

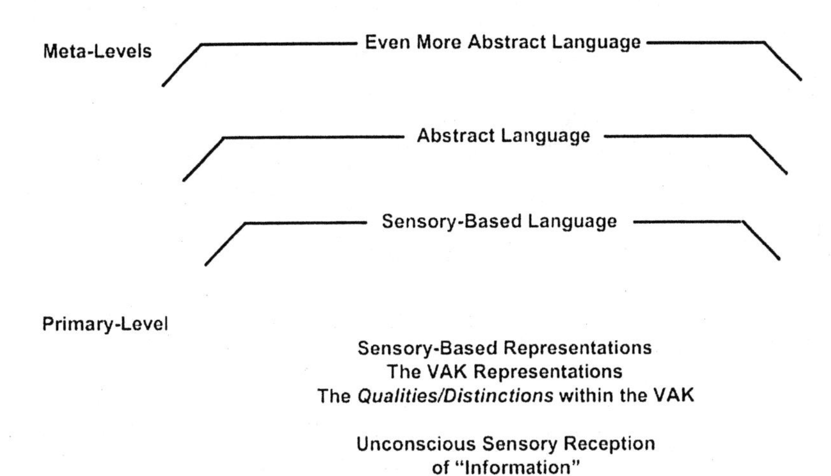

All of this makes frames and framing incredibly powerful, does it not? Our freedom of choice, creativity, and ability to change things and experience transformation emerges from our frames. In this, we are only as free as our frames permit us to be. If we have frames that allow or encourage ongoing growth and development, if we have frames that validate our ability to intentionally "think" and to set new frames-of-references—the future is ours. If we don't, we're dead in the water.

> We are only as free as our frames permit us to be.

No wonder our frames play such a crucial role in everything in our lives! What we call a thing or person, whether "an argument" or "a search for mutual understanding," whether "a bitch" or "a person really persistent in discovering things," determines the quality and intensity of our experience. Our reality arises from our frameworks.

Frame Games For Resilience

No one in public life has played the *Resilience game* more effectively than Christopher Reeves. What a tremendous example of playing a very different game with the cards that life dealt him with his spinal chord injury! What were the inner games that actor Christopher Reeve played for ten years which kept him so resiliently positive and hopeful?

Paralyzed in a fall when thrown from a horse in 1995, Reeve absolutely refused to wallow in his misfortunes, but in a way that surpassed the Superman role that he played, he continued to live life to the full, taking effective actions in doing what he could, playing in movies, creating a foundation for research, becoming a spokesperson for that cause, raising a son, etc. Amazingly he continued his film career with his performance in a wheelchair in the TV remake of *Rear Window*, made appearances in the TV series, *Smallville,* directed several movies, just to mention a few of the things. And he continued working at regaining his health.

> "At the beginning, I could only move my jaw. Now I'm able to move my diaphragm. All that's lacking is signals from the brain. All I have is a little 28 millimeter gap that is causing all the damage. That makes me a prime candidate for recovery. And, as [spinal cord] regeneration is achieved, I'll be in very good shape. It's a game of patience now, but there will be a great reward coming."

Did you detect the frame games in that? What frame games are there? He took the progress of being able to briefly breathe on his own and counted it as highly significant, rather than discounted it as nothing. In doing that he played the *Let's Count Every Step of Progress as Significant* game. He played the game of *Focusing on Potential Solutions*. As a result, he became involved in taking actions that reflected these frames.

> "Last spring, Reeve began special therapy in which he's put in a parachute harness on a treadmill. As the treadmill moves, his spinal cord instinctively transfers weight without input from the brain, and he walks. 'I do this at least once a week. I'm up for an hour and walk about 3 or 4 miles. All the assistants have to do is make sure I don't trip over my feet.' As a result, Reeve gets a cardiovascular workout, and his muscles don't atrophy."

Does this mean he never felt down and depressed? Don't believe it.

> "I limit the amount of time I'm allowed to feel sorry for myself. Right now it's between 6 a.m. and 8 a.m. I tend to wake up at 6, and it's hard to come back [to reality]. Because, at night, when I dream, I'm always on my feet, like I was for 42 years. When I wake up I realize I can't just get up and go for a walk and do the things I used to do. I sometimes say to myself, 'I don't deserve this.' Then at 8 a.m., my son, Will, comes in and gives me a big kiss and hug, and I think, 'What can I do today to take a step forward.'"

By limiting the time he plays the *Ain't it Awful!* game, Christopher refused to let it have much sway in his life. It also empowered him to turn toward the day and ask the implementation question of *the Aim frame*, "What one thing can I do today that's going to put me in the direction I want to go?"

The Frame Awareness Game

In this chapter we have begun to play one of the most important of all games, the *Frame Awareness game.* We have been using our *game eyes* to consider the games that we have been playing in our lives.

- Given any event, person, or idea, what's your frame of reference?
- When you use that experience, thought, idea, feeling, person, etc. as a *reference*, does it improve things?
- What *game* does it initiate for and recruit you to play?
- Are you playing an enjoyable game? Does it make life more of a party for you?
- Has it been a productive one for you? Has it made you rich and wealthy in mind, body, relationships, spiritually, financially?
- Has the game enriched your sense of self and others?
- Has it endowed you with a strong sense of self-efficacy, self-esteem, and self-confidence?
- Has the game increased your effectiveness and efficiency? Does it give you a sense of power?
- Do you find yourself repetitively playing a game that you feel sick and tired of and want to quit, but it keeps playing you anyway?

Summary

- It's frames all the way up because we have a frame brain and think by framing. In answer to the question, Why do we play *frame games*? It's because that's how our mind-body-emotion system works.

- The challenge today for each of us is to *wake up* to our frames and to become aware of how we create meaning frames and the Matrix system that results from our framing.

- While we're always in some *frame of mind*, we have control over which frames we choose and play. Unless you play the *Doom and Destined as Life's Victim* frame game, you have complete control over the kind and quality of games that you play.

- This means that just because we grew up in an environment, family, school, or experienced certain events—such does not *doom* us to keep playing those *frame games*. First games, like first impressions, can be seductively influential, yet they are not destiny. They are not unless you set that as your frame and so close the door to new learnings.

- We take a step in human development when we begin playing the *Frame Awareness* game because it will greatly expand our sense of choice, control, and options.

End Notes:

1. See the book *Movie-Mind* (2002) for a simple overview of this NLP description of how we "think" and create our sense of reality. *MovieMind* presents this without any of the usual NLP jargon.

2. The Matrix is the virtual reality that we create from all of our self-reflexive framing. Overall, it is the model of the world we have created or the mapping that guides our navigating of the territory.

Chapter 3

WE ARE THE FRAMERS

"What exists today are only messages
about the past which we call memories,
and these messages can always be framed and modulated
from moment to moment."
Bateson (1972, p. 233)

It's difficult to see the picture
when you are inside the frame.

If it is frames all the way up and if we are the framers of the Matrix we live in, then to a greater extent that most of us have ever even dared to dream, *we can set meaning frames in our mind that enable us to then experience a tremendously higher quality of life and achievement.*

Do you believe that? No, this is *not* just "positive thinking." It is much richer and much more involved than that. Nor is it just "running our own brain." While it begins with running your own brain, it involves more, it means taking charge of your entire multi-layered framing system, your Matrix, and becoming the master of your Matrix, of the meaning universe you live in.

Let me explain. If *the way we interpret* things set ideas in our mind at a higher level so that those ideas become beliefs or frames of mind, then it is not merely our thoughts that govern our mind-body system, it is our second thoughts. And it is our third thoughts that govern our second thoughts. And beyond that, it is our fourth and fifteen thoughts. It is always the thoughts "in the back of the mind," the thoughts *about* the previous ones that create the mental *contexts or frames* that then self-organize our entire mind-body system.

No wonder these states-about-states or meta-states are so much more powerful, pervasive, and determining than our everyday states. We all know that our mind-body states are pretty powerful. Get into a robust state of playfulness, confidence, excitement, curiosity, persistence, etc. and we know the power those experiences create. We also know the power of depressive states, states of anger and frustration, states of fear and timidity. States powerfully determine our experiences and the quality of our experiences. That's why state management skills are so critical in taking control of ourselves and experience self-management.

> *We can set meaning frames in our mind that enable us to then experience a tremendously higher quality of life and achievement.*

Yet these are nothing compared to meta-states. After all, what is the quality or nature of your anger? Is it *thoughtful* anger, *considerate* anger, *calm* anger, *respectful* anger, even *gentle* anger? What about your timidity? Is it *courageous* timidity, *playful* timidity, *mindful* timidity, or what? The *quality* of your state reflects the meta-states frames that govern the state. The properties and features of our states arise from our meta-states.

What is a meta-state? Structurally, it is a state-*about*-another-state. It is one mental-emotional state that operates at a *meta* or higher relationship to the first state. As such, a meta-state operates the *frame* or *mental context* for the first state. What is important about this regarding frames and framing? Precisely that the *inner* games that we play involve setting meaning frames. We do so by meta-stating resourceful thoughts and emotions so that as they become our higher frame, they actually construct our meanings and classifications of reality.

What's Your *Inner Game* about Learning?

> ***The Name of the Game is to Name the Game.***

To make this extremely practical, let's look at what you are doing right now as you read and learn. What *inner game* are you playing this very minute as you read these words? How do you think about reading this book (or any book)? What's in the back of your mind?

To engage in effective *reading*, we use words as symbols to create representations. We take the words and use them to create an internal *movie* of what we see, hear, feel, smell, and taste. If we're reading a book about business effectiveness, we may imagine seeing a business office and hearing the boss speak. We could then edit into the movie a resourceful self speaking with more persuasion and effectiveness to take our career to the next level.

That's what we do with the *content.* Let's now step back so that we can examine this from a higher level and see the *form*. If that's where the higher magic occurs, then let's go there and look at how we *frame* or structure our thinking. How do we do this? We shift from examining *content* to examining the form, shape, and structure of our thinking—*the frames as the frameworks of our mind.*

- What's your frame about reading something to become more effective?

- Do you believe that reading can enhance your skills?
- Do you believe it is worth the effort?
- Does your personal history make you think it's a waste of time?
- Do you worry, question, or doubt whether it will really change things?
- Do you think in the back of your mind, "Why am I kidding myself? Reading another book has never really helped in the past. It never really changes things."
- Or do you use your personal history to think, "Reading and applying new insights will further my career success, expand my creativity, give me lots of new ideas, and keep refreshing my purpose!"?

Examining the *frames* and the *inner* games that we play is challenging because typically the more we are *caught up* in the game, the less awareness we will have of the game. Yet we can play a higher or meta-game. To do so we only need to ask, "How well does it serve me?"

What are the common *frame games* for reading a book or for learning a new model? Here are some of the typical ones. Do any of these ring a bell?

The frames you set govern the games you play.

- *Book Learning Doesn't Count* game. "If an idea came from a book then it is just academic and can't be practical, useful, or real."
- *Book Learning is all Academic* game. "If an idea comes from a book, then it's hard to understand, theoretical, conceptual, and therefore impractical for real life."
- *The Book Worship* game. "If it's written down in a book, it has to be true. Anything written in black-and-white cannot be questioned."
- *Getting to Dialogue with an Author* game. "Reading a book is like dialoguing with an author about a subject that he or she may (or may not) be well versed in and offers ideas, insights, and procedures that may enrich my life."
- *Reading is a Waste of Time* game.
- *Reading good books Provokes Insights and Expands Consciousness* game.
- *Reading stimulates me to Action* game. "I never leave the scene of a great idea without doing something about it to get my body and neurology to *feel* that great idea."

As a meaning-maker and "a semantic class of life" (Korzybski), we always and inevitably operate by frames as well as we put *frames* around things. It is the *meanings* that we attribute to things that set up our frames-of-reference which, with some repetition, will become our frame-of-mind. The practical questions are:

- How are you specifically framing X [some particular subject]?
- Does it empower you to frame it in this particular way?

- If it doesn't, what frame would make your experience richer?

If you are ready to learn more effectively and efficiently, to accelerate your learning of frame games, then the following questions are designed to get you to take action and begin to create some better frames so that you can get the most from exploring frames games. If you're genuinely committed to your own personal success and happiness, take time to answer these questions.

- What frame of mind have you brought to the activity of reading this book?
- To what extent do you aim to use this book to enrich your life? What will that do for you? And why is that important?
- How much time, energy, attention, and focus do you bring to this experience?
- What frame of mind *could* you use that would greatly enrich and empower your experience of reading, studying, learning, and integrating the information here?
- Would you like to play an entirely new game in how you read to use and integrate as part of your skill development and personal enrichment?
- What other games could you choose to play that would enrich your reading experience?
- What's the quality and nature of your *inner game* of reading? Is it a fun game? Playful? Intense?
- What does it mean to you? What could it mean?
- What are the rules of the game?
- How do you score points in the game?
- What's a win in the game?

Most of us *know* far more than we *practice*. This creates a gap between our knowing and practicing. This tells us that it is possible to stuff our brains full of information without letting it do us much good. Do you know that one? That is a formula for becoming an egg-head—informed about effectiveness, but not effective. We could play the *Educated Fool* game, *Look at How Much I Know. It Doesn't Change my Life, but At Least I Understand How I'm so Messed Up.*

Personally those games don't appeal to me as useful or fun at all. I'd prefer to play it differently. How about you? How about an entirely new and different game?

Suppose you decided to use your reading to understand *and* to immediately implement in order to turn it into a competency? For just a moment, imagine that game and how it would play out. The basic idea is this: You would first read something, then you would incorporate the principles, ideas, and processes that you find into your own life. You apply first to self. So, *if* you did that, what *frame of mind* would you have to be in?

Here are some ideas:

- I can and will learn new principles and insights and make them mine!
- I will personalize my reading by underlining, highlighting, taking notes, creating my own index of the book, journaling my learnings and decisions, and tracking my practice.
- I will never leave the scene of reading a page or a chapter without taking some action. My aim always is to get the truths and concepts into my muscles so that I can feel them in my body.
- I will suck out all of the hard-learned lessons from others and avoid having to do trial and error learning. I model the experts to learn from their mistakes.

Imagine fully shifting to the game of *Reading Expands My Mind and Choices,* or the game of *Reading Gives me Mental Exercise for Greater Intelligence.* What would you have to think, believe, or value? How about one of these?

- I'm a ferocious learner.
- As I feed my thinking with noble ideas, so I will become.
- A little practice using what I learn makes it *mine.*
- Learning from the lives of others saves me the trouble and pain of "trial and error" learning.
- You only need to go to the School of Hard Knocks if you don't use your intelligence to learn from others.
- I experience *accelerated learning* by turning on my motivation, interest, commitment, and decision.
- Learning the strategy of success and excellence by modeling the experts saves lots of time and trouble. It alerts me to the paths that go nowhere, and gives me the secrets to excellence.

"Good God, Man, Do you Hear the Frames You're Spouting?"

If we are the framers, then frame detection is the first inner game skill. We have to tune up our eyes and ears to recognize the invisible frames around us. Suppose you play the inner game, *It's Shameful to Have Negative Emotions,* then you have no other choice but to deny, repress, guilt yourself, shame yourself, hate yourself, get angry at yourself, fear yourself, etc. when you experience this most neutral and amoral of all experiences—emotions.

Yet so many people, perhaps most of us, play that game. We get it in our heads that somehow it is a bad thing to experience a "negative" emotion. It's not only the case that we want to experience the positive emotions: love, joy, peace, fun, playfulness, contentment, excitement, relaxation, etc., but that we hate experiencing the negative emotions. Perhaps we think that only the positive ones are valid and the negative ones mean that we are wrong or bad.

However a person structures the game, thereafter every "negative" feeling becomes a signal to reject, refuse, guilt, etc. Yet this only makes things worse. When we frame a "negative" emotion as "bad," we turn our psychic energies *against* ourselves as we refuse to straightforwardly experience or explore a negative feeling. I recently met a gentleman who did this with extreme vigor. If an anxiety or fear come into his consciousness he would be all over the place.

> "I'm really screwed up! I can't believe that I'm so messed up. I'm so intelligent that I know I just make it worse on myself. I thought that after spending three years in therapy, I would be over this. But now that I realize how much my dad has messed up my life, I feel even more messed up."

"Ah, Todd," I said, "It sounds like you're playing the *Ain't it Awful that I'm this Screwed Up* game while simultaneously playing, *If it Weren't for Dad . . .* Game."

"Yeah. That's what I mean. Look at how screwed up I am."

"Good. Take a deep breath and as you stand back and appreciate, really appreciate, the *problem frame* and the *blame frame,* do so in the growing realization of your awareness of those old games, and that you can bring them to a complete and final end. In fact, let this awareness empower you to say *'No!'* to the old frame games. Are you willing to do that?"

"But I don't know how . . . and I'm afraid . . ."

"Does it really help you to go there?"

"Go where?"

"To start this whining litany of your inadequacies and fears of not knowing how. Do you really want to play that game about your other games?"

"No, but . . ."

"Ah, the *Just Try to Help Me, Yes, But . . .* game! Is that what you want to play? I'll present a suggestion and you figure out how it won't work, how you've tried that, how you're stuck, how you're beyond everybody's help? Is that the game you want to play with me this afternoon?"

"Is that what I'm doing?'

"Check it out for yourself. What do you think? I'm no wizard. I have no powers beyond your own in detecting frames. You can catch and name your frames just as well as I can. The power of human magic simply lies in these *stepping back moves.* What would you call the frames that you've been playing?"

"Probably the same as what you've called them, the *Blame* frame, the *Be Sorry For Me* frame, the *Yes, But* frame."

"Okay, so let's now check them out. Do they serve you? Do they enhance your life? Do they make your life a party? Would you want to install them in your head? Do they bring you honor or respect?" [The *Quality Control* frame]

"No they do not."

"Are you definite about that? Any doubt or question about that? Maybe they do serve you well?" [The *Confirmation* frame, then the *Exploration* frame]

"No, no question about that. They stink."

"So are you ready to say *"No!"* to them? Are you ready to utter a loud, bold, and definitive *"No!"* to them?"

"Yes I am."

"Then say *'No!'* to them and blow them out of the water. Refuse them so completely that they don't have a chance to take up any space in your head."

Let the Learning Games Begin!

If no one has ever told you that you can take charge of your mind and emotions, then let me have that honor. *You can* take *charge of your mind and emotions.* You can set that mind elevating idea in your head as your frame of reference. And when you do, something magical will happen. As *managing your own mind* becomes your *reference point*, it will cause all of your powers of thinking, emoting, speaking, behaving, and relating to self-organize in service of that idea. How about that? Slowly or suddenly, you will begin to look upon the world, every conversation, every relationship, every book, etc. as an opportunity to practice and enrich your own skills at running your own brain. Would you like that?

Yes, I know that you did not receive a *User's Manual of the Brain* when you were born. Richard Bandler, co-founder of NLP, says that it was probably lost in the placenta. Yet today you can learn to "run your own brain" for the simple reason that brains run on the "thoughts" that we use to set frames.

You can take charge of your mind and emotions. You can set that mind elevating idea in your head as your frame of reference. And when you do, something magical will happen.

For now, *set this frame* in your mind and give yourself a chance to believe it. (You can believe something else later on, if you so choose.) Write the following words in your own handwriting and begin to feed your mind on these words as juicy and enriching thoughts:

- I can take charge of my own brain and run it with efficiency and choice.
- I can, and will, detect the *frames* that I've been living by and take complete charge of setting the frames that I want to set—frames that will enhance my life and serve my values.
- I can and will learn this information by simply applying my time, energy, and motivation to it. As I do, it will increase my intelligence and enable me to play *inner game of learning* and becoming a ferocious learner in a way that will revolutionize my life.

> ***When you find the frame, you can change the game.***

Whatever challenges or difficulties arise in life to put you to the test, the problem is never the event or circumstance, nor is it merely the thought, the emotion, or the behavior. *The problem is always the frame.* When you learn how to intentionally play frame games, you'll be able to think any thought, experience, or emotion without it dominate you. There are safe frames for trying out any thought, emotion, and behavior. Nor are *you* ever the problem. When we're misbehaving, going crazy, being stupid, acting immoral—there's always a frame that's driving the game and doing the damage.

It's paramount that we distinguish person and frame, person and thought, emotion, behavior, etc. We are more than our frames. And yet, our frames govern our thinking, emoting, behaving, speaking, relating, etc. We live our lives by referencing, and we do so *inside of frames.* The frames work as frameworks— frameworks for experiencing. Now that you know about frame games, you know that *you can take charge of the games that you play.* This initiates a whole new dimension in human experience, does it not? Are you ready to play?

Summary

- *We are the framers.* Yet while framing is how our mind works, we typically do so without awareness of this truly magical process. Yet as we step back to recognize this incredible power of mind, we move up a level to a choice point where we can begin to truly choose the frames that we want.
- At the heart of *framing* is the process of *meta-stating.* It is by meta-stating that we frame and set frames.
- It is never the environment, people, family, school, or experiences that we go through that determines or controls our experience, it is the conclusions, understandings, interpretations or frames that we construct. In this we have total freedom if we wake up to our Matrix and take charge of our frames and framing. This is the heart pulse of *Winning the Inner Game.*
- By stepping back and moving up the levels of our mind we play the inner game of *Frame Awareness.* And that's where control, power, choice, and options begin. It is frame awareness that puts us at choice point.

Chapter 4

FRAMING SECRETS

"He grew up with the honest confusion
of a man who didn't understand the rules
by which the game of life was being played."

*"The game of life is not so much in holding a good hand,
as in playing a poor hand well."*
H. T. Leslie

Where there are games, there are rules. There are rules for how to play and how to win. Is that also true for the inner games of our meaning frames? Are there rules for how we can more effectively and joyfully play our *inner* games that will give us more power and performance in our *outer* games? You bet there are. Would you like to be let in on these secrets?

The Rules of the Inner and Outer Games

If our frames create the inner hidden structure of our lives, then within those frames are rule-like structures for how to play, when to play, with whom to play, how to score points, how to win, how to end a game, etc. If we look closely within our frames we will find *the rules* that govern our inner and outer games. The frames reveal the secrets for understanding the games: how to play them, who wins, how to score, how to quit, how to celebrate a win, the motivations, etc.

***Where there are games,
there are rules.***

Consider *the Blame Game.* In this game the rule is that when things go wrong, do whatever you can to avoid taking responsibility. With that intention, it's best to distract attention from yourself by accusing others, circumstances, fate, genetics, your upbringing, anything other than you as the cause of the problem.

An effective player of the Blame Game will get into an accusatory, even an angry state, point with the index finger, and start sentences with "You . . ." What's the payoff in this game? You win points by feeling that you are off the hook and excused from any accusation. When you score several points, you can feel blameless, even self-righteous. That's what you win. To win at *the Blame game,* you protect your innocence and so avoid any punishment, apologies, or corrective behaviors. You're home free to do keep doing what you've been doing, and, of course, getting the same old results.

Contrast that with the rules of the *Power Zone* game. To play this game, you always default to taking ownership of your personal powers that contribute to effecting and influencing people and events. You step into a state of feeling empowered to use your thinking, emoting, speaking, and behaving and you look around to see what you can do to make things better. What a different game! In this game "blame" never occurs, only the power state of feeling response-able—feeling the power to respond. Playing "It's My Brain and I'll Run it as I see fit!" sets us up for looking for opportunities for learning, growth, refinement, response-abilities, and success.

> ***#1: Frames govern everything: it is always a matter of frames.***

Now while every game has operational rules, only those who know those rules well are able to play them to their fullest capacity. Further, only those who go on to *master* the rules will be able to play at the masters level. It is in mastering *frame game* rules that we learn *the secrets* of the masters. Then we can use the rules to play with skill, finesse, and elegance.

The key to excellence lies in knowing, practicing, and mastering the rules of the inner and outer games. Learning these rules enables us to learn some of the higher level principles, or secrets, for making the rules work for us. The following offers some of the first secrets about our inner and outer games that we've already covered. These secrets show how the rules operate and what we can do when we know them.

#1: Frames govern everything: it is always a matter of frames.

The frames that we set, that are set for us, and that we buy into *control* our whole mind-body experience and usually do so outside-of-our-awareness. The more outside of awareness the frame, the more it *plays* us. Conversely, the more awareness we develop, the more control we have over the game. Mindfulness of our frames puts us at choice point.

#2: Whoever sets the frame controls the game.
Whoever changes a frame— alters the game.

Someone always sets a frame and whoever sets a frame for a context, area, domain, field, interaction, etc., governs or exercises the most influence over that area. Awareness of frames empowers us for frame setting, changing, and rejecting. If someone is playing a mind game with you, look for the governing frame that you've bought into. What frame has recruited you? How has it recruited you?

> While every game has operational rules, only those who know those rules well will be able to play them to their fullest capacity.

#3: It's never the person, it's always the frame that's the problem.

This rule is also known as, "It's not you, it's the frame, stupid!" To think symptomatically (in terms of symptoms) is to become focused on the person, behaviors, and emotions that result from the frame game. Yet the person and the expressions of the frame are never really the problem, not the ultimate problem. "Problems" only and always arise from *frames*. Where there is "fault," the fault, my dear Brutus, lies not in ourselves, but in our frames.

#4: Frames create and direct focus and perception.

Frames control the shift and concentration of our focus. The structural format of a frame calls attention to the *cognitive content* inside of the frame as it *foregrounds* some ideas, and at the same time, *backgrounds* the shape and form of the frame itself, making it less and less conscious. In this way frames *magically* foreground content and background structure.

> ***#2: Whoever sets the frame controls the game. Whoever changes a frame— alters the game.***

We increase our appreciation of the power and pervasiveness of *frame games* as we realize that they are everywhere. They are as extensive as our thoughts. Even this very moment, as you read these words, how you make sense of these lines occurs within, and through, several frames. You can develop *frame awareness* by asking lots of exploration questions:

- What frames have you brought to this task?
- What frames about reading, learning, and understanding serve you well and which ones do not?
- What frame game would you prefer to be playing?
- Does anything stop you from setting that frame in your mind?

Deepening Understanding of the Rules

We begin with the awesome realization that *frames govern experience (*Secret #1). In this, it's all about frames. This explains the importance of who or what does the frame setting. Because, *whoever sets the frame controls the game* (Secret #2). What's more determinative than a frame? The *person or persons* who set a frame. And those who set the frame may have done so a long time ago, years ago, hundreds of years ago, even thousands of years ago. That's because frames can get set and incorporated in external things: social structures, rituals, in books, laws, inventions, etc. Social norms set frames, so does the very structure of language. Yet since frame setting eventually always goes back to a person, or group of people, any of us as a person can reset a frame. The possibility of experiencing a personal revolution is always that close!

When it comes to most things in human nature that put us to the test and challenge us (i.e., problems, difficulties, mis-communications, etc.) while it may seem that "the problem" is some person, thought, emotion, behavior, etc., that's an illusion. *The problem is always the frame* through which we view and interpret the events.

As our mental and emotional frames structure our perceptions they govern the focus of our attention. What we see and focus on is a function of our frames. Take any situation and notice what you focus on, then step back to ask what others are noticing. What makes the difference? Each person's frame.

I did this recently as I worked with a young man who stuttered. Having heard about the successes of numerous people using Neuro-Semantics to move from stuttering to fluency,[1] he sought me out when I was in his city doing some trainings. When the day of the scheduled consultation came, I asked Adrian, "What's on your mind when you begin to stutter or block your flow of words?"

> *Adrian:* I've got to stop. They won't consider me professional if I stutter and make a fool of myself.

Michael: So you want to stop and you want to come across as professional. [Yes.] That's good. So these are the motives in the back of your mind and you really want this? [Yes.] So when you do begin to get stuck at some word and can't say it fluently, what's on your mind?

> Well . . . What I want to avoid, you know, the stuttering.

Great And how do you represent this?

> I don't know. I just feel tension and a feeling of dread that I'll stutter again and that I don't want to do that.

Where is the tension?

> In my throat . . . And there's a nervous feeling here in my stomach [pointing to his stomach].

Good. Do you feel that right now? [He nodded his head 'yes.'] And if I could peak into the movie theater of your mind at that very moment, what would I see?

> Ah [long pause] . . . Oh yes, you'd see me looking embarrassed and feeling awkward.

You are seeing yourself at that moment? [Yes.] What about the person you're speaking with and seeking to influence? What state is that person in?

> Ah . . . well, no. I just see myself . . . and feel myself in that tension state. I don't see the other person at all. That's weird, I never have noticed this before.

Great. So now, just to explore this, switch the foreground and background around and put the person you're speaking with in the foreground and yourself in that tense, awkward state in the background. . . . [Pause] Have you done that? [Yes.] Good. So what is the color of that person's eyes?

> I don't know. I was thinking about Jim, who is the owner of the company I work for, I always get nervous and stutter with him, and I guess I have never looked at his eyes. That's amazing!

Let's pretend that he has light brown eyes and I want you to look at the color of his eyes *in your mind* and just imagine watching his eye movements, face color, changing facial muscles as he speaks and listens and just imagine talking to him.

> Hum . . . That's really different. The tension has gone away, it's like I'm not focused on me or my stuttering.

Here's the game I want you to play in the next couple of days. I want you to talk with Jim as many times as possible, invent some reason if you have to, and when you do count how many times his eyes move up, move down, and do lateral moves. Are you game?

He was game. Then as he did that in the days that followed, he found that his stuttering and blocking reduced considerably. Later I invited him to do the same with some others in whose presence he felt nervous because he thought they were intimidating, except this time he was to imagine them in a big white diaper and shaking a rattle. Holding that image in his mind while talking with them put him in a very different state, one in which he was able to talk more fluently.

In Gestalt Psychology, a *gestalt shift* occurs when we shift our focus of attention from what's in a frame, or in the center of a picture, to what lies in the background and what has been unattended. This frees us up from the over-control of our frames. After all, it is our frames that bracket some things in and other things out.

When we look at a wood or metal frame of a picture on a wall, the frame itself is typically neither part of the content of the picture, nor part of the wall. Yet if someone picked the frame for both the wall and the picture, the frame may itself play a paradoxical role where it both sustains and confuses the borders and boundaries, inasmuch as it is both inside and outside and at the same time, neither. This can lead to frame ambiguity and confusion. It can elicit a framing dilemma.

In everyday life we experience this whenever we find ourselves in a situation and don't know what it *is,* what it *means*, or what it *asks* of us. "What is this?" we ask, not quite sure about how to take things. Is this a formal occasion, a set-up for a joke, or what? Is this a criticism or a "roast" set up in our honor?

The fourth secret says, "frames create and govern focus and perception." This highlights the fact that our focus results from, and is a function of, our frames. What's your focus of attention? Whatever it is, it comes from the frames you are using. Notice the specific elements and factors in the Old Woman / Young Woman picture. What draws your attention first? If you notice the big nose and tight lips and chin on coat—the gestalt perception of an old woman emerges. If you notice the feather at the top of the hair and the eyelash looking to the left, then the gestalt of the young woman emerges. These facets of the lines operate as attractors —attracting and focusing attention.

#5: It takes frame detection skills to master the inner and outer games.

Awareness of the frame exposes the frame game. It is by shifting from *content* to *structure*, from the thoughts *within* the frame to the shape and form of the higher level *thoughts* that we are empowered to shape and control the inner and outer games. This involves moving *above* and *beyond* the content to the structure or form which operates the higher thoughts *about* the lower thoughts.

#6: The name of the game is to name the game.

When we *name* the game, we expose the *frame* and it typically changes everything. Generally, it's very difficult to continue a toxic game when it has been exposed. So the name of the game regarding sick, toxic, and dis-empowering games is to name the game. Doing so exposes the dragon. In *Dragon Slaying* (2000), we discovered and explored the power of exposure— frequently just naming the dragon is enough to vanquish it.

> ***#3: It's never the person,***
> ***it's always the frame that's the problem.***

Some time in the future when you have finished this book, come back to this chapter and to re-read these pages. As you do, you will find that you will do so with some new and very different frames. When you do this, it will enable you to see, hear, and feel some different things in this text. You will not only have new frames from which to operate, but also the ability to see, hear, and detect *frames*. Perhaps you will even notice some of my frames, the frames that I used in writing this text.

This will open up a whole new world of awareness. It will increase your intelligence and, even more importantly, give you more choice and control over the quality of your life.

Without frame detection skills we live blind to the governing frames that control our lives. As a result, the structural formats of the frames that we absorb and unmindfully accept control our perceptions, thoughts, feelings, behaviors, etc. It scripts for us the roles that we act out, the games that we play, and the possibilities open before us.

#7: Where there's a frame, there's a game nearby, that is, a mind-body state. Where there's a game— there's a governing frame overhead.

Frames create the mental and emotional states that we feel. The thought-and-felt experience of a *state* operates from governing frames. A *state* of mind-body-emotion, as an attitude functions as a holistic mental-emotional energy field, is self-reinforcing. We call this "state dependency," which means the state colors what we see, hear, feel, remember, act, imagine, talk, etc. When *in state,* we see the world from the frame and perspective of that state. States have *energies* which we can learn to see, hear, and feel.

What does any given act, word, tone, or stimuli mean? The frame determines the associative meaning and the conceptual meaning as well as induces a corresponding state. The *meanings* that we experience emerge from the way events and experiences have become associated with other events, ideas, understandings, feelings, etc. Sometimes things get linked together accidently and coincidently, sometimes it happens by design. Sometimes we see and recognize the linkage, sometimes it happens apart from our awareness. However it works, once the association is made, it puts us into *a mind-body state.*

#4: Frames create and direct focus and perception.

At this point, the *state* develops "a life of its own." When that happens our states interpret all other signals and symbols and color them through the frames that drive our states. This explains the rampant subjectivism that we find inherent and inescapable in all human experiences. This subjectivism is "rampant" because we interpret and experience the world *through our own personal states.* Our subjectivity dominates our thinking, feeling, reasoning, and so on.

Without frame detection skills we live blind to the governing frames that control our lives.

At our most "objective" best—we still see, hear, feel, perceive, and experience the world *from out of our subjective histories, perceptions, and emotions.* Yet all too often we don't even recognize our states, our rampant subjectivity, or our states that color the world of people and things that we experience. That's because when our states habituate, we lose awareness of them. We then think and feel that we are experiencing the world objectively for what it is. We don't know, or we have forgotten, that our experiences are all *state-colored.*

It's not the Experience,
It's the Game you play with the Experience

While we think by referencing and representing our experiences, it is actually *not the experience* that determines our beliefs, attitude, skills, or life. Some people experience a traumatic event like being raped, mugged, unfairly imprisoned, or exiled to a concentration camp, and it ruins them. They suffer Post Traumatic Stress Syndrome. Others become stronger, bolder, more resolute, resilient, and even enriched. Yet it is not the experience that determines the reality of what we experience, it is our framing.

Some people grow up in impoverished, toxic, and dysfunctional homes and become "victims," alcoholics, drug users, welfare cases, etc. Oprah Winfrey was raped and violently mistreated in her youth, yet what a different game she plays today and has played most of her life. Sharing her experience, she focuses on her determination in touching the lives of millions and turning people around from victimhood.

> **It's not the experience that makes the difference, it's *the game you play* with it which depends on the frames you set.**

Viktor Frankl noted this principle in his experience of a German Concentration camp during the Second World War. Out of that experience, he set the frame, "They cannot take my ultimate freedom of choosing my own attitude." Giving himself to daydreams about "life after the war and after the concentration camp," he went on to create an entire field of psychology, *Logotherapy,* the healing power of meaning. Believing that experiences do not have to control meaning, he framed the experience as something to conquer.

> ***#5: It takes frame detection skills to master the inner and out games.***

In this, there are no "bad" experiences. And, for that matter, there are no "good" ones. There are just *experiences. Good* and *bad* are our judgments and evaluations about such events—evaluative frames that initiate different games. This is true of our evaluative terms that we can apply to experiences, events, interactions: function/ dysfunctional; supporting/ sabotaging; traumatic/ empowering. These are the *frames* that we bring to our experiences.

Now there's something truly great and wonderful about all of this. It is this principle: *Our experiences do* ***not*** *determine our future.*

Our past experiences do *not* have the power to control our destiny or to fate us to a certain way of thinking, feeling, or acting. Above and beyond *any experience* is *the frame of mind* (or meta-state) that we put on the experience. The creative magic in this realization is that we can rise above our experiences. Like thousands and millions of others, we can *refuse* to give away our power, peace of mind, and future to a historical event—no matter how horrific or dehumanizing.

While doing that may not be easy, it is possible, and is always the way of human empowerment. To do so all you need are the basic *frame game skills* as described throughout this book. You may want to learn how to stubbornly refuse to buy into some default mental program for how to think about a trauma or hurtful event. You may want to learn how to utter a resounding *"No!"* to a certain frame. After all, there are many sick and morbid frames that can undermine personal resourcefulness. You may want to learn the mental skills of changing a frame and setting new frames.

You may want to engage in some discovery of your current frames and then some analysis of what those frames have done for you.

- What experiences have you been through?
- How have the experiences been memorable, significant, and impactful in your life?
- How have you used these experiences for good or ill?
- What games have you played, or are you playing, with those experiences?
- Do they enhance and empower you?
- What game would you be willing to play with those experiences?

From Rules to Mastery Secrets

The *rules* of the games describe how the game works. When we use the term *rule* for the inner game, we simply mean, "This is the way a given kind of thinking, believing, valuing, etc. (framing) works." The rule arises from the nature of our mental mapping, not from an outside authority. Because it is *our* rule, *we* are the authority who sets and enforces it.

> ***#6: The name of the game is to name the game.***

From these *rules* we develop insight and wisdom about how to use the rules in a masterful way. It is this knowledge that describes *the inner secrets* for how to truly win and master our inner and outer games. With practice and continual improvement, we shift our focus from merely following the rules to using our highest insights and wisdom for learning to play the game like a master in that field. These secrets contain the wisdom about how best to play the game using the principles. These secrets are like an insider's understanding about the *frame games* work and how to work them with more finesse and elegance.

Summary

- Everyday we play *frame games.* Setting frames for our inner game enables us to express those frames in the actions of our outer game. This is how our brain and neurology work together. Frame games describe how our minds and bodies work to generate our personal frame world or Matrix.

- Because there are secrets for how *frame games* work, learning them and applying them empower us to get on with taking charge of our inner and outer games and learning to master the games we long to play and win.

- The empowering rules of the inner game are the structural principles that inform us about *how to think or frame* about our mental and behavioral responses as games, how the games work, and how to work with them.

- The *frame games* that we have inherited and learned have tremendous power over us until we develop awareness of them. Awareness moves us to a new place so that we can begin to become a master of our frames. When we master our Matrix of meaning frames—entire new worlds of possibilities open up to us. Are you ready for these openings?

End Notes

1. See the book, *Mastering Blocking and Stuttering: A Cognitive Approach to Achieving Fluency* (2005) by Bob Bodenhamer.

Chapter 5

MULTI-DIMENSIONAL FRAMING

"We call it 'self-awareness'
or *the ability to think about your very thought process.*
This is the reason why man has dominion over all things in the world
and why he can make significant advances from generation to generation.
This is why we can evaluate and learn from others' experiences...
This is also why we can make and break our habits."
Stephen Covey (1987, p. 66)

Here's something that you may or may not know, and yet which is absolutely critical for winning the inner game. *The inner game of our meaning frames is not one-dimensional, but multi-dimensional.* There are layers upon layers upon layers of frames in our inner games. It's this very factor that makes our *inner* games so rich and complex. Yet once we know that they are simply made up of frames within frames, and are able to see the single thread that weaves this dynamic complexity, we are able to suddenly discover the simplicity of the game.

Take, for example, the *inner* game of thinking of yourself as a responsible person. At first glance, it sounds pretty simple, right? After all, how complex could the state of *being responsible* be?

Well, as it turns out, it is very complex. What's required in creating a batch of *responsibility*? First, awareness of our *abilities* to *respond.* To that we then add the state of *willingness* to take ownership of these abilities. Next we add taking *ownership* of thought, feeling, speech, and action. After that comes the willingness to *accept* the consequences for what our responses elicit. To all of that we then add the self-definition that "I'm a responsible person." The formula also includes the willingness to *discipline* oneself in exercising such responsibility. Then we will probably want to add the belief that this is valuable and important. For good measure, let's add *long-term thinking* to project it into our future, and maybe the *joy* of being thought of as a responsible person, etc.

That's a lot more complex than our first thought suggested, isn't it? This also quickly demonstrates the many layered and multiple-dimensional nature of a complex meta-state like "being responsible." Yet while there's obviously some dynamic complexity that makes the state rich with its own uniqueness for each of us, there's also a single simple strand that puts it all together. The whole was put together by simply *meta-stating* each resource as we apply each one to the original and do so until a synergy arises that creates the gestalt state that we call "being responsible."

All of this layering gives us a *simple complexity.* Yet it is by our awareness of the creative itself, and how it works, that we are able to make sense of the detail complexity. Actually, it is only one single process that organizes the many layers of resources. While it's all made out of the same stuff of any ordinary state (thoughts and feelings), and only that, the complexity arises from the weaving. We *weave* these mental-and-emotional states together into a whole as we embed one as the frame of another. In this way we create the multi-layers of our inner games.

By understanding these powers and the pervasiveness of our multi-dimensional frames our understanding expands and so gives us insights about how to work with our frames and games. Then, understanding the *frame games* at play in our lives, we are alerted to the higher levels of mind, levels which typically disappear from our sight. Yet understanding this enriches our sense of *appreciation* for frames and their power.

This appreciation begins as we understand that our basic *referencing* leads to the creation of our *frames.* Then, as we repeatedly use them, they grow up to become our *frames of mind,* and eventually the higher *frameworks* of our reality and personality, the Matrix world within which we live. Understanding this developmental model about referencing and framing deepens our appreciation of the power and influence of our multi-level frames. It heightens our awareness of these higher level structures as we use them as leverage points for transforming frames and playing the games that we choose.

Frame appreciation is an crucial ingredient for remaining open, curious, and positive in our explorations of a matrix. If we resent, hate, or fear frames (ours or another's), we then create an internal battle for ourselves that wastes energy and misdirects focus.

It Takes a Semantic Class of Life to play Frame Games

In mapping distinctions about our *meaning making* powers, Korzybski described us as a "semantic class of life." This phrase describes how we operate as *meaning-makers* due to our lack of pre-programmed instructions ("instincts"). We have the freedom and power to create, invent, and construct meanings. It is in our nature and destiny to *make meaning.* We do this first by simply *linking* things together. We associate internal things with external things. Since meaning does not exist "out there" we create it as a product of our brain and neurology by interacting with the world. Meanings *only* occur in a mind as part of our internal mapping of the world—how we *frame* things. This makes every frame a *meaning* frame.

On the first level, we engage in meaning making by *linking.* We associate a stimulus with some response so that the "stimulus" (S) comes to "mean," equal, or lead to a "response" (R). Similarly, the more intelligent animals create this kind of *meaning* as well. The dogs in the original experiments by the Russian physiologist, Pavlov first saw and smelled a piece of meat. As they did, their autonomic nervous system *reacted* with an instinctual, automatic, and unprogrammed response by salivating. The saliva glands prepare the dog's stomach and organs for eating the meat.

While this was occurring, sneaky Pavlov *rang a bell.* The first time the dog may not have linked up the ringing of the bell to his aroused state of experiencing a full-body response of salivating and therefore not make the connection between bell and meat. Yet, it only takes a few of these events of "bell and the presence of the meat" for the bell to become *associated* with the saliva response. By ringing the bell with the exposure to the meat "at the same time," or in close approximation, the dog's nervous system links the sound of the bell (new stimulus) with his unconditioned response (the salivating). After that, the bell alone can trigger the salivating. Now, for that dog, the ringing *"means"* or "is" food. We call this associative conditioning, learning, meaning, or anchoring. It is the first level of meaning-making.

Framing—Programming for Reactions

After the first level of perception and representation of information and basic structuring of understanding using associations, we move to higher levels of meaning. After the basic level structures of mind and body link, associate, and connect things, we use these associations as *reference points.* Doing so creates our first *frame-of-reference.*

Even dogs do this. Fido now "thinks" of the sound of the bell in a new way. His original experience *sets the frame* for him as he now comes to view the bell as the *signal* for meat. In doggie-think (from what we can tell), Fido treats the bell sounds as being "equal to" and "the same as" the food, and responds as if the bell *equals* the meat. The sound *is* meat. In this, he *confuses* his associative map with the territory. He *identifies* the map (how he codes the bell) with the meat. This confusion shows up in his full-body neuro-semantic state of salivating. Imagine that! A dog salivating to the sound of a bell. How silly! That dog can't eat the bell.

Nor is the dog wanting or intending to eat the bell. The bell *means* something significant to the dog. As the bell now *stands for* the meat in the dog's mind, it operates like a symbol of something else. We humans not only engage in this process as well, but we take it even further. We link things together so that things can now "ring our bells" and get us to react.

In *Mind-Lines: Lines for Changing Minds* I wrote about the following as an example of associative meaning.

> "In one of the big earthquakes that shook southern California in the 1980s—just prior to the quake, a mother became upset with her little five year old for slamming a door in the house. Just as she began a new rebuke and stated that "something really bad will happen if you keep doing this," the little boy slammed the door and then the whole house shook and trembled, dishes crashed to the floor, lamps came tumbling down, etc. This absolutely terrified the little boy—who *in his nervous system*—connected "slamming the door" with causing an earthquake. He also connected, "arguing with mom" as leading to an earthquake."

A very special kind of *"logic"* arises inside our nervous systems when we *associate or link* things. This linkage does not have to fit the criteria for "logical" in any formal sense. It is the "logic" of the primitive mind. It "makes sense" of the world in terms of making simple associations or linkages.

> "This X happened (sassing mom, talking back) and then this Y happened (earthquake, house devastated, emotional state of intense fear, even terror). So X must have *caused* Y. Speaking up to mom is really dangerous, threatening, terror producing."

This kind of thinking in a five-year-old in response to *those events* reflects the best thinking that a child of that age can do. Twenty-year-old minds would not create that map (at least not typically). An adult mind would map it out with a more mature understanding as it could apply other frames-of-references to the situation: knowledge of earthquakes, the ability to separate events that occur sequentially or simultaneously in terms of the concept of "causation," etc.

Yet this is the "logic" of our *psycho-logics*—the "logic" of how we reason to create various classifications and categories in our mind.[1] "This is an example of X." The five-year-old reasoned, "Sassing mom is a member of the class of end-of-the-world-terror," and so it became to him. As the child so maps it out, so he or she *thinks, feels,* and *"knows"* it to be real. It *is* "real" inside the reasoner's body. His very neurology experiences it as "real." The *semantics* that he maps out in his mind, "sassing mom *makes* bad things happen," creates powerful *neurological effects* throughout his entire body, brain, physiology, and nervous system. It induces a *neuro-semantic state of consciousness.*

Now suppose this five-year-old in the earthquake story receives no help for how he maps out the traumatic event of the earthquake. His first mapping might have led him to think and believe that "sassing mom leads to devastating results and ultimate terror." Yet he will not leave the framing there. He will continue generalizing about that event and generalizing about his generalizations. He will layer thought upon thought about things.

"Speaking up is not only really scary, but also physically dangerous."
"It's best not to speak up or do anything that exalts one's will against those in authority."
"To feel safe against the capricious nature of the world, I must "Play it safe, keep quiet, don't cause any ripples."
"I'm just a fearful type of person; I don't have what it takes to stand up for myself in a courageous way or to take risks."

With each belief and conclusion *about* the previous experience and conclusions, he sets yet another *frame* for himself. Each creates a new level of *meaning attribution*. Each constructs his "sense of reality," his model of the world, his cognitive map for how to think, feel, act, speak, relate, etc., in other words, his Matrix. As each embeds all of the others in yet another higher frame, it confirms and validates the others. In this way, the thinking-and-feeling that created the first map becomes more and more entrenched, confirmed, "real," believable, "logical" to that person, and the "program" or game that governs his everyday experiences.

Figure 5:1

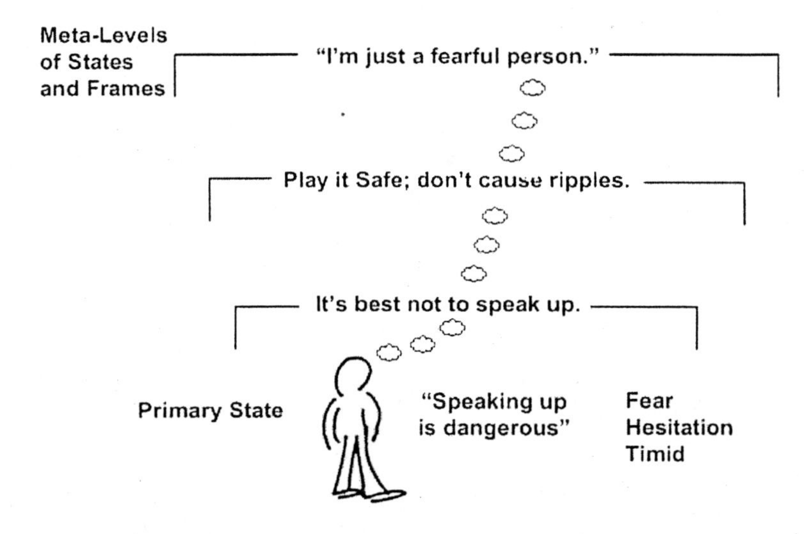

This creates a more complete *frame game*. In this case, we have a terrifying, limiting, non-enhancing, toxic, and non-productive game. It builds up the game *It's a Terrifying World Out There.*

Now imagine the life that Jim (let's go ahead and give him a name) will have as he heads out into the wondrous, bright, and abundant world full of opportunities. Yet with *the* map that Jim has created, with the frames he will use, we can count on Jim will not "see" the world as wondrous, bright, or an abundant world full of opportunities. He will not be able to do that. Not with the frames that he has set in his mind. That will not be *the game* that his *frames* will allow him to play. No way.

With those frames, Jim has to play a very different kind of game. He has to play *a Game of Fear*—fear of speaking up, of asserting himself, of taking chances, of being weak, of "knowing" in his very gut that existential dread can happen to him at any given moment, that insecurity dominates and that it's a terrifying world. His entire neuro-linguistic state, at all of its levels, programs him to *"know intuitively"* that this is so.

How free are we?
We are as free as our frames!

Suppose at this point we ask some philosophical questions. "How free is Jim to change?" "How much will power does he have to choose a new way of being?" The answer is relative, is it not? Jim is only as free as his frames allow him to be.

- What can he do?
- How could he change any of this?
- How could he ever step aside from all of these higher frames and re-program the game so that he doesn't have to salivate in this way?
- How can he rise above this dog's life of stimulus–response?

Not only is Jim *as free as his frames allow him to be,* so are all of us. Frames have that much power. How much freedom do your frames give you? How much choice? How much fun? Love? Power?

Appreciating the Stuff of Framing

To answer these incredibly important questions about our framing, consider how we create our frames.

- What *mechanisms* empower us to "set a frame" in the first place?
- How do we do so? What is the "stuff" out of which we create our frames?

The answer is seductively simple:

> The power to frame and to set a frame begins with our powers of *representation* and extends to our powers of *referencing*.[2]

Our nervous system and brain enable us to make maps or facsimiles *of* things out there in the world. While I know that this over-simplifies the neurological and cortex mapping, it does outline the basic structure of our framing. Given the make-up and construction of our nervous system and bodies, we *take in* the form, shape, and structure of the world out there via our eyes, ears, skin, etc. and construct "an internal map." This becomes at multiple levels, our representing or thinking.

Obviously, the map we construct on the inside is *not* the same as, equal to, or even very accurate to the way things are "out there." Our experience of "seeing," "hearing," "feeling," "smelling," "tasting," etc. depends more on the structure of protoplasm and our nervous system than "the reality" out there. There are all kinds of energies out there that we have no neural mechanism for detecting or recording—such as the electro-magnetic field, ultraviolet light, radar, gravity, electricity, etc.

Actually, *how* we encode and "sense" things inside our minds frequently have little correspondence with what exists "out there." Via our nervous system, we create qualities that do not exist "out there" at all like color. From the differences in the energies that impact our skin, the cones and rods of our eyes generate the phenomena that we experience as "color."

Yet while we inescapably live in a phenomenological world (i.e., world of mental, emotional, conceptual, and neurological phenomena) of our own making, to the extent that our mapping provides us a way to interact effectively with the outside world, it works. To the extent that the structures we create inside enable, facilitate, and empower our navigations in the real world—we have some useful maps and can go places.

At the foundation of mapping is representing. So we *represent* and do so (at the macro-level of our awareness) by using sights, sounds, sensations, smells, tastes, and words to create our internal movie. This describes the first level of mind where we use the sensory-based languages.[3] We *represent* also by using words, symbols, sentences, metaphors, stories, etc. This moves us out of the world of the higher level animals who use *signals* and initiates us into the world of *symbols*. What's the difference?

An animal uses *signals,* not *symbols.* The growl *is* the threat. The showing of the teeth and the snarl *is* part of the threat and so *signals* it. The bell *is* or *signals* the eating response. Our consciousness has allowed us to graduate to the level of *symbols* where we can use completely arbitrary signs, gestures, and stimuli *to stand for* something totally unconnected to it. This allows us to build and use arbitrary symbol systems (languages, music, mathematics, diagrams, scientific formulas, theoretic models, etc.).

When we point with our finger, we usually do not invite the other person to look *at* our finger, but to look *at* our referent—the object our finger is pointing at. In the movie, *City Slickers,* we laughed when the rough and crusty trail boss, Curly, told Mitch, the middle-aged guy from New York City (played by Billy Crystal), who wanted to find his purpose for living, that "the secret of life was one thing." He held up one finger as he said this. That was the cue for actor Billy Crystal to ask, "Your finger?"

With our *representational power* comes our ability to use our symbols *at multiple levels.* So from the "language" of images, sounds, and sensations, we graduate to the symbolic use of linguistics and then onto words about words as we move up into higher and higher levels of abstraction. We begin with *names* for see, hear, feel, smell, taste referents: apple, banana, and grapes. Then we *categorize*: fruit, food, perishable goods, organic substances, agricultural items, etc. As we generalize, we can construct higher level *concepts* and conceptual understandings and then manipulate these "understandings" just in our minds.

Yet the composition of the stuff of our "thoughts" at the higher abstract and conceptual levels remains the same. Regardless of the greater sophistication of our symbolization at the higher levels, we continue to use the same "languages" of the mind. Our pictures may become more like diagrams or formulas, our words may become more obtuse and "thick," and our body sensations may become more subtle, yet they are still pictures, sounds, sensations, words, etc.

***#8:* Our brain frames with the "stuff" of thoughts.**

There's nothing mystical about frames. Frames are made out of the stuff of thoughts. The *material* out of which we *construct* our world of meaning, communication, significance, etc. consists of the fairly fluid and malleable "thoughts" or representations that we entertain. Your *frame brain* frames, and it frames at multiple levels.

Frame Transformation using Thought Stuff

- How can this help Jim to stop playing the *Fear Frame game* and shift to something more enhancing and positive?
- What does all of this have to do with changing the higher frames of Jim's mind which create so much fear and limitation for him?

Everything. Because the very *stuff* that makes up his frames of mind, that makes life painful, torturous, and limited for him, puts into his hands *a most powerful mechanism* for transforming his frames. His "thinking" (which means his full neuro-linguistic processing) creates his distress. So he needs *a different kind of thinking* to change it. None of it is "real" in any ultimate sense anyway. It's all constructed. He mapped it all out in the first place, he installed it in his body as his "reality." This makes it malleable, changeable, and alterable.

He can stop the *frame game* that he has invented for himself and set new frames. How? You'll discover the answer to that in the coming chapters as we detect, shift, refuse, and set frames.

It's important to realize that the problem with Jim is not Jim. There's nothing wrong with Jim as a person. Jim works perfectly well. He built a frame out of the earthquake experience when he linked sassing, speaking up, expressing his frustration, etc. with earthquakes, fear, terror, etc. While it was a "logical" association, it was not useful, enhancing, or empowering. It made sense when he created it at five. It made perfect sense. It just did not serve him well. Nor did it take many other things into account.

With our kind of *frame brains,* we cannot but associate things. Nor can we stop setting conceptual frames *about* that frame. Get use to it. We're a semantic class of life. We play *frame games.* But (and this is a big *but*), we do not have to play any given frame game. No. Actually, we have the freedom to play *any* frame game that we choose to play. If a particular game is not obtaining the results we want, we can alter that frame. Of course, to do so mindfully *detect* our frame games and appreciate that they are but frames and that we're not the problem—the frame is the problem.

> ***#8:* Our frame brain *frames* with the "stuff" of thoughts.**

Summary

- To win the inner game, we need the ability to *appreciate* frames. Appreciation empowers us to enter into the fray of the most intense *frame games* that we inherit and construct.
- The neat thing about frames is that all of our frames are made out of the stuff of thoughts. It's *thoughts* all the way up. It's beliefs all the way up. It's *frames* all the way up.
- Since you have a *frame brain*, and your frame brain *frames,* the quality of your life and experience lies in *the quality of your framing*. You, like, me, are an inevitable frame game player, there's no escape from that. So make the most of it as you play the frame games with courage, mindfulness, and choice.

> ***We have the freedom to play any frame game that we choose to play.***

End Notes:

1. The term *psycho-logics* refers to the face that we are not so much logical as we are psycho-logical in our thinking and reasoning. We reason according to the *logics* that we create via our framing. However we *classify* something determines how we define our sense of what's real and what things mean. This leads to how we interpret and explain things, our exploratory style.

2. At the heart and soul of NLP is representation. The model primarily focuses on what and how we *represent* things. That's why it explores the sensory representation systems and the language representation system in great depth. By way of contrast, the heart and soul of Neuro-Semantics is reference and referencing. It concerns the contextual reference structures or frames within which our representations operate.

3. We have *visual* representations made up of sights, pictures, images, movies, etc. We have *auditory* representations of sounds, tones, volumes, pitches, music, voices, etc. We have *kinesthetic* representations of sensations, touch, pressure, movement, etc.

Chapter 6

FRAME MAGIC

"*Magic is hidden* in the language we speak.
The webs that you can tie and untie are at your command
if only you pay attention to what you already have (language)
and the structure of the incantations for growth . . ."
Bandler and Grinder (1975, p. 19)

If all of life is a game played within a frame which is embedded in yet a higher frame so that it is frames all the way up, and if the quality of our life and performances is a function of our framing, then within the heart of success lies the ability to *see* and to *transform* frames. Success in our *outer* games depends upon our *inner* games. This is great news. It's great news because as framers in our own Matrices, we can take complete charge of our framing.

Now in taking charge of our Matrix, we enter into a very strange world. When Neo was invited to begin to discover the Matrix and learn what *it* is, he was told to "follow the white rabbit." Later when invited to take the red pill, Morpheus said that he would show him "how deep the rabbit hole goes." He then went for a trip into an Alice-in-Wonderland type of world where many of the rules that governed the world he had known no longer worked. He discovered that he had to be trained to learn how to handle the Matrix, to learn a whole new set of rules —rules that sometimes seemed crazy, irrational, non-sensical, and paradoxical. In that world, "there is no spoon" and there is no bending the spoon, there is only our own bending.

This isn't far from the way *the world of mind* works. And that's why there's a disturbing sense of *magic* in our frame games. That's why sometimes the solutions to problems are paradoxical and counter-intuitive. Does this use of the term *magic* seem strange as part of the vocabulary of NLP and Neuro-Semantics? So why do we use this word? It's actually pretty simple. It refers to the quality that seems magical in contrast to our thinking, representing, believing, and framing being *logical*. Bateson (1972) noted this property of "magic" regarding the world of communication, mind, and information in these words:

> "This, I think, is what people mean by magic. The realm of phenomena in which we are interested [psychological, mental, communicational, etc.] is always characterized by the fact that 'ideas' may influence events." (p. 229)

There it is! *Ideas may influence events.* This formula obviously does *not* work in the external world of forces and energies. You can say *Abracadabra* to the side of a mountain until you're out of breath and it will not cause a secret door to open. You can say, *"Let there be light!"* when you walk into a dark forest, but that will not turn the light of the sun on. Nor does the *idea,* wish, or prayer of winning the lottery make it so. Wish for a million dollars all you want, but wishing alone will not increase your assets. In these areas, *ideas* alone, ideas without action, will *not* influence events.

> "The realm of phenomena in which we are interested is always characterized by the fact that 'ideas' may influence events."
> Gregory Bateson

Yet in the world of thought, communication, and meaning, *ideas can and do influence events.* How we think, and the ideas we entertain do effect our sports performances, emotional states, health, relationships, and a thousand other things. We can worry ourselves into illness and disease. So what did Bateson mean when he used the term "magic?" I'll let him answer for himself:

> "It might well be sufficiently confusing to be told, that according to the conventions of communication in use at the moment, anything can stand for anything else. But this realm of magic is not that simple." (p. 230)

In reference to the realm of communication or mind, he used *magic* to refer to the cognitive-neurological understanding about how *ideas can influence events.* Why does this seem magical? Because in the realm of symbolization we can *turn some things into other things* by simply calling them by new names. Since the classes and categories (frames) only exist in human minds in the first place, we can perform *mind magic* by exchanging symbols and reclassifying events. This enables us to *spin* things around to create a new perspective.

- That's not laziness; that's the exquisite ability to relax under the most harrowing of pressures!
- That's not insult at all; that's being ruthlessly honest.
- Betrayal? That's not betrayal, that's the wisdom of recognizing a higher priority in the midst of a crisis.

When we don't like the magic, we say, "Ah, yes, the spin doctors have been at it again!" When the magic transforms our lives and gives us a new lease on life, we say that we have attained a higher truth and have gained a transcendent insight and wisdom.[1] In both cases we use the magic of words to frame or reframe reality, and so our world transforms.

As a symbolic-class of life we can so manipulate symbols in the process of mapping and navigating life, that a wide range of things (although as Bateson noted, not "anything") can *stand for* many other things. This symbolic flexibility explains a great deal about our "psycho-logics." It explains how radically our meanings, experiences, understandings, and emotions can shift and change as if they were completely fluid. When that happens, our Matrix bends and sways to our command. In *The Matrix* movie, Morpheus said that there was a man born when the Matrix was first created who could change it at will. This explains the wide range of experiences people can have with the same event. It explains the extremes that we can create in our meaning making, from the pathology of psychosis to the excellence of genius.

In a dimension where so many *things can stand for other things* and where *ideas* influence events, we have to shift our expectations about how our *psycho-logics,* and those of others, work. The structuring that we experience "on the inside" emerges almost entirely from our thinking and framing. We *invent* it! The world of communication with its "dynamics" (which we experience somatically in our body as "emotions" and "motivations") operates from higher and higher levels of "magic." Again, Bateson (1972) wrote:

> "All communication has this characteristic—*it can be magically modified by accompanying communication."* (p. 230, italics added)

How can we *magically modify* one communication message or representation? We do so by simply using other communication messages and putting one into a meta-relationship to another. One message then relates to another as *its frame.*

For example, we do this when we speak with our fingers crossed behind our back. The crossed-fingers *stand for* and mean, at a higher level, that we do not mean and won't stand good for whatever we're saying. As a meta-message *about* the words, the crossed-fingers modify the lower-level message. Every meta-level thought, emotion, or state performs this kind of magic, it is the transformative power of the governing frame that makes reframing and meta-stating so powerful. If I tell you, "I've had my fingers crossed when I said that," I am commenting on my crossed-fingers meta-message which, in turn, sets a new frame.

Inviting a Game that will Improve Things

Shirley was the kind of person who loved being the fastest and the best and she had certificates to prove it. Yet she also did so at the expense of skipping some of the rules, especially whenever she thought they were unnecessary or just plain stupid. Her inner game? *Rules are for Other People.*

Then the day came that she got caught. One day a supervisor inspecting her work discovered that she had violated the company rules about leaving her government postal vehicle running during a stop while she left to grab some food. That was a major violation of the rules.

What was her frame of mind upon getting caught red-handed doing something that violated the rules? Anger and frustration. She was mad as hell and turned her fury loose on her supervisor as she got into a yelling match. Why? What frame drove that response? "I can't be wrong." The rule to this game was, "To be wrong is to be a bad person."

So she adopted the worse type of "union attitude" in her place of business and tried to shift the focus to the supervisor having no right to boss her around or discipline her and that they were violating her rights as an employee. These were her defensive games.

So when one supervisor lowered the boom, telling Shirley what was and what was not acceptable, the exchange escalated into a yelling match. In this, the games were getting worse as they were becoming less productive. Now she was playing, *"Nah, nay, nay, nay, nay!! You can't make me!"*

It was at that point that Cheryl, another supervisor, called Shirley into her office. The first thing Cheryl said was, "Shirley, how can we improve this issue? What would make things better for you?"

Using this *defusing frame,* the supervisor then sat back and just let Shirley unload all of her complaints and gripes. At first this caused her to become even more emotional, so the supervisor asked,

> "I find it really interesting how you're behaving right now. And I'm wondering, are you doing this intentionally or have you lost control?"

This framing question completely interrupted Shirley. In fact, it interrupted her so much that she temporally couldn't say anything. And even though she was almost at a pitch of hysterics, the question caught her off guard. In interrupting the old state and game, it simultaneously launched a new game and Shirley was clueless about how to play, whether to play, or what to do to begin.

Shirley's first impulse was to say that she couldn't help herself . . . but she knew that if she said that she was "out-of-control," well, that was not exactly the way she wanted to present herself given the circumstances. As she thought about it, she eventually eked out in a mild little voice that she guessed it was intentional.

> "Then obviously, if you decided, you could lower your voice and allow us to solve this like two professionals looking for the best solution, couldn't you?"

And that's exactly what happened. Cheryl later commented to me that the almost instantaneous change in Shirley was so shocking that it was "as if some magic had been conjured up."

The Magic of Framing and Reframing

Have you ever experienced *magic* in a new meaning? Have you ever heard something that changed your mind so suddenly and profoundly that everything changed in a moment? In that instant, your emotions changed, your perspective shifted, you became different in your very personality. Perhaps you thought your best friend betrayed you and took you to the cleaners, and then you found out that he had been tricked in the same way so that yet another person was the responsible culprit.

You thought the jerk who sped past you in traffic on the interstate, weaving in and out of traffic was "an idiot who should be locked up." Then you hear on the radio that a good Samaritan had rescued three wounded children from a shoot-out and raced through town to the hospital with them in the back of his car. This happened to me once while driving in St. Louis. The "idiot" who zoomed past me on the interstate and flew across three lanes of traffic to dash off on an off-ramp got my blood boiling. "Did anyone see how he was driving?" "Where are the cops when you need them?"

> "All communication has this characteristic
> *—it can be magically modified*
> *by accompanying communication."*
> Gregory Bateson

I continued my trip downtown to a meeting and then, three hours later, while returning home along the same highway and listening to the news I discovered something about that "Idiot Driver," who he was and what he did. Talk about a shift of perspective. One moment, I thought about my experience using "the idiot driver" frame, a moment later I shifted to the "Good Samaritan" frame. One moment I was angry, the next in awe of the person as well as ashamed of my knee-jerk reaction that was so fast to jump to such conclusions.

Suppose you are tired and on a long international flight of fifteen hours and then there are two children immediately behind you crying, kicking, constantly moving, making noise, etc. Imagine feeling angry and irritable and getting to the point where you just can't take it anymore so you voice your anger only to find out that the children have just lost both parents in an accident and are being taken to a foster home. Would that change your frame?

Our *frames of mind,* by which we reference things govern, modulate, organize, drive, and control our *experiences*. They govern and organize the way we think, feel, talk (language), behave, and respond. When we set a frame, the frame creates a conceptual context that determines the consequences that follow. A *psycho-logical fate* inevitably follows. This effect of frames not only makes them crucial and determinative, but endows them with what can sometimes seem like "magical" powers.

Many use the *History is Fate* frame and play that game. For them, they can only see today and the future only in terms of what has been. Ben was like that.

> "I just can't see how that will work out. We've tried at least four times and it never has succeeded. And I don't want to go through the disappointment again."

What a different frame game comes into being, along with new experiences, if one uses *The Future is Wide Open* frame. Here one's thinking and feeling is magically different:

> "What I do today really counts. It creates the future. The choices I make and actions I take empower me to be the architect of a new future."

As long as we operate from one frame of mind, certain things inevitably follow. We feel, experience, talk, behave, etc. in a particular way. It fits the frame. That's the game we play. When the frame changes, or we use a different reference system to make sense of things, it results in behaviors, talk, feelings, and thinking that radically differ. When the frame shift occurs quickly, the results can seem miraculous or magical. The resulting transformation may seem to defy explanation. At such moments we sense that reality ought to be more solid, secure, and less amenable to such disruptions.

Playing the frame game of *"Give Me A Quick Fix"* sets into motion a very different kind of set of choices and actions than does the frame, "Let's Invest the Time and Energy to do an Excellent, High Quality Job." It costs less in terms of time, trouble, and energy if we put some effort into it than if we want to find the easy and quick tricks, "The Path of Least Resistance."

Because we use the "languages" of the mind to encode our frames, especially the linguistic systems, when we suddenly hear a powerful expression that totally transforms a *frame game,* it transforms our meanings at a higher level. A new frame pops into mental existence which calls forth new perceptions, experiences, and skills. This change creates an effect that seems like magic. Everything transforms. New realities pop into existence. There's now a *new game in town.*

The Magic is in the Higher Frames

The magic is in the framing and, as noted, in the higher framing we think and reflect back onto ourselves. We think *about* our thoughts, experience feelings about feelings, concepts about concepts, etc. By simply reflecting back onto our previous states we create meta-states, new layering of states-*about*-states which sets up new framing.

What state of mind, emotion, or body do you typically experience when you get frustrated? Whatever your answer, you just set a higher frame of *that* thought, feeling, or physiology *about* the previous state.

- Anger about your frustration: angry frustration.
- Guilt about your frustration: guilty frustration.
- Frustration about your frustration: frustrated frustration.
- Depression about your frustration: depressed frustration.

In each of these responses we have set a *negative emotional frame* of judgment, attack, and insult to the experience of feeling blocked or frustrated. And, more often than not, bringing a negative evaluation *against* ourselves in this way, creates even more internal stress and makes things worse. This creates various games:

- The *Self-Contempt* game
- The *If It Wasn't for Me, I'd Be Just Fine* game
- The *Look at What an Ass I Am* game
- The *What's Wrong with You that You Can't Be More Perfect* game.

In these games we reject, taboo, despise, and judge various facets of our self and personality. This, in turn, leads us to use various "defense mechanisms" to *not* know the truth about ourselves. It leads to denying, repressing, projecting, internalizing, etc.

"Magic" happens when we detect and transform our meaning frames.

But suppose we set some different frames about frustration. Suppose we reflexively bring back some positive ideas regarding frustration. Suppose, that instead of bringing some negative thoughts-and-feelings against ourselves, we set a more neutral or positive frame of reference.

- *Acceptance* about your frustration: welcomed frustration.
- *Curiosity* about your frustration: learning about frustration.
- *Anticipating* what *good* will come out of this frustration: anticipatory frustration
- *Calmness/Relaxation* about frustration: calm frustration.
- *Loving self and others*: thoughtful, considerate frustration.

How about those frames? These would establish very different frame games. Do you think of them as strange altered states of consciousness? Would you like to go there? Would accessing such frames give you a more resourceful handle on things? What game would they create?

If we play the *I'm Okay* game, or even better, the *My Self-Esteem is a Given* game, then we don't move through life feeling that either we or others are broken, defective, or substandard. We're just perfectly fallible human beings. Nothing more; nothing less.

All of this leads to the next secret of frame games, a secret that I think you'll want to integrate until it becomes part and parcel of how you think and operate.

> ***#9: "Magic" happens when we detect and transform our meaning frames.*** Words can magically make frames appear, disappear, and re-appear. Reflectively thinking about our thinking patterns (meta-thinking, meta-emoting) empowers us to set any frame that we choose. We can now use this power for tearing down frames, loosening frames, switching to better frames, and setting higher frames, etc. Our *word magic* which creates frames can also deframe, reframe, and outframe. We can now tap into the neuro-semantic levels of meaning making.

Summary

- Shifting a frame works *magic-like* transformation, giving us a new lease on life. As a semantic-class of life, we inevitably and inescapably use symbols which, in turn, completely govern the kind and quality of experiences that we experience.

- The magic lies in the framing and the meta-framing that creates new psycho-logics for our meaning-making and explanatory style. Are you ready for some new psycho-logics? What new frames would you like to set to create a new logical system?

End Notes

1. For more about this kind of communication "magic" within our inner Matrix, see *The Structure of Magic (1975), The Source Book of Magic (1997),* and *Communication Magic (2001).* Given that Bill O'Reilly puts forth the possibility of *no spin*, you might want to check out an article on "The Spin of the 'No Spin Zone'" on the website, www.neurosemantics.com.

Chapter 7

FRAME DETECTION

Once you see the bigger picture of the patterns
at work in your life, *the game can't play you.*
Catching the frame games robs them of their power.
Awareness breaks the spell of the hypnotic induction.

"Frames organize more than meaning,
they organize involvement."
Erving Goffman

Here's a thought experiment. Imagine that you and some friends have decided to play a game on someone and that you've decided to *not* let that person know what you're doing. You designated them as *the target*—the patsy. In game terms, they are *it.* Yet they don't know that they are *it.* As you play the game with them, you make moves with each other by the way you talk, signal, act, and relate. Both the meaning and impact of this game occurs entirely outside of the patsy's awareness.

The story is told, whether apocrypha or not I don't know, of a psychology class that decided to test Pavlovian conditioning principles on their professor. When he stood on the left side of the room, the students all acted disinterested. They slowly moved their attention away from him. They yawned and acted restless. When he moved to the right side, they perked up their attention, looked more interested, maintained eye contact, took notes, and asked questions. Of course, with that interplay of reinforcements, it wasn't long before they conditioned their professor to go to the right side of the classroom.

While this was a harmless game, the students fully delighted in it. They especially delighted in *the power* that they discovered in providing positive and negative reinforcements for a piece of behavior outside of the learned professor's awareness. And this delight was magnified by the fact that the very professor who taught them the reinforcement principle didn't see it happening. In this, the students learned how they could subtly shape another person's behavior. As a *frame game,* they played the *Reinforcement game.*

This illustrates one of the ways that we learn to play the *inner and outer games.* Here the students learned something and consciously used that learning to *set a frame.* They collectively set up an outcome (shaping the professor's behavior) along with a set of actions (reinforce the right side, negatively reinforce or extinguish the left side responses).

Becoming conscious of higher level patterns, frames, meanings, intentions, etc. enables us to design and play the games we want to play.

Unaware of *the meta frames* guiding the responses of his class, the professor did not have a clue as to what was occurring at that higher level of structure. He didn't see *the pattern* as it was occurring. Why did he not see it? Caught up in the *content* of his subject, he detected no *pattern* in the interest or disinterest of the students. Such did not even cross his mind. It's funny how we can see what we care about and focus on and miss what we don't. Yet while the professor was not conscious of the pattern, he was simultaneously *responsive* to the positive and negative feedback as the class shaped his behavior without him being any more the wise to it.

This story tells about the power of awareness and of unawareness. Becoming conscious of higher level patterns, frames, meanings, intentions, etc. enables us to design and play the games we want to play. Lack of such awareness makes us puppets to the frames that families, cultures, societies, governments, schools, advertisers, marketers, etc. establish. That's when some Matrix *has* us. That's when we need to wake up to the Matrix of frames that we live within.

Frame Detection Skills

Do you want to become a master in developing your skills in *detecting frames*? The challenge is to learn to think in terms of meta-level patterns. We develop this skill as we use our self-reflexive consciousness to reflect on our frames and those of others, and to *step back* in our mind to consider what *frames-by-implication* are also present. Every time we step back and reflect on our thoughts, feelings, states, etc., we cultivate this ability of mindful awareness of our experiences.

Learning to think in meta-levels empowers us in stepping aside from the juicy content of the details and the story to view things in terms of structure, pattern, shape, and form. This is truly a different kind of thinking and a different kind of intelligence. Yet in the end it lifts us to a whole new level of perspective and enables us to transform our frames from a structural level.

Game Consciousness: Tools for Detecting Games

Alfred Korzybski called this ability to detect frames, "consciousness of abstracting." It's a higher level awareness, a thinking about our thinking—what we today call *meta-cognitive skills*. With this higher level awareness we are then able to detect the content, form, shape, nature, and quality of our thoughts. We are able to hear and see frames and their derivative games.

- How do we become aware of the *frames* and *games* that we're playing?
- How do we become better at *frame detection* in our communications and interactions with others?
- What tools, processes, and techniques can we use to flush out the *frame games* incorporated in the corporate culture at work, the culture of our family, or even those incorporated in our minds from our youth?

The miracle of detection begins as we pay attention to and look for frames. When we do, we begin noticing them everywhere. This allows us to begin taking inventory of our frames.

Becoming a Meta Detective

To become skilled in frame detection you only need the ability to *step back* (in your mind) from your thinking, feeling, and experiencing to take a larger and broader perspective of things. What happens when you conceptually step back from your immediate experience? Your awareness is shifted from *content* to *structure,* and that initiates the adventure of beginning to see and hear the Matrix.

After you have stepped back, ask questions about the form, shape, process, and structure of the thinking and framing.

- What kind of thinking are you (or another) doing?
- What is the context of the thinking?
- What factors are influencing it?
- What frames may be in the background of the mind?

"I'm just ashamed of my anger, that's all." Ah, here *shame* (as an emotion and a state) stands in a meta-position to anger. The shame is *about* the anger. The content is anger, but the meta-frame above and beyond it is shame. So while we first note the anger, the step back and meta-perspective begins to identify the person's feelings *about* the anger. Relationally, as shame is meta to the anger, it sets the frame for it.

Next use the meta-states diagram to sketch this out for yourself. Do it on paper or just in your mind. Sketch out a diagram of the relationship by first noting the beginning state, then the second as a higher classification of it.

- When you feel shame about your anger, what does that bring out in you?
- Is anger shame in itself or is there something about your anger that you believe is shameful?
- How shameful is this anger? What would make it more shameful? What would make it less shameful?

Figure 7:1

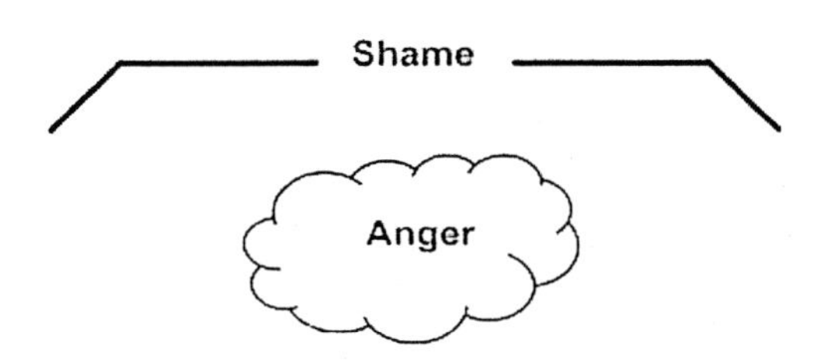

To *detect meta-levels,* look and listen for "meta" terms. The key ones include: about, of, relating to, in terms of, first, second, then, higher, back of the mind, what's uppermost is, on the whole, etc. These are the kind of terms that cue us about a meta-level or position that classifies that embedded experience and creates its psycho-logics.

> What happens when you conceptually step back from your immediate experience? It shifts your awareness from *content* to *structure.* And with that, the adventure of beginning to see and hear the Matrix is initiated.

To flush out the meta-levels, use a series of "about" questions. The first about will inquire about the person's first level reference ("out there"), then it will invite the person to a second level reference ("in the mind"), and then on up the levels to the embedded frames.

- What are you angry *about*? (Primary level)
- What do you feel *about* being angry? (First meta-level)
- And what do you think or feel *about* that? (Second meta-level)
- Okay, when you think or feel that, what do you believe *about* that?
- Hmmm, and what do you value *about* that?

About questions give us a special ability to move up into the Matrix of a person's meaning frames to explore the ever higher levels of thinking and referencing. With each jump we move up into the more influential frames. In the *Diamond of Consciousness* diagram, there are 26 categories of terms that give us hundreds of meta-questions that you can use as a meta-detective.[1]

All of this allows us to move to a position from which we can reflect on the layers of embedded frames that create the mental contexts of our framing. Doing this uses the basic meta-stating process for discovering the next highest level and the frames that govern that level.

As a meta-detective our ability does not stop with the first level, nor the tenth, nor even the hundredth. We can always access yet another thought, feeling, awareness, etc. *about* a previous thought. We can always say something else about whatever we have said. We have that much flexibility within our self-reflexive consciousness. Within it we can find an infinite regress of responses as we also create an *infinite progress* of new frames.

With every jump to the next higher level, we flush out and can detect even *higher frames.* Typically, however, usually within five to seven levels we begin to loop around, moving up and then down and then up. This typically indicates that the person is using synonyms for the same meta-level state and is at the top of his or her Matrix. We have come to the end of our mental mapping about that particular subject. Having not mapped things any further, we have come to *the edge of our model of the world.* At this point, you will hear *edge of the map* words:

- "That's just the way it is."
- "There's nothing more."
- "It's just ..."
- "I don't know."

Playing the Meta-Detective Game

The first time that I consciously played *the Meta-Awareness Game,* and knew that I was playing it, I was riding with my colleague Dr. Bob Bodenhamer. We were out for a drive in the Appalachia mountains of North Carolina as Bob was showing me the area. During the drive we decided to explore our governing and operational frames. So from time to time, regardless of what we were talking about, one of us would ask the reference question:

- What frame-of-reference are you using as you say that?
- What are you referencing now?
- What ideas or principles are you assuming are true to say that?

Such questions would stop the conversation at the content level as we would then move up to our higher frames. Sometimes it would evoke memories of experiences (the memory frame). Sometimes it would elicit references about ideas, principles, concepts, and learnings (conceptual understanding frame). Sometimes it would evoke emotions as it would put us more in touch with some strong values, beliefs, or memories (value frames). As we talked, we knew that it really didn't matter where the conversation would take us, we were more interested in the process. So we would then repeat the meta-questioning of our frames:

- Okay, and given that, what references do you have for that?
- How do you know that you know, feel, believe, or value that?
- What has to be true in order for you to think that?
- What class or category is this an instance of?
- What generalization have you created about that?
- When and where did you come up with that?

This enabled us to explore the higher ideas "in the back of our minds" about health, exercise, faith, investment, career, relationships, the seminar business, writing, etc. Use these meta-questions as you begin. They will give you the ability to flush out higher frames and to detect them.

Jill's Spiraling Meta-Muddle

Jill was angry (level 1). In fact, she felt extremely angry because she lost her job as a teacher. They said she was too rigid and harsh with the children, too perfectionistic, and demanding. Yet because she didn't think this was accurate, she disagreed with their evaluation. She didn't see it that way at all. For months before the firing, she defended herself by saying that she was "just demanding high standards." Eventually, however, they fired her.

The firing put her into a real funk: angry, frustrated, ashamed, upset, and confused. In that state, she wasn't very pleasant to be around. Her boyfriend Fred said that she seemed like "a real bitch" to live with. Again, she didn't think so.

"Why doesn't he understand? Why can't he be more sympathetic?"

So, in an attempt to make things better, they argued. Eventually the arguing turned into just straight out yelling which again didn't help matters. Things were in a negative downward spiral and getting worse. Jill even knew that her anger was making matters worse, and she tried to cool it, but she couldn't. Eventually Fred had enough and left.

When that happened, Jill felt *ashamed* of her anger. She also *hated* her anger (level 2). But in shaming and judging her anger, that only caused her to start to hate herself (level 3). "Why am I this way? What's wrong with me?" These were the questions she mused on. "Why can't anything work out for me?"

Eventually she decided that she was inferior, that she was deprived and abused as a child, and that her father was her chief reason for being the way she was —perfectionistic, hard, demanding, etc. (level 4). Of course, he was dead, so she blamed her mother.

On each level Jill framed things and so played different *frame games*.

- Level 1: she played *"I'm Damn Angry and Have Every Right to Be!"*
- Level 2: *"It's Such a Shame to Suffer From Such an Uncontrollable Anger!"*
- Level 3: *"Woe is Me! I'm So Messed Up, Always Have Been/ Always Will Be!"*
- Level 4: *"If It Weren't For Dad, I'd be Okay!"*

When Jill eventually showed up for therapy, a psychologist stuck the label "manic depressive" on her which then allowed him to play the medication game with her. Given that experience, she set yet another frame, *"It's All True—I Am Screwed Up and Don't Deserve to Live."* At first this was not a conscious awareness. It was more of a feeling, a vague sense that something was not right. Frames are like that. We *feel* them long before we recognize them consciously and understand them. She also began acting out that frame of desperation as she engaged in some futile and pathetic attempts at suicide.

Figure 7:2

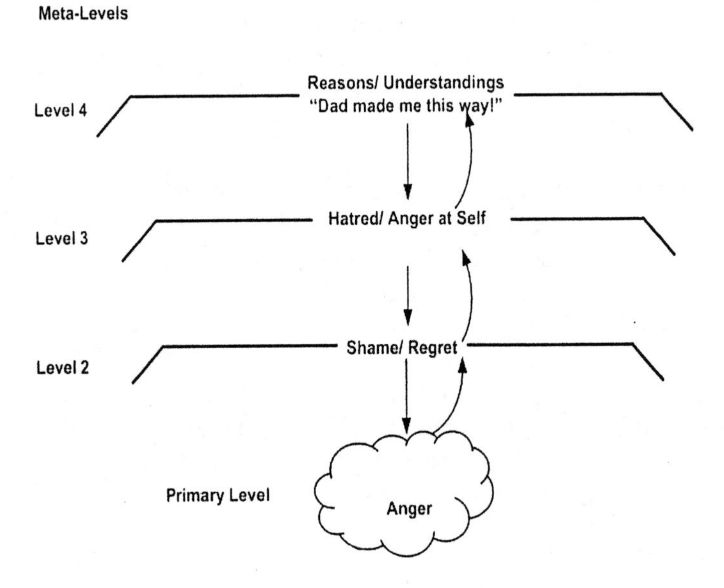

When I first met Jill, my sense was that the central problem was *the way she thought* about all of this. The style of her thinking itself not only made the problem worse, *her framing was the problem.*

Her learned and practiced way of framing was her biggest problem. The more she thought that way, the more she went into state, the more her thinking became even more state-dependent or *frame-dependent.* This means that once in that state or frame of mind, we *see* things through the filter of that frame. The frame then governs how we perceive. It runs our attention filters. All of this traps us in a double-bind. The very *kind of thinking* by which we created the problem now governs and prevents us from engaging in a different kind of thinking. Talk about framing oneself into a corner!

Jill's demanding and perfectionistic frame of mind[level 1] led to her harsh judgments of shaming herself[level2], which led to her even harder judgments of her "self"[level3], and which led to her demanding and judging attitudes[level4]. This frame of mind then made her very quick to reject, discount, and downplay any small improvement, any small success, any small anything. In fact, she was highly skilled at discounting. No one could have beat her at the *Discounting* game, she was a true master!

With every family member, friend, and therapist who even broached this subject, Jill would see, hear, perceive, reason, and feel *from those frames.* She heard their advice as "put downs." She read them as implying that she was "defective." This gave her more reasons to feel bad. Caught up in this negative spiral of frames made her seem like a tough customer.

Eventually, however, she set an even higher frame as she found one source of pleasure, namely, she could defeat the most skilled clinicians from helping her! Her *game* at that point was an advanced version of *"Yes, But..."*. It was:

> *"Try in Vain to See if any of Your Feeble Maneuvers Can Help Me, You Son of a Bitch!"*

Of course, this wasn't conscious either. Though she was feeling completely unloved and powerless, she was doing the best she could given her frames. It is recognizing this that enables us to see the real problem—*the frames* in which she was caught. Yet, since higher frames govern lower ones, all of this allowed very little possibility of transformation. It locked her into a Matrix of pain and despair. She was not really "a Manic-Depressive." The problem was not Jill. It was her frames. If I used those frames, I'd be just as miserable, stuck, and crazy as she felt, and I would behave in similar ways.

The name of the game is to name the game.

What's the end of the story? You'll find out in a later chapter when we will return to Jill. For now our focus is on the skill of *detecting frames.* Later we will specify some powerful *frame games* to counter that one in order to transform even a "reality" like that.

Frame Detection through Naming

Naming frames and naming games is a great way to detect, identify, flush out, and remember frames. Bob and I have found it very effective when we counsel, consult, or do a demonstration in a training. The simple act of *giving a frame a name* somehow gives it more reality and makes it more tangible. This highlights one of the key secrets and principles of *frame games. "The name of the game is to name the game"* (#6). It's the closest we can come to putting a finger on a frame.

- "Ah, look! There it is. *The Blame Frame.* See it lurking around on the edge of consciousness!"
- "Say, isn't this the *Play it Safe* frame?"
- "You know, this sound kind of like the *Ain't our Aches and Pains Terrible?* frame. What would you call it?

- "Is this the *Path of Least Resistance* game that's going on?"

There's one really neat thing about *naming a frame*—you don't have to get it right. If a name doesn't work, try another. Keep doing this until you find one that fits. This frees us to take the risk, give it a name, and then see if the name fits. It may not. If it doesn't, no big deal. You'll correct it or the recipient will correct it.

"That sounds like the *Ain't it Awful!* frame."

"No, it's not that. I'm just feeling down today and, I don't know, I just need to get this off my chest. That's all."

"Oh, the *Blowing off Steam* frame."

"Yeah, that's it. Just blowing off steam."

I used to do this all the time when I saw couples in my private counseling practice. I'd begin with something like, "Terri, that sounds like *the Blame Frame* to me."

"The what?"

"You know, *the Blame Frame* like there has to be someone to blame and so the game that you have to play with Todd is one where someone has to become the bad guy."

"Yeah, Todd is always blaming me and trying to make me feel bad."

"So you play *the Blame Frame* right along with Todd? Well, that makes sense. After all, it takes two to play *the Blame Game.*"

"But he always starts it. I wouldn't do it at all if he didn't start it."

"Ah, so you play *the Blame Frame* about who's the bad guy who starts it?"

Silly grins started to appear about this point in the conversation. It's like we have put a spotlight on the culprit—we blame *the Blame Frame.* The culprit is neither person, it is the *frame.* It's the game that's messing up the intimacy and love. Then comes admissions:

"Yeah, I guess we do play *the Blame Frame* with each other."

"So do you get a lot of mileage out of it in terms of being the loving intimates that you wanted when you first got together? Does it make your life a party? Does it cause you to melt into each other's arms?"

"Yeah, really!"

"So would you like to give *the Blame Game* a severe kick in the butt? Would you like to boot it completely out of your intimate conversations, love making, and creative problem solving?"

"Sure."

"No really, I'm serious here. You're going to lose a lot and give up a lot if you do some serious butt-kicking here. If you decide to stop playing *the Blame Game,* you won't get the juicy delight of making the other wrong and feeling the self-righteous superior feelings over the other. That's a lot to give up, you know. I mean, what will you replace those feelings with? I don't think you're ready to just be loving and thoughtful or to lust after each other's bodies, or learn to enjoy some recreation activities that might make you grow.What do you think?"

In all of this, the name of the game is to name the game. Name and confirm the *frame games* to first of all detect it. Enjoy the process as you.

> "So you're playing the *X* game?"

The "What Comes to Mind" Detection

- When you think about confronting someone with something unpleasant, *what comes to mind*?
- When you consider exercising, *what comes to mind?*
- How about criticism? What *frame games* emerge and rush into your awareness using that question?

You can also use the *What comes to mind . . . ?* question as a discovery tool. Sigmund Freud happened upon this *thought intrusion* technique. Relax and just let whatever *comes to mind* emerge without censoring it. Just notice what bubbles up into your awareness.

The thoughts and feelings that *come to mind* then indicate some of the outside-of-awareness references that influence and govern our lives. It's a great detective tool. I used it once with Brad when he offered an explanation of his internal dread. Notice the open-ended invitation to just allow the old frames, mental frames and emotional frames to emerge with no judgment, nor even trying to fix them. The governing frame was not detected with the first or second question, but the fourth, which I then highlighted through the use of exaggeration.

> Brad: "I know that I probably look successful on the outside, and in some ways I am. I have a real knack for making money, lots of it. I have friends, but inside I feel like I'm always on the precipice, ready to fall into a deep cavern. Sometimes the stress and anxiety gets so bad that I think I'll have a heart attack."

From?

> "I fear that I'll be more successful than my dad."

And?

> "Well, that would be betrayal." [Breathing heavy, feeling agitated.]

Oh, really? How so?

> "It would show him up."

So that's what you think? And your dad has said that he would not like or appreciate it if you became more successful than him? Is that what you're recalling?

> "Oh no. He would never say anything like that. He would deny it. But I know that it would devastate him."

Devastate him, huh? That's pretty strong stuff. He would fall apart, commit suicide, or do something destructive if you allowed yourself to become more successful than him? I guess his very life really is in your hands. If we were to name this game that you're playing, what would you call it?

Well, that did it. Brad didn't even have to answer the question. A silly grin appeared as he suddenly heard what he was saying and with that realization, the frames went pop.

Detecting Frames through Behaviors

As a skilled Frame Detective, you know that the *inner* game of our frames inevitably leads to the *outer* game of our actions and behaviors. So we can start with the behaviors and backtrack to the frames. Obviously when someone has slumped shoulders, downcast eyes, mumbling voice, vacant look, and so on, there's a high probability of reflecting a depressive frame unless the person is on stage as an actor in a play. A clinched fist, tight neck and vocal chords, restricted breathing, and flushed face probably indicates a stress or anger frame.

Not only do *frames drive behaviors*, but *behaviors* can also induce, elicit, and can even create frames. Because mind-body operates as a system of interactions, we can use actions and behaviors to backtrack to their frames. After all, we act, move, behave, relate, speak, etc. due to our understandings and perceptions. But what? What frame drives a given behavior?

We can not only set frames via overt symbols that we encode through a complex symbolization system like language, we can also set frames by gestures, tones, movements, actions, rituals, humor, etc. In this, there is a whole domain of principles for learning how to "calibrate" to a person's sets of behavioral responses as we read one's body language.

We have to use "language" here very carefully. "Body language" does *not* represent a systematic and well codified system like English, German, Spanish, or other true languages. The "language" that any given person communicates through his or her body is entirely unique to that person. So we have to ask, "What do *you* mean to signal or symbolize when you use that tone, posture, gesture, etc.?"

Then we have to calibrate to *that* person. We have to pay lots of attention to how *that person* uses his or her body, hands, eye gaze, lateral eye movements, breathing, gesturing, movements, posturing, etc. Next we pay attention to the larger actions and behaviors that reflect internal thinking and feeling. How does a person greet people, shake hands, affirm, assert, disagree, negotiate, etc?

Typically (perhaps stereotypically) people in Western cultures who don't maintain good eye contact, who lower their head and slouch their shoulders manifest in their muscles the *"Woe is Me"* game.

Here we ask questions about the meaning, significance, associations, etc. of the behaviors.

- What does that tone mean to you?
- If your posture were a statement, what would it be saying?

Frames Detecting Through Working Beliefs

While we begin with representing things, above our representations are our belief frames. And from there it is *beliefs all the way up.* Every frame implies a belief which is simply *a represented thought embedded inside a frame of validation.*

This separates a mere "thought" from a "belief." Without this distinction, we could not *think* without believing. Yet we can. We all know that we do. Every day we *think* lots of things that we do not *believe.* We read and understand the local newspaper's editorial without believing everything we read. If we could not think without believing, we would end up believing everything we heard, saw, or read. Yet we do not.

So what creates a "belief?" When we *believe* a thought, beyond representing it, we mentally *confirm* it. To the thought we say, "Yes, I validate that as true and real." To *disbelieve*, we embed the thought inside of a very different kind of frame. We put it into a frame of *dis-confirmation.* "No, I do not believe that. That is wrong. That is not true. I can think of lots of examples that invalidate that idea. The thought does not hold up and does not adequately describe the state of affairs."

The simplest structural analysis of a belief lies in this higher level confirming or dis-confirming, validating or dis-validating, saying "Yes!" or saying "No!" to a thought. In other words, we have to "go meta" in order to believe. Beliefs do not exist in the world "out there." They are *frames of mind* about other ideas.

Belief/ Disbelief FramesThis means we can detect a frame every time we hear someone *confirm* an idea or representation, or talk about something that think is true, validate, or real. When we hear that kind of a thought, we hear a belief. This holds true for all concepts, understandings, values, self-definitions, decisions, etc.

- Beliefs in the importance or significance of something: *Values.*
- Beliefs in what causes or contributes to something else: *Causation.*
- Beliefs in the meaning or definition of something: *Meaning.*
- Beliefs in what one should do: *Morality, Ethics, Right/Wrong, etc.*
- Beliefs in what one will do: *Decisions, Choices, Commitments.*
- Beliefs in how to define oneself: *Identity, Self-Esteem, Self-Image,* etc.

- Beliefs in how something works: *Causation, Function, Process.*

One secret for frame detection is the realization that all of our mental frames are beliefs.

- What do you believe about feedback?
- What is your thinking about conflict between people?
- How do you feel about that?
- What leads you to such concepts?
- How important is this to you?
- What have you decided about this?
- How much validity do you give to this idea?
- Are there many things that give rise to doubt about this for you?
- What if there were?

Figure 7:3

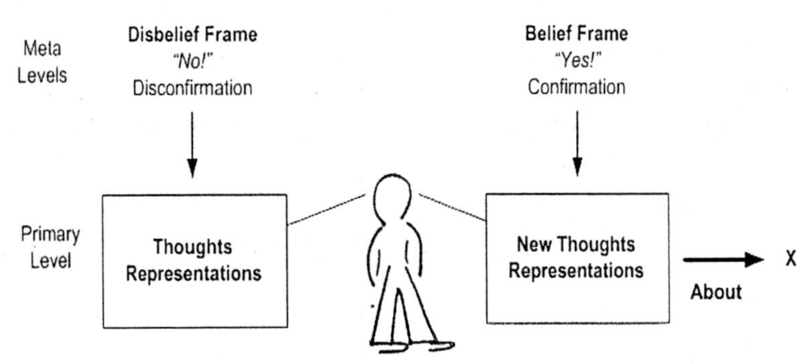

In a way, the word "belief" makes frame detection more difficult. When we *confirm* a thought—the synergetic state they results is a *confirmed thought.* As a gestalt which involves a sense of something more than the sum of the parts, the "confirmed thoughts" seem so real and actual that it is easy to forget that it's just a mental construct. That it's just a map! It's easy to forget that it is just a frame, because it feels so real.

Frame Detection through Experiencing

Once you detect a frame, you can gain further knowledge of it as you flexibly *step inside* and *outside* of it. When you do this, you obtain a double-description of the frame. You then get to see it from both the inside and the outside.

Just for the purpose of discovery, temporarily *step into* the frame so that you allow yourself to feel it deeply and allow it to work on your emotions, body, mind, etc. Immerse yourself into the frame and imagine moving through life with it.

Now step out. As you stand back from the frame and notice it, just witness the *you* who had stepped into it and from this broader perspective allow your awareness to expand about it. You may want to step back yet again, taking numerous other perspectives, each time allowing more richness and wisdom to accumulate. Do this with the memory of a conflict.

Once you do this, you may want to step back in again for the purpose of this exploration and see what the frame now evokes and how you feel when operating from the first frame of mind. As you do this, use the following sentence stems to enrich and expand it:

- When I view things within this frame I see, hear, and feel . . .
- When I view things from outside this frame of reference, I become aware . . .
- When I hold both of these descriptions simultaneously, it enriches my understandings so that . . .

Figure 7:4
Stepping In and Out of Frames

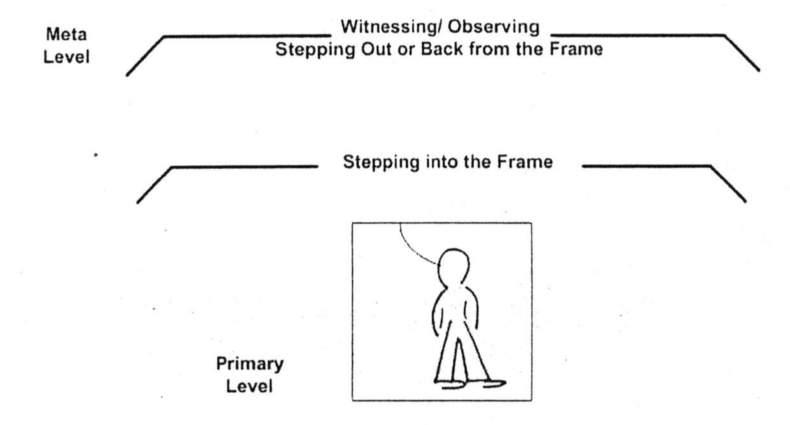

Frames Detecting through Assumptions

When we move to the top of our mental frames and come to the edge of our maps, we reach our reality strategy. This identifies what we have mapped as real. As our ultimate frame, it specifies our *ontology*—our beliefs about what exists, the level of beingness, and our *epistemology*—what we "know," and how we know that we know it, our common sense or studied understandings about "knowledge" and knowing itself. It also specifies our *teleology*—our understandings and maps about where we and the universe are going, the end (*telos*) of things.

In all of this we have many *unquestioned* beliefs, ideas, concepts, etc. about the world, people, themselves, morality, etc. that sets the frame. To become a *Meta Detective*, flush out the higher, hidden frames by inquiring about assumptions and presuppositions.

- What are you assuming about what exists?
- What are you assuming about criticism?
- What are you assuming about people when they differ?
- What do you just take as real without questioning?
- What has to be true in order for you to say that?

Frame Detection through Word Awareness

Because the smallest and simplest of words can set a frame, keep your eyes and ears open for terms, labels, metaphors, and semantically loaded terms.

1) "Now I have to clean up that mess."
2) "This is so boring."
3) "It burns me up the way Bill puts things off to the last."
4) "There I go again. I'm so screwed up."

What frames are nicely hidden away in these phrases? Did you catch the frame of necessity (1), passivity (2), victim of another's actions (3), and harsh self-judgments (4)? What *words* do you use that set frames that you may prefer not to set?

Words as symbols highlight certain facets of experience and simultaneously de-emphasize other aspects. They *foreground* some things and *background* other things. As a meta-detective, step back from language itself, recognizing that all words and statements are but linguistic maps. As you do, you can then ask:

- What lies in the *foreground* of our awareness?
- What lies in the *background*?
- How are we linguistically highlighting things in the foreground?
- What elements cause something to *stand out* and become *salient* on the screen of our mind?
- What processes and mechanisms enable us to *background* other facets?

The power of single words to set frames is easily recognized by contrasting the effect that the *connective* terms, "and, but, even though," and the verb tenses that relate to "time" (the temporal verb tenses; past, present, future, etc.). Consider and feel the simple connective terms in the following statements. Especially pay attention to the foregrounding and backgrounding that the terms invite you to use in your representing of the following:

1) "I know she means well, *and* she really hurt my feelings."
2) "I know she means well *but* she really hurt my feelings."
3) "I know she means well *even though* she really hurt my feelings."
4) "She really hurt my feelings, *and* I know that she means well."
5) "She really hurt my feelings *but* I know she means well."
6) "She really hurt my feelings *even though* I know she means well."

The same ideas with just a slight twist in the connective terms and suddenly we have a different focus, emphasis, and feeling, do we not? What happened for you? How did the change of one term affect you? When we used an entirely different order (or syntax) of the sentences (the last three), how did that change things? With the word *"and"* we have two equal sets of representations that we encode as side-by-side with neither *in an about relation* to the other. "This *and* that." So we process and represent two equal items.

With the word *"but"* we shift logical levels. The second statement now shifts *upward* and takes *a meta position* to the first statement. It outframes the second. It becomes dominant as it stands out in the forefront of our mind as *the most important* piece of information of the two. So in sentences 2) and 5) we have first *"she hurt my feelings"* as the dominant and higher frame . . . regardless of her good intentions, *she hurt my feelings!* We re-sequence this in sentence 5). Now *"she means well"* stands out as the most salient piece of information. It operates and governs as the higher frame. So, in spite of the hurt feelings, she means well.

Figure 7:5

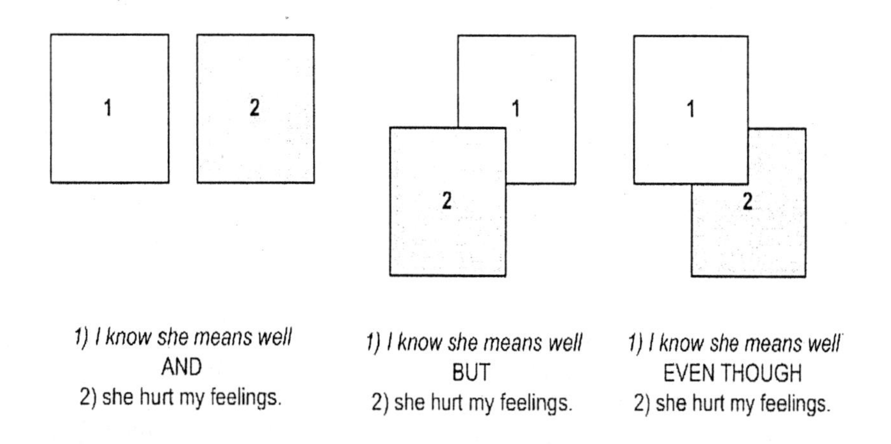

With the phrase *"even though"* we create a focus on the first statement and display, de-emphasize, and perhaps even discount the second. Now the first becomes more prominent *even though* it has not become a higher frame. What *frame games* can we play with this linguistic understanding about these connective terms? Consider the impact in conflict situations, disagreements, negotiating, influencing, etc.

1) You've got a good point there *and* I don't agree.
2) You've got a good point there, *but* I don't agree.
3) You've got a good point there, *even though* I don't agree.

Recognizing how *small words and terms* connect our ideas, beliefs, wants, and experiences, we can then more smoothly slide into setting even higher frames.

> So you want X *while* I want Y *and* I'm wondering if we can come to a meeting of our minds on this so that we don't ruin our business relationship over this X or Y?

With this type of verbal framing, we can take any two or three or more portions of experience and link them together to create an implied cause-effect relationship. Suppose we take the following ideas:

1) You can achieve your visions of greatness
2) If you take this one with energy and discipline.
3) And apply your skills every day.

Now notice the different emotions, thoughts, and experience that it generates in the following:

1) You can achieve your visions of greatness if you take this on with energy and discipline and apply your skills daily.
2) If you take this one with energy and discipline, and daily apply your skills, you can achieve your visions of greatness.

Which is put into the foreground of your mind as you read the statements? What do you hear emphasized in each?

Framing with Time Words·

Consider the tiny words or word fragments that indicate *verb tense.* The way we *code* the action terms that we use to describe processes (verbs) sets a "time" frame that then governs representation and emotion. Read each of the following slowly and pay attention to how you represent each, noticing what happens to your internal pictures, sounds, and sensations.

1) I *went* for a walk.
2) I *am going* for a walk.
3) I *will be going* for a walk.

Now do the same with the following set of statements.

1) So you *have* a problem with this?
   So this really *is* a problem for you?
2) So you *have been having* a problem with this?
   So this really *has been* a problem for you?
3) So you *are having* a problem with this?
   So you *will have* a problem with this when you set it up?

***Modus Operandi* Frames and Games**

A *modus operandi* refers to your basic mode or style of operating. It's your M.O. Linguists use a form of this term to describe words that encode some of the key personal, mental, and emotional *modes* of operating. They call these *modal operators*. They come in an assortment of various sizes and shapes. There are:

- Modal operators of *necessity:* must, have to, forced to.
- Modal operators of *desire*: want, desire, get to, can.
- Modal operators of *possibility:* can, may, possible, options, choices.
- Modal operators of *impossibility:* can't, not possible.
- Modal operators of *obligation:* ought, need to, demand, should.
- Modal operators of *choice*: choose, get to, want.

Each of these terms identifies a different M.O. game that we have framed for ourselves or that someone else framed for us, and that we play. Those who play *the Necessity game* move through life assuming that life is a bunch of rules and obligations and that they *have to* follow them, abide by them, and comply with them. Will, choice, options, and wants have little to no reality in this domain. You *have to* go to work. You *must* take the garbage out. You *have to* finish everything on your plate.

Others play *the Desire game*. They move through life doing what they *want* to do. If they play this game in an exclusive way, then they can *only* do and choose things that they desire. This turns every undesirable task into an impossibility.

Yet others play the *Possibility game.* What's possible? How can I turn this into a benefit? What's possible to learn from this? What's valuable or important about this? Others play the *Impossibility game.* Nothing's possible for them. They *can't* learn, grow, succeed, lose weight, become fit, parent effectively, develop communication skills, etc.

> "I really hate it that I have to put up with his grumpy attitude. It really irritates me."

So it seems that you have built a necessity frame about putting up with your boss's grumpiness. Does this mean you're playing, *I'm Such a Martyr?* What game are you playing? Maybe its, *I'll Give All Power to Your Grumpiness to Totally Control My Emotional Responses?* Is that it?

> "You don't understand. He is *so* grumpy. He acts like a peevish little boy always demanding his way."

It's kind of like a big boy in diapers and a rattle, and throwing his whining tantrums at work and hooking the Parent in you that wants to spank him and send him to his room or the Child in you that wishes that you could get by with such fussing and fuming. And that's why you *have to* feel irritated by his grumpiness. You are choice-less. It's the Law. You *have to* feel irritated and upset.

> "Well, what am I suppose to do when he's so grumpy? Just put up with it?"

No, you don't *get to do that*, that would give you too much resourcefulness to deprive his grumpiness of its power over you. As you said, you *have to* put up with it and you also *have to* put up with it as a victim. You're not allowed to feel good about yourself while he's having his tantrum. It's the rule. You're not allowed to play, *I'd Rather Have a Moment of Resourcefulness*. [In this I played *"Let Me Provoke the Hell out of You so You'll Resist My Prescription that You Have to Keep Playing the Same Old Sick game."*]

Linguistic Frames

All of this reveals that the very structure of our language sets frames. Linguists have long argued that language does not play a neutral role in life, but comes loaded with assumptions and presuppositions. We explain this with the next secret for the frame game mastery.

#10. Brain Frames thrive on Symbols.

***#10:* Brain frames thrive on symbols.**

What do you feed a *frame brain?* As a semantic class of life, we set frames in our brain-and-body by using symbols (both linguistic and non-linguistic symbols). This means that even the tiniest little word can sometimes fully establish and set powerful frames-of-reference and frames of mind that control perception, memory, experience, behavior, emotion and even skills. The secret of word magic is that *as we represent, so we encode our mind and neurology.*

Lacking the innate and "instinctual" coding that animal's have, we have to construct maps of the world to navigate our journey. That's why we use *symbols*. As we feed our levels of mind various symbols, and then symbols of symbols, our mind becomes increasingly structured by symbols. The symbols powerfully order our consciousness as it constructs our inner world, our inner game, our Matrix of frames.

Meta-Program Filters

Another source of frames and process for detecting frames involves meta-programs. As our perceptual filters, these describe the lens we use in looking at the world and processing information. As such our meta-programs are our solidified meta-states, meta-states that have coalesced into our neurology so that they get into our eyes as our way of perceiving things. Detecting and working with meta-programs is the focus of the NLP domain, Meta-Programs. This also explains the name of our Meta-Program board game, *Meta-Detective.*[2]

Summary

- While frames operate outside of our awareness, we can learn to become a skilled frame detective by stepping back and tuning up our eyes and ears to notice the invisible framework we live in.

- Because frames are made out of the stuff of "representations" and "thoughts," raising consciousness about symbols, symbolic systems, linguistics, etc. increases our ability to detect frames.

- By becoming mindful of our frames we increase our sense of choice, empowerment, sanity, and control over the games that we play and that we invite others to play.

- By giving us more choice, frame awareness makes us more wise and powerful. All we have to do to develop *game awareness* is to *step back* from our thinking and step up to engage in some meta-thinking. This empowers us to then transform the reflexivity of our mind so that it becomes a powerful ally, rather than a tormenting dragon.

End Notes

1. The list of *meta-questions* arose from modeling using the Meta-States model. You can find them in *Coaching Conversations* (2004) and *Coaching Change, Meta-Coaching Volume I* (2005). Also, see Appendix A.

2. *The Meta-Detective Game* is a board game that you can play with 2 to 8 people to learn meta-programs.

Chapter 8

FRAME ANALYSIS

Exiting the Matrix
To Discover Game-Scape

First there was Freudian Psycho-Analysis.
Later there was Transactional Analysis (TA).
Today we can move up to Frame Analysis.

If frames, and our framing, lies at the heart of all of our meanings, interpretations, emotions, and experiences, then here are three critical questions:

- Is it possible to create a *frame analysis* of our frames and games?
- Is it possible to take our *game eyes* and look at our lives in a rigorous way to see the invisible structures holding it together?
- Is it possible to use our frame analysis to launch a transformation in the games that we play?

The answer is a resounding *yes*. *Yes* we can use the game metaphor that we've been exploring to more thoroughly understand our patterns. And *yes*, by this analysis we can transform old frames and old games into new ones as we step back and use our meta-cognitive powers to see the structures that make up our inner and outer games. We can redesign life's games for actualizing our potentials.

As we learn how to engage in *Frame Analysis* using our frame awareness, we will be able to use our self-reflexivity to rise above the game, detect the frames, and mindfully transform them so that they serve us.

- Are you game for this?
- Do you have the knowledge base for frame analysis?

Ultimately, knowledge is only powerful when we know *how* to use and apply it. Mere knowledge in itself is not powerful. Not at all. What we call "head knowledge" is merely academic if it is not relevant and practical. It is the skill of converting information into *how-to* knowledge that makes it powerful. To this end, *frame analysis* offers practical know-how in using our frame understanding and detection skills to analyze the meaning frames of our Matrix.

Frequently in *Frame Game Workshops* we spend a half day running a *frame analysis* around various challenging and complex human dilemmas. People usually choose to analyze work conflicts, personal conflicts, complicated and nasty divorce situations, major life decisions, etc. We have even had people apply *frame analysis* to "personality disorders." Once I even sat in and watched a group run a game analysis on the "manic-depressive" disorder, schizophrenia, and an obsessive-compulsive disordering. I mention that to highlight the flexibility of frame analysis and that it can provide insights for even the most complex and convoluted of human experiences. After all, these too are games driven by frames.

In this chapter I will pull together the key facets of *Frame Game Analysis*. In this, the game analysis summarizes what we have covered and forecasts things to come. By putting these components together, we can use them as a system of analysis and transformation. At the end of the chapter, you will find two worksheets for keeping track of the Frame Game Analysis as you diagnose an old game and design a new game.

Frame Analysis offers practical know-how in using our frame understanding and detection skills to analyze the meaning frames of our Matrix.

Frame Analysis

In *Frame Analysis* we put on our game eyes and look at any aspect of life as if it were a game.

> *If your life, job, relationship, health, etc. were a game, what games are you playing, what are the rules of the game, how do you score a point, what penalizes points, how do you win, who do you play with, when does a game begins, when does it end, and so on?*

Frame game analysis gives us a way to summarize the skills and tools that we've described under the category of frame identification and detection, as well as those that we will describe under game transformation. Game Analysis allows us to now take things to another level by providing *an organizing structure* for how to think about our life and relationships in terms of the inner and out games that we play. All of this is based on the one mechanism that most essentially enables us to do frame analysis—*meta-awareness.*

To *analyze* our frames and games we use our self-reflexive awareness to think about our thinking-and-emoting. This puts us on a quest for the structure of our meaning-making and the Matrix of frames that we've created. It gives us insight into the organizing system of our matrix of frames. By using the organizing principles and dynamics of frames that we have explored, frame analysis pulls all of that together in a way that we can use to see the actual structure of our lives.

Using the following *Game Analysis* gives you a way to detect, flush out, and identify the key patterns that govern our thinking, feeling, speaking, and behaving. It provides a way to organize the confusing and chaotic mess of thoughts and feelings, beliefs and values, decisions and memories, imaginations and concepts.

The meta game of *Frame Analysis* offers advanced practical know-how in using our frame understanding and detection skills to analyze the meaning frames of our Matrix.

The center of gravity in all of this are our *frames*. Yet all frames are not the same. Frames occur on different levels and dimensions. At the primary level we have our representational frames, the movies that we play on the theater of our mind. Above and beyond that level, we look at all of the meta-frames: imagination, dreams, visions, possibilities, fears, worries, decisions, understandings, etc.

In the mind-body-emotion system, frames make up a dynamic mental structure influencing our perceptual and attentional filters, how we think, and a whole range of frames: historical, conceptual, intentional, identity, pain, pleasure, etc. They involve the frames that comprise our *frame of mind.*

The challenge for frame detection and analysis is when our meaning frames lie outside-of-conscious awareness. Once we set the *frame*, it simply operates as our sense of what's real so we then take our beliefs for granted. In this way we develop frames and meta-frames as the *organizing principles* of our mind and emotions.

Metaphorically, they make up our internal world or Matrix, so that we experience our frames as our mental *atmosphere.* Then, like the atmosphere, we seldom notice the canopy of the sky. We live and breath and have our being within our meaning universe hardly noticing its influence over our experiences, emotions, states, and perceptions. We continually frame our thoughts-and-emotions as we move throughout life, continually embedding our frames in ever higher frames until we construct a whole system of frames.

Figure 8:1

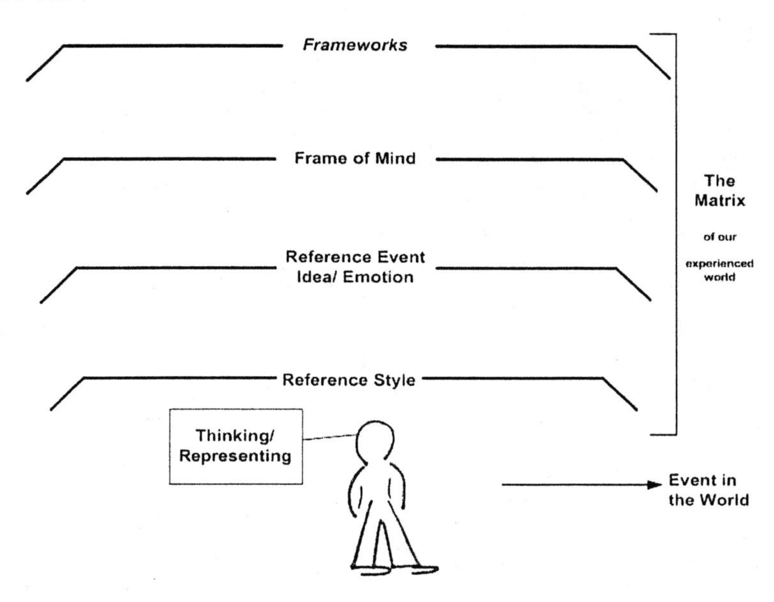

The Levels of Frame Analysis
The multiple levels of our frames endows them with a rich complexity which contributes to making *Frame Analysis* tricky. That's because we have to move to a level *meta* the whole frame structure to *analyze* the structure. So as we reflect on our frames and framing we create yet another higher executive state of mind. Yet all these layers do not stay neatly separate; they blend, merge, coalesce, reflect back on themselves, and spiral up and down.

While I have sorted out the levels of meaning-making from representation up through to intention and metaphors, it's critical to realize that this is only a way of *talking* about these processes. These are just words and in reality all of our swirling thoughts spin round and round simultaneously. This makes *thinking* itself dangerous and calls upon us to be aware of *what* we think. Every thought lies *within* a frame, and at the same time, *sets* a frame. In this double-service it *reflects* and *generates* frames.

Frame Games at Work
Let's flush this out with a practical everyday experience. Suppose that while at work tomorrow, *something goes wrong,* suppose something major goes wrong, something that's going to cost a lot of money and time to fix. As you imagine that, step into the experience. Good.

- Now what's your first thought?
- Where does your brain go?
- What are you beginning to feel?

Typical responses to a catastrophe or a major mess-up include:

- Who did it; who's at fault?
- Why did this happen?
- Why does this always happen to me?
- What's wrong with me?
- What's wrong with him, her, or them?
- What shall we do about this?
- What can I learn from this that's going to increase my effectiveness?

Which frame did you go to? Did you go to *the Blame* frame, the *Recreating History* frame, the *Poor Me* frame, the *Solution* frame, *the Self-Contempting and Self-Questioning* frame, the *Looking for Creative and Insightful Solutions* frame? How many of the frames did you entertain almost simultaneously? What other frames popped into your mind?

> Awareness of frame games
> allows us to play something brand new
> and entirely different—
> the game of *Frame Game Analysis.*

We inevitably construct and use various *frames* and we cannot *not* do this. So, given whatever frames we set, we play out our thinking, emoting, speaking, behaving, and relating according to that frame. Sometimes we do this to our benefit, sometimes to our harm.

Knowing that our frames control our experiences, we know that what and how we use our *references* in response to the scenario of something major going wrong at work structures the *inner* and *outer games* that we play. Because frames operate as our assumptive reality, whatever we assume to be true and real, whatever we assume about what a thing "is," what we "are," what something "means"—*so it becomes to us.* It makes up our conceptual Matrix.

- If you think people are out to get you; that you can't trust them; that people always operate from hidden agendas; that people won't like you; etc.—somehow you will seemingly find or attract such things. *The Paranoid Frame.*
- If you think that people are friendly, have good motives, are trustworthy, will like you—somehow it seems that life will prove this to be true for you. *The Friendly Frame, The Rosy Glasses Frame.*

In this way, our *framing* initiates the systemic process of self-fulfilling prophecies. This establishes the filters by which we see the world. In terms of self-organization theory, our frames establish a *set* (i.e., a mind-body-set) so that what we believe organizes our mind, emotions, body, relations, etc. and thereby invites, attracts, and constructs life after the image of that belief.

Frame Induced States

What drives our emotional states? What defines our states of mind and the matrix of frames we live in? How and what we reference as we frame. From the first level, our framing induces us into various states. If we reference dangers and threats, we will probably experience a state of fear, anxiety, dread, etc. Frames induce states and we don't need to be aware of the process for it to occur.

Yet because our *higher frames* exercise the most power in influencing our feelings, perceptions, and behaviors, they determine our destinies. These meta-states are much more complex than just regular, primary states—they involve feelings *about* feelings, thoughts *about* thoughts, mind *attending to* mind. When I fear my anger and dislike it, I'm in a state about a state. We commonly refer to meta-states as "beliefs," "values," "understandings," "concepts," "decisions," "self-definitions," etc.

If when something goes wrong at work, we first think about, remember and reference getting in trouble at home with dad which puts us into a state of feeling dread, apprehension, "like a little boy," stupid, inferior, etc., then we may also have developed a *dread* of things going wrong, being "made wrong," or being called to give account. This frame about a frame describes how we *meta-state* ourselves with these thoughts and feelings. The original referent experience has "grown up" to become a meta-state of *dreading mistakes*. What could be just a B-rated movie is now used as a self-organizing filter to define oneself and predict one's future—a terrible misuse of a historical referent.

These frames are also "commands" to the nervous system. As "orders" for our body to carry out, they set up the games we play. Once set, we can count on them to operate automatically and outside-of-conscious awareness and to feel real. All this is great unless the frame we set creates a self-sabotaging game, a toxic game for self or others, or a childish out-of-date game. Then it will just run repeatedly, automatically, and unthinkingly undermining our health, effectiveness, relationships, and happiness. It will run until we catch the game and engage in a new frame game.

The Meta-Game or the Frame Game[2]

Because we inevitably move up to higher levels as we play frame game after frame game, and games about games, we regularly jump "logical levels" in a single bound. Conscious awareness is not required for this. That's why 99% of our framing is outside-of-awareness.

Yet as we recognize this, we are able to play a higher *game*. Awareness of frame games allows us to play something brand new and entirely different— the game of *Frame Game Analysis.* The meta-awareness of recognizing the power of frames and detecting them allows us to *step aside* from the game. This gives us a moment to pause and creates the space wherein we can initiate an entirely new game.

The *Frame Awareness Game* is so powerful that sometimes it can totally transform old games. The old *Insight Therapies* of Freud, Rank, Adler, etc. were built on the idea that "Awareness is curative *per se*."

> "Oh, that's what was going on! I never knew. I thought you didn't like me. How could I have guessed that my tone of voice reminded you of a cousin who raped you?"
> "So you mean that my dad did not graduate from Parenting #101? You mean he was doing the best he could given what he knew about raising kids?"
> "Oh, you mean that I got 'harsh tonality' connected with 'pain,' and 'getting into trouble,' and I don't have to necessarily link up those meanings with that stimulus?"

Sometimes it is. *Awareness* of what has been happening, the mechanisms creating the experience, where something came from, why we made the map we did, etc. can sometimes "pop" an old belief frame in an instant. Then the meaning that we experience from the representations and embedded frames dissolve. The awareness exposes the framing giving us an "Ah ha!" moment.

The point is that there are no *frame-less* meanings. Where we have an emotion or experience, we have a frame. Our *meaning* frames establish the internal "contexts" of our mind by which we can determine significance. Meanings always occur in multi-layered frames:

- *Time frames:* Past, Present, or Future.
- *Configuration frames:* Foreground/ Background.
- *Language frames:* sensory-based representations or non-sensory based: sights-sounds-sensations or words.
- *Intentional frames:* Higher levels of mind that seek to achieve some goal or objective: This answers the "why" of intention question.
- *Belief frames:* What do you believe about this or that facet within the meaning? Yourself? The World? Etc.
- *Size frames:* life size, smaller, larger.
- Etc.

The Frame Analysis System

With all of that in mind, here's the system of *Frame Game Analysis.* The following sections and questions correspond to the worksheets at the end of this chapter. Each section ends with a set of questions that you can use as a guide in conducting your own *frame game analysis.*

1) What is the Game?
What sub-games are also involved inside the Game?
If we set a blame *frame,* then blaming becomes the *game*. We access a state of mind wherein we see and detect "wrong" and feel the need to accuse, find-fault, judge, correct. So we set out to find someone or something to blame. Add the either/or frame to *the blame frame* and we have a game that motivates a single-focused awareness. "Someone has to be the problem, someone or something caused this and needs to pay for it." Get two people playing this game and you have each one wanting to be the inquisitor, and judging the other for blaming!

- What is the game? What kind of a game are you playing?
- What set of mental, emotional, verbal, and behavioral interactions does it initiate?
- What states and meta-states are you experiencing?

Because our frames activate our mind-body system and create our mental and emotional states, *frames get into our neurology*. We not only have our references in our "mind," we also incorporate them into our body, into the very muscles and organs and nervous system of our body.

- What state, mood, feeling, attitude, etc. does this reference elicit?
- How does this reference make you feel?
- What state-about-a-state does it call forth?
- What larger gestalt state or synergetic state emerges?

Primary states have an outside reference, something "out there" in the world, whereas a *meta-state* will have an internal reference, something about a previous state. Primary states are typically more kinesthetic whereas meta-states are more conceptual and deal with ideas. Ask, "Where do you feel that?" If the person can point to a body part or organ (lungs, heart, stomach, etc.), it has more chance of being a primary state. If the person has to point to his or her head, it's more likely a meta-state.

"I feel dumb." Where do you feel that?
"I feel judged." Where do you feel that?
"I feel like I might cheat on that test." Where do you feel that?
"I feel like such a nerd." Where do you feel that?

2) Who are the Players?

- Who's involved in this game? How many people?
- Any invisible players (phantom players) in the background? (i.e., divorced spouses, influential ancestors, employers, etc.) Who?
- Any larger level family, cultural, historical players?
- How are they a part of the game?
- What part of the game do they play?

3) Quality Control
Checking the ecology of a system involves analyzing the consequences and long-

term results and health of the system in terms of how one thing affects and influences other facets and relationships. This provides one of the most profound and pervasive interventions. In checking the ecology, we can evaluate its usefulness, empowerment, service, productivity, reality, likeableness, etc.

- Do you like the game?
- Does it serve you well? Does it serve the others well?
- Does the frame of mind describe the game that you really *want to play?*
- Does it enhance your life or empower you personally?
- Does it lead to any consequences that you don't like or want?

4) Hooks, Triggers, and Baits (Anchors)

- What hooks you into the game?
- What bait is used to seduce you?
- What triggers the cues for the games to begin?
- How does the game itself hook others to jump in and play out their roles?

5) Cues and Clues

- What are some of the cues whether in language or in the environment, or personal (the way the other person talks, gestures, etc.) that indicate that the game has begun?
- How do you know?
- If others deny the game, what would give you a clue and convince you that you're in the game?

6) The Rules of the Game

Games operate by rules, procedures, and set-ups. The rules of the game tell us how to play it, when, with whom, how to set it up, what payoffs to expect, how to account for exceptions, etc. The rules of the game of Win/Lose differs radically from Win/Win.

- What are the rules of the game?
- How is the game set up?
- How do you play the game?
- What are the moves in the game?
- How does a person score points or win a game?
- What do the rules say is important in the game?
- How do you end a game?
- Are there any rules for changing the game's rules?

7) Name the Game

Realizing that every thought, emotion, behavior, intuition, idea, etc. occurs *within* a frame and is *governed by* a frame, initiates our exploration for detecting and identifying the specific frame-of-reference and gives us the ability to just come right out and name the frame or name the game.

- What are you referencing?

- What is the frame?
- If you gave this frame a name, what would you call it?
- What ideas, concepts, evaluations, values, beliefs, etc. code this frame?
- What focus does this frame create?
- What mind-set arises from it?

The key to understanding yourself and to figuring out other people lies in the frames being used. Knowing the *frame* allows us to recognize and appreciate a person's way of reasoning and feeling. To follow anybody's "train of thought" or understandingly enter into his or her emotional world, we have to know what frame drives it.

- What's the name of the game?
- Are there any sub-games? If so, what are some of them?
- What would you like to call this game?
- Can you find a colloquial way to summarize the game?
  For example, Mine is Better than Yours! Why Can't You Ever Do Anything Right? Peace at Any Price. Why Don't You, Yes But . . ." So' s Your Old Man! It's All You! Let George Do It. The Blame Game.

8) Frame of references for the game

All *references* are not the same. Our minds give us the ability to both remember and imagine. We can construct representations of what has been, and representations of what we imagine will be. This distinguishes between whether we are using past or future referents, or in what order. References can also differ according to the following dimensions:

- What is your referent or references?
- Is it a literal and physical reference (a person, place, thing, event)?
- Is it a conceptual reference (an idea, concept, principle, belief, decision, understanding, value, etc.)?
- Is it an imaginary reference (a hope, dream, vision, intuition, etc.)?
- Is it a vicarious reference (movie, book, ideal, etc.), a reference about someone else?
- Is it a personal reference (unique experience of the person)?

Then there are higher level references.

- What do we believe, think, feel, etc. *about* past events and future possibilities?
- What kind of a reference do I have in mind?
- What is the nature of the reference?

The kind and quality of our *referencing* determines the quality of our intellect, emotions, and life. What references do you *prefer* using? We all have preferences. Some people reference use past references, others focus on the future, others reference ideals. And yet others practicality, a religious faith, a political view, some value, family, etc.

9) Style of referencing

- How are you referencing?
- What's the quality and characteristics of your style?

As we can make distinctions about the *nature* of a frame, so we can distinguish between different referencing styles. When some people reference things, they sort for "the big picture" while others sort for "the details" (global / specific). Some sort for what they think and feel while others sort for external sources of influence: parents, family, culture, experts, etc. (internal / external).

Some reference things in their minds and emotions by matching what they're experiencing with what they already know, others by mismatching (sameness/ difference). Some run their referencing very fast, others very slow (fast / slow; active / reflective). Some sort for visual qualities, others for sounds and auditory facets, others for sensations and feelings, and yet others for words (VAK and words).[1]

Some engage in referencing in a very rigid way while others do so with lots of flexibility (rigid / flexible; options / procedures). The frame games we play will differ in terms of flexibility versus inflexibility. This, in turn, will govern the degree of creativity and playfulness we can exercise within a game. All of these *styles of referencing* or sorting information are called *meta-programs.*[1]

- How rigidly do you or another play?
- How much flexibility do you have in using a given frame?
- Are you stuck in a frame?
- Can you shift your frame on your own?
- Are you or another looping round and round?
- Can you take new information into account and make internal adjustments?
- How are you referencing in terms of your perceptual filters?
- Do you look for the big picture or specifics?
- Do you match or mismatch?
- Do you reference internally or externally?
- Do you attend mostly to yourself or to others?

10) The agenda and intentions of the game—Game Pay-offs

All frames are *motivated.* We establish them to achieve something that we value and want. On the surface we may not have any conscious awareness of *why* we play the games we do or what original positive intention we had. We may have to ask the intention question numerous times in order to find the original positive intention.

- Why are you playing *that* game?
- What are you intending to accomplish by playing that one?
- If you achieve your objectives, what will you have?
- What will you win? What's the pay-off?
- What is the outcome of the outcome?

11) The emotional and somatic intensity of a game

Every game has some degree of emotional intensity and somatic involvement. This determines how much we get into the game, how much psychic energy we invest in it. It generally governs the dominance of a game. The more emotional intensity it has, the more it runs our motor programs, then the more dominance it can hold. We feel obsessed or compulsive about the game. We have to play it.

- How intensely are you playing from 0 to 10?
- How obsessively and/or compulsively?
- How does the intensity show up somatically in the body?
- Can you see the game in the person's face, posture, and movements?

12) Leverage points in the game

Every game has a leverage point because every *frame* has edges, boundaries, and structures. When we frame things, we structure information and format it in a certain way. Changing how we encode the information changes the frame which changes the game. We can always modify the information in one frame by another frame (the meta-stating process).

- Where is a leverage point in the game?
- Where could we create and install a leverage point?
- How can we most easily alter the frames and the nested frames?

Look for un-used references:

- What references does the person never use?
- Are there any references that are tabooed or prohibited?

As we all have our favorite and preferred, or just habitual, referencing style and references, we all also have references that we will never use. These totally unacceptable, tabooed, or just never used references map out boundaries in the person's mapping of reality.

- What beliefs do you never use?
- What decisions do you never consider?
- What values would you never choose?
- What questions do you never ask?

13) Preferred frame game

- What game would you prefer to play in the place of the old game?
- What is a compelling game that you would love to play?

Summary

- Playing the *frame game*, rather than having it *play* us, is kind of sneaky. It's sneaky because we use the very stuff of consciousness (i.e., our thoughts and emotions) to frame our thoughts, and then frame those thoughts with yet more thoughts.

- This can change everything and can change everything in a moment. The layering of thoughts upon thoughts, emotions upon emotions, states upon states puts into our hands a higher level power that can totally reframe meanings and transform even our own personality, character, and destiny.

- *Frame Analysis* enables us to flush out frames and work with the very organizing principles of our mind-body system. This allows us to use our *frames* as a meta-state structure by which we can identify and use as leverage points for transformation.

- The *quality* of our life (mind, emotions, perceptions, skills, etc.) can't be any better than our referencing and framing. This makes our referencing critical and central to our well-being and sanity. People who become experts and excel in a given area simply use better references. Modeling them entails replicating the references they use as well as their referencing style.

End Notes:

1. See *Figuring Out People* (2006) for an entire work on meta-programs as well as the board game, *Meta-Detective.*

Diagnosing a Toxic Game
Worksheet #1

1. *What's the Game?* Describe the game being played out in terms of states meta-states, and gestalt states. *What's the script of the game?* What sub-games or sub-frames are part of it?

____

____

____

2. *Players:* Who plays the game? With whom? Who else has games going on? What's the larger social system of the game? (Use a separate worksheet for each person in the game).

____

3. *Quality Control: Do you like this game?* How sick is this game? Are you ready to transform it?

____

4. *Hooks (triggers, baits):* What hooks you into the game? How does the game hook others to play this game?

____

____

5. *Cues and Clues:* What are some of the cues (linguistic, physical, environmental, etc.) that indicate the presence of a game? How do you know? What cues you?

____

____

6. *Rules of the game:* How is the game set up? How do you play? What are the prohibitions? What's forbidden? What's demanded?

____

____

7. *Name the frame game:* Give it a funny colloquial name.

____

8. *Frames of references that you use: What are you* referencing?

Literal and actual   Conceptual   Imaginary
Vicarious (referencing what happened to someone else)
Personal   Meta

9. Style: What is your frame of mind or style of thinking? What perceptual filters or meta-programs are operating?

_ Matching / Mismatching
_ Fast / Slow
_ Aggressive / Passive/Assertive
_ Options / Procedures
_ Judger / Perceiver
_ Internal / External
_ Reactive / Thoughtful
_ Rigid / Flexible
_ Self / Other
_ Global / Specific
_ Counting / Discounting

10. *Agenda of the game:* What's the intention, motivation, or payoff of the game? What's the payoff?

---

11. Emotional intensity of the game: How intense (0 to 10)? Are there any somatic responses or symptoms? What psychosomatic effects result?

---

12. Leverage points: Where is the leverage in this game to stop it, change it, transform it?

---

13. Preferred frame game: What game would you rather play?

Design Engineering a New Game

Worksheet #2

1. Desired *Game:*

____

[Questions 2 through 6 summarize worksheet 1]

2. *Target:* Name the person/s you want to influence.

____

3. *Current frame games:* What is the current game and frames? What is its quality? How sick is it? What consequences does it generate? How significant (0-10)? What frames do you need to break it?

____

____

4. *Evidence of the current frame game:* Symptoms, cues, evidence, source of evidence?

____

5. *Emotional motivation:* What concerns, him or her most? Values? What's really important to this person? What would hook X into this game? Vested interests?

____

____

____

6. *Players:* Who plays the game? What's the larger social system of the game?

____

____

7. *Objective and outcome:* What do I want in this? What do I want for the other/s in this?

____

____

8. *Description:* What frames best describe the new game?

____

____

9. Process: How can I set up these frames? How can I implement my persuasion process?

---

10. Leverage points: Where is the leverage to interrupt, stop, or change the game? What frames will best create leverage for this person?

---

11. Patterns for shifting, loosening, and transforming the frames: Which patterns or techniques would provide the most leverage?

---

12. *Patterns for installation:* Which patterns would work best for installing new frames?

---

13. *Solidification:* What accountability process will you establish to monitor the new game until it becomes habitual? Who will support the new game? How will you celebrate the wins?

---

14. How will you test and refine the new game to make it increasingly more robust?

Chapter 9

END GAME

Games Over.
Everybody to the showers!

To fully and completely say **"Yes!"** to Life
you have to be able to say **"No!"** to toxic things.

One day while I was writing this book, I received a call from a hypnotherapist on the east coast who told me about a particular client he was working with. It seems that a particular woman had developed a phobia about *the possibility* that someone might "die on her." Over the years this terrifying idea grew larger and larger in her mind. As it became a dominant idea that she couldn't get away from, the idea began to control her lifestyle so she was terrified to even walk down the street.

The therapist inquired, "Has anyone ever died 'on you?'" Yes, indeed. When she was a young nurse, she lost a patient.

Being NLP-trained and knowing "The Phobia Cure,"[1] he decided to help her step back from the experience and restructure her representations. He asked her to go "in your mind to the end of the trauma as you remembered it. When you get to the end, then stop, create a snap-shot of some event when it was all over." That's when he was stumped about what to do next.

> "It's never ended. It's still occurring. That's the problem, there's no end."

When I heard about that, I thought, "Wow! 'No end!' That's great! What a frame! This lady has actually framed her experience with the idea of it being *'Endless.'"* What a great way to *solidify* the continuance of a frame so you can keep it with you for the rest of your life. I was impressed.

But not so the therapist. While he confirmed that this was precisely what she had done, he was worrying and fretting about what to do with her or how to help her. Her "endless" frame prevented him from using the usual Movie Rewind pattern. So, I then asked about when this happen. He said that the patient died in 1970.

So here's a woman who used that original experience as her frame-of-reference, until it eventually grew up to become her *frame of mind*. Then through repetition, she habituated it until it began operating as the very framework of her personality. Now she has *eyes* for looking around her everyday environment to see if someone might "die on her." Would you want to orient yourself like that in life or play that game?

That's not the *game* I want to play in life. How could we deframe that reference structure? Since she had *solidified* her framing with *Endlessness*, with *No Ending*, *Still Going On and On and On* . . . that's the first piece I'd go after. The conversation I would have with her would go something like this.

"When did that first patient die?"

"1970."

1970? My God, and you're still remembering it in 2006? I can hardly remember *anything* that happened to me in 1970. What else do you remember that happened to you in 1970?

"Well, not much else . . . mainly having that patient die on me?"

He died "on" you? My God! That's horrible. He clunked over and fell *on top of you*?

"No, I don't mean that. It was on my watch. He died during my watch at the hospital."

Whew! Thank goodness. I was afraid we had a real trauma on our hands with a dead man falling on you and your watch, and you not being able to get him off of you.

"But it's continuing. It has never ended."

"Really? He's still dying on you? That's absolutely incredible. He certainly has more lives than a cat! How do you do this? If you were to teach me how to run my brain like that so that I could take something from thirty-six years ago and keep it going on and on, tell me how to do that? There's lots of things that I can think of that I'd like to set up as a perpetual movie in my head."

"You don't understand. I'm trying to stop this."

"Yeah, yeah, I know. But before we change that, I first want it. How do you know to frame your experience *without an ending*? How do you not just close the door to the event at the end of a day, or at the end of a pay period, or when you left that job? You've got a tremendous skill here. Most people see things ending, chapters closing, doors shutting, flights taking off, people de-planing, that kind of a thing. Do you know what I mean?"

While I would not want the *content* of the lady's framing, I am incredibly impressed with her awesome creativity and inventiveness. As a modeler, researcher, and trainer constantly seeking for new patterns for empowering people to make a change and *keep it for the rest of their lives*, this was an incredibly powerful lasting frame.

Yet suppose we are working with something like that, how could we then do the opposite and *stop* that frame game? How could we bring an end to that kind of framing? As already noted, deframing offers one choice, as does questioning the current framing to loosen it. In this chapter we will explore these questions to gain insight and skill in how to call an end to an inner game that we've had enough of or an outer game that is no longer producing the results we want.

Stopping a Game

What is *frame refusal* but the exquisite ability to bring an end to an inner and outer game that we no longer need or want? It is the ability to blow the referee's whistle and yell out, "Games over, everyone to the showers!"

The Art of Ending a Frame Game

1) Deframe
2) Question the frame
3) Quality control the frame
4) Substitute a new contradictory frame
5) Release the old game
6) Set a paradoxical positive negative frame
7) Power up to say, "Hell No!" to the old frame and game

1) Deframe the old Frame

Whenever we explore the make-up and structure of an experience by asking lots of precision questions of an inner or outer game that doesn't enhance one's life, we inevitably de-frame that matrix. You undoubtedly have noticed this in previous examples. If not, begin to do so with the examples that follow. Deframing is a powerful tool when handled correctly.[2]

2) Question the Frame to Undermine it

Take a moment to think of some old frame that you're fully ready to reject.

- Do you like that frame?
- Does it serve you well?
- How has it played a destructive and hurtful role in your life?
- What price have you paid for it?
- So, do you really believe that it serves you well?

There's nothing like *questions* to question the validity, usefulness, and even the reality of something. There's an undermining power within questions. If you question anything sufficiently enough, you'll begin to doubt it. So, apply lots of questions to the toxic frame to pull apart its fabric.

- To what extent do you find this frame ridiculous and absurd?
- How is the frame ridiculous?
- How does this frame of reference undermine resourcefulness and create personal limitations?
- Where will this frame take me if I keep using it as my reference point?

Questions that index the specifics of an experience that we dislike empower us to thoroughly explore the idea, belief, or understanding. Such questions empower us to look reality in the face and to develop a greater understanding of what's happening, how, and what we can do to transform things. Questioning also give us a more scientific orientation so that we do not blindly accept something. Especially use questions that elicit pain. This will give you a powerful leverage over the old frames and games.

- What price will you pay for this emotionally? Inter-personally? Financially? Physically?
- Have you had enough of this or do you need five more years of this crap?

3) Quality Control the Frame

Another fabulous way for stopping a frame game that's unproductive or destructive is to quality control it. Every time we step aside from our matrix of frames and run a *quality check* on it, we are in a powerful position to say *No* to that frame and to construct another frame that we can affirm.

Adolf Eichmann, as a Nazi calmly shipped tens of thousands of people to the gas chambers. His frame? Did he want to be an evil or bad person? No. In other environments, he would have been viewed as an upright pillar of a community. He played from the frame of *unquestioning loyalty.* Apparently he never checked the ecology of the system he was within. The rules prescribed:

> "Be loyal to those in control. Be faithful to the rules of the bureaucracy. Don't ask questions. Conscientiously make a well-ordered system work. Treat the rules of your superiors with respect and the Organization as sacred. Don't rock the boat."

How could he have refused that frame? If he could have stepped aside and gained a larger perspective, he could have checked the quality of that frame, and look at its long-term consequences. He could have shifted to question this unquestioned loyalty.

Napoleon (1967) tells the story of Thomas A. Edison who was thrown out of school in the early grades after his teacher decided that he had an "addled" mind and could not take schooling.

> "This then was the impact of another person's voice upon Thomas Edison—to let him know with the voice of authority that he didn't have what it takes to absorb even a primary education! Where would he have been if he had allowed this directive to take charge of his thinking?" (p. 10)

In terms of frame setting, it's pretty powerful when *a voice of authority* rejects us as "not having what it takes." Yet in spite of that, Edison somehow was able to decide to live his own life and to refuse counsel from that authority. Hill says that "he learned that he had a mind that he could control and direct it toward any desired end." In touting the power of setting a definite goal, Hill described the "affirmation" that he gave to Senor Quezon who became the first President of the free Philippine Islands. Here's a frame that establishes a boundary *against* certain thoughts.

> "I will allow no person's opinion, no influence to enter my mind which does not harmonize with my purpose." (p. 12)

4) Substitute a New Contradictory Frame

Sometimes awareness of the shift from an old game to a new one is lost because we're so caught up in doing something new, positive, and empowering, that we don't even notice that we've stopped the old game. The new game that we're discovering is so fascinating and enhancing that the experience simply makes the old inner game redundant.

For example, for most of us we fully realize and accept (intellectually) that nobody can *make* us angry. Our anger is our own. It arises from our angry thoughts and angry state. What's difficult is to practice this higher level of consciousness in the presence of someone who seems to know how to "push all of our buttons" and get under our skin. Further, how can we refuse the *blame game* when it feels so pleasurable to blame?

Here clarity informs, intensifies, and reinforces our strength. Being crystal clear about owning our power zone and having mentally, verbally, and behaviorally practiced a set of effective responses enables us to refuse to default to the blame frame.

Certainly, others can *invite* us to feel angry and upset. To do that, they have to communicate or act in such a way so as to provoke us into thinking upsetting thoughts. If we then buy their frame, it becomes inevitable that we will feel upset. Others can provide incredibly powerful stimuli that invites, urges, provokes, incites, and elicits upsetting thinking-and-emoting responses from us. Yet our response is always that—*our response*. It begins with a mental response and it shows up as a behavioral response.

We can only play the *blame game* by failing to distinguish between *the stimulus* that others offer and *our response*. There is a difference. One is trigger, the other is response. When I *think* that I have no choice, that I *have to* get angry, I give my power away. I become the other person's slave, doing his or her bidding. It dis-empowers me so I become a victim.

Listen to the frames that people set that sends them into *the Blame Game*:

"My boss makes me so angry that I can't stand it."

"I know that he uses that tone of voice with me in the board meeting just to make me feel put-down and degraded. I just hate the way he controls me."

"I had to retaliate in the way I did, she made me feel worthless."

Talking this way operates within the implied frame that the speaker has no power, no choice, and no response-ability. No wonder we become *reactive* when we frame things that way. We have no other choice. Framing this way induces us to live in a deterministic world and as long as we *frame* others as controlling our responses, we will play that game. Yet how different things become when we get turned on about the personal *empowerment game* and wake up to the fact that using the word "make" in reference to someone else robs us of our own power.

Oh, so he *makes* you angry. Is that right?

"Yeah! Make him stop making those faces and using that tone!"

So you *have* to feel mad when he does that? You have no choice. You are his puppet and he totally pulls your strings, is that right?

"Well . . . I . . ."

Come on, you know that you're just a weak wimp of a slave boy and that you can do nothing about it but *react* with anger when he does this [mimicking the facial expressions] or when he talks like this [mimicking the tonal qualities], you have to. Even when I do it, you *have to* feel angry and bad and sad. You are now my slave, ha, ha, ha! Submit you worthless scum!

"No, never. You can't make me!"

No, no! Don't tell me that you are taking ownership of your response-powers? That's terrible. Help someone! I'm losing my slave boy! Surely you don't yet realize that your responses of thinking and feeling result from the way *you* think and emote. Don't tell me that you're in charge of you and your responses. You're robbing me of my magic spell and making me depressed!

5) Release the old Frame

How else can we stop a game or give up on an old inner game that we don't need? What if we just *release* it? What if we meta-state our frame of mind with the sense of *letting go*? Would that work? Could we make that kind of adjustment within?

> From this day forward, I let go of the need to blame others. Blaming never makes things better and usually makes things twice as bad; while I've been an excellent player of the Blame Game, that was good for a five-year old, but as of today, I let it go as a childish way to act. Every time I think about blaming and playing the Blame Game I will breathe in that feeling, notice it, and then breathe it out as just a silly thought or feeling from childhood.

6) Set a Paradoxical Positive Negative Frame

If we need to develop a strong stand against frames that would not serve us well, what else can we do? We can tap into the paradoxical power of meta-stating. We do this by mindfully applying a *negative* frame or state of mind, like negation, refusal, stubbornness, intolerance, and rejection to set up a paradoxical relationship. In doing this, the higher negativity actually sets a limitation frame of a boundary. Here are some examples:

- *Hating* hatred creates a new synthesis of caring about people being treated fairly and equally. I hate the intolerant hatred of prejudiced people! I'm prejudiced against their prejudice.
- So the meta-intolerance at a higher level of intolerance nullifies the intolerance at the primary level.
- Do you accept rejection as negative? What if you rejected the negative framing about rejection?
- Suppose you became stubborn about your right to reject negative frames? You could then solidify your firmness to choose your frames.

In this way, we can set up higher level frames that can safeguard the frames of mind that we desire to keep. If a doubt arises that undermines our self-confidence, we can doubt the value and usefulness of that doubt. When we *doubt* our doubt we feel more certainty. To refuse procrastination, we can decide to procrastinate on our procrastination and put it off until a better time.

Have you had it with the old frame game? Has the pain and distress pushed you past your tolerance threshold? Will you take it no longer? In a real decision, we "cut away from" (de-cision) the range of our choices and options those which we refuse to tolerate any longer. We decide by saying *"No"* to some alternatives so we can say *"Yes!"* to others.

Access a total *intolerance* about the old frame and then apply that intolerance to your game to blow it away.

> "I refuse to tolerate this one more minute!"
> "I stubbornly refuse to tolerate this as a way of living."
> "I absolutely and stubbornly refuse to tolerate this another instant!"

As we become more aware of frames, and especially the *frames* we default to, we can decide to stubbornly refuse to accept any label, definition, point of view, idea, belief, focus, or reference that doesn't serve to enhance our lives. Are you ready to refuse to cooperate with the frame game requirements? Are you ready to retire an old game as no longer fun or useful? Good.

7) Power Up to say *"Hell No!"* to the Old Frame Game

Can we actually just refuse a frame and say *No* to it? Can we say *"No!"* to an alternative way of looking at things and reject the frame? Yes. There's all kind of ways of rejecting a frame. Many times you've done it by saying things like:

"That's crazy! How can he think like that?"

"What's wrong with her? Nobody in her right mind would believe *that!*"

What a tremendous power this is! Knowing how to reject a *frame* or a *game* is essential for mental and emotional health precisely because some *frame games* sicken. Some devastate hope. Some destroy skills. Some limit and imprison. To allow some *frames* to play out in our minds and emotions will toxify our thinking, perceiving, talking, acting, and relating. They lead to no productive results.

So as a way of mentally mapping the territory, the frames in some games not only do not enhance life or empower people, they actually undermine effectiveness and even sanity. When they operate at a higher level of mind, as one's programs, beliefs, and orientation in life, they attract influences and forces that undermine well-being, inner peace, effectiveness, and sanity. They self-organize mind, perception, emotion, and life to fulfill a negative frame.

Refusing an inner frame game gives us the power to control the influences in our minds and emotions. It enables us to *push away* destructive and limiting influences. Frequently we cannot play a new game because of the presence of an old frame that prevents it. You may want to succeed fabulously, but suppose you have the frame, *Don't Fool Yourself, Dreaming about Success is for Fools.* If those frames are well installed in your mind, they will undoubtedly sabotage your best efforts.

The good news is that we have lots of effective maneuvers for refusing old *frame games*. Your ability to say *"No!"* in a definitive way gives you the foundation for this. Can you say no? Is there anything in life to which you can utter a strong and powerful "No!"? How about —

Here, eat these worms.

Here, let me cram this finger up your nose.

Here, grab that gun and put it to your head.

Do those suggestions induce a strong kinesthetically felt *"No!"* to well up inside you? If they don't, then what does? Then, once you detect a pathetic frame that sickens your spirit and creates a crappy attitude, you can access your own particular definite and resounding *"No!"* and blow it to smithereens. This is the most direct route to stopping a game. The *No* enables you to say, *Stop this sick merry-go-round game, I want off.* How's your definitive **"No!"**? Do you have a powerful one? With it you have the mental-emotional power to refuse, to set boundaries, to establish limits, to differentiate ourselves from others, and to individualize your own identity.

Developmentally, we all experience two periods of life where we have to engage in saying *No* in order to individualize and differentiate as we learn to become our best selves. First during "the terrible twos" and then during the turbulent storms of adolescence. These developmental stages enable us to differentiate to create the kind and quality of *independence* so that later we can become healthily *inter*-dependent.

Of course, parents who didn't graduate from *Parenting 101* and don't know about the importance of differentiating, take personal the child's *"No-ing!"* read it as meaning that the child is rebellious or "selfish," and so squelch it. They may even try to beat it out of them. They forbid their kids the right to say *No.* Then, growing up with a taboo rule about saying *"No"* they play non-assertive game and may even fear their own independence of thought. That frame would forbid them from knowing their own mind, emotions, values, strengths, etc. Permission to do this is taken away. Years later they will find themselves feeling like wimps, beaten pups, jello personalities with no fiber of will, no will power, no determination or persistence to go after their own visions and values. And because it undermines sanity, it's not a very fun game to play.

- How strong and definitive is your ability to say *No!*?
- Do you need to reclaim this power and right?

If so (or just to refresh this frame), begin by giving yourself permission to know and own your own *responses*. When you develop the *ability* to *respond* at your will and choice, you become response-able. Set the frame that you, and only you, stand responsible for what you think, feel, say, and do. Totally own and acknowledge this as your *power zone.*

Powering Up for your No

It takes power to refuse an old familiar frame game. It takes energy. What are the most fundamental powers that we experience at *the primary level?* What powers at this level can we then use at higher levels for frame-setting and mind-managing?

The *powers* that make up our fundamental *power zone* are four. Two of these occur deep inside and comprise our private powers and two occur more outwardly as our public powers. Each of us have these *four* central and inescapable *powers* and by them we have the ability to respond to things. Two of these human powers operate very privately (thinking and emoting) and two operate as our public contributions to the world (speaking and behaving). Within these lie our ability to cope and master the challenges that we face. Herein also lies the essence of our *response-ability*.

In the private recesses of our mind we *think-and-feel.* Thinking and feeling make up the central *engine* that drives all of the rest of our responses and gives shape to our personality. As nobody can "make" you think a certain way, but can only invite you to try on a way of thinking, so nobody can "make" you feel a certain way. People can invite, evoke, and provoke, but that's all.

We express our thoughts and feelings by *talking and acting.* These two public powers describe *how* we express ourselves. This gives us the power of *action* —the ability to give our thoughts and emotions a tangible and felt influence in the world. Herein lies our power to affect events, people, systems, etc.

Figure 9:1
Power Zone

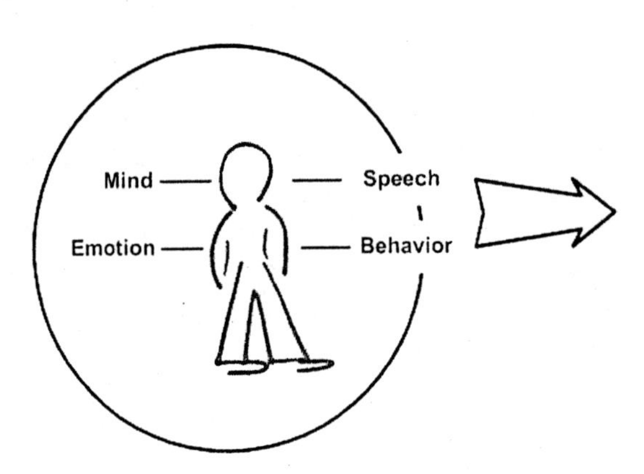

- To what extent have you fully owned and accepted your *powers*?
- To what degree have you cultivated and developed these powers?
- How much of your powers do you give away to others?

To play the *Empowerment Game* you have to first of all own your *powers* of thinking-emoting. Say this:

> I, and only I, ultimately determine what I think and feel. Nobody can *make* me think or feel anything . . . I always play a determinative role about what I let into my mind and what I give attention to.

Saying *"Yes"* to these mental and emotional powers builds up that higher quality that we call *ego-strength.* This gives us the ability to affirm our values and visions and to dis-confirm things that do not fit or that violate what we consider important. Uttering a *"Yes"* and/or a *"No"* to the experiences, thoughts, choices, emotions, and responses available to us puts into our hands the dynamic-duo of affirmation and dis-confirmation. As we now say *Yes* to some things, we say *No* to other things.

What's the very first on the list of things to *Yes* and *No*? The *content* of our consciousness. What do you want to say *Yes* to in terms of what frames you set? What do you want to say *No* to?

- What beliefs will you *Yes*, which will you *No?*
- What values and visions?
- What decisions and commitments?
- What self-definitions and identifications?
- What ideas and frames?

When we say *Yes* to our power zone, we also say *No* to blaming, excuse-making, and irresponsibility. This shifts us from playing the *Blame Game* to the *Solution Game*. We focus on what we want to achieve—our aims, our desired outcomes and solutions. When we don't get the responses we want, we treat it as feedback (the feedback frame). We then go into a learning mode (the learning frame) to discover what we can learn about how to do things differently. Then we shift our responses (the flexibility game) and keep varying our speaking and acting responses until we get the response that we want (the persistence game).

Cranking up your *No!* to *"Hell, No!"*

With all of this in mind, identify five different items to which you feel a strong, powerful, and definitive *"No!"* Access each of these experiences separately and as discreetly as possible so that as you re-experience them you can fully and completely feel that sense of "No!" everywhere in your body. Feel it in your muscle tension, facial muscles, voice, breathing, posture, etc. Then, as you do, anchor each "No!" with a gesturing of your hands and arms that shoves the undesired referent away from you and your "space."

Upon accessing this *"No!"* each time, amplify this experience or state so that it begins to feel stronger and stronger in your neurology. Continue to do so until every fiber of your being wants to shout out with all of the energy that you can muster, *"Hell, no!"*

When you get all of that definitive energy pumped up so that it energizes you thoroughly in mind-and-body, take a moment to *enjoy* this power of refusal, disconfirmation, rejection, and stubbornness. *Relish* in this power of self-determination to have the final word about what you will, and what you will not, admit entrance into your mental and emotional space. This power enables you to create your personal boundaries.

Now, *holding* all of these feelings of *"No!"* constant, begin to direct them to every idea, thought, activity to which you want to utter a final and definitive "No!" Bring this neurological *"No!"* to bear upon various toxic ideas, beliefs, behaviors, and habits and as this *"No!"* becomes a *meta-**no*** to the state that you will no longer tolerate, repeat the *"No!"* until you feel it pushing away the unenhancing state . . . do so until this neurological *"No!"* becomes a matter-of-fact "No." "No, of course, not. Are you crazy? Why would I want *that*?"

Doing this will now allow you to apply this reference as a refusal frame for any experience, idea, etc. that you want to forbid entrance into your experience. In this way, you can refuse morbid and toxic frames that limit and sabotage.

Summary

- Isn't it really good news that we can reject and refuse frames? But don't *just* say *No.* Say *No* with power, strength, firmness, and definitiveness. Access a strong neurological state of rejection, stubbornness, and intolerance and apply these boundary defining experiences to the things that you refuse to give one inch in your mental and emotional world.

- We can learn to insightfully guard our heart and mind as we refuse to let toxic frames that spread disease and create negativity in our head. Frame refusal allows us to take a strong stand against letting thought viruses and frames-of-reference that don't promote our well-being.

- The skill of seeing and detecting a frame gives us the opportunity to then take the courage to refuse to be played by some frame that doesn't serve us well. So, what old games and frames will you bring to an end and make no longer an option?

End Notes:

1. See *The Sourcebook of Magic,* 1997) or *MovieMind* (2002) for the Movie Rewind pattern.

2. See *Mind-Lines* (2005) for an entire chapter on the art of deframing.

Chapter 10

FRAME TRANSFORMATION

"Men are not disturbed by things,
but by their estimate of things."
Marcus Aurelius

"Be transformed by the renewal of the mind."
The Apostle Paul

Lou Ann Walker (1999) wrote about Erik Weihnmayer of Denver, one of the toughest and best rock climbers in the US. At 31, he had scaled El Capitan in California's Yosemite National Park, the world's tallest exposed monolith. He has climbed Aconcagua in Argentina, South American's highest peak (22,834 feet).

Yet one thing stands out making Erik special among climbers—he can't see. Literally! He can't see anything because he is blind. He learned to hike in the Rocky Mountains with his dad and hated it— until he found trekking poles in an outdoor store.

> "That's when I decided blindness is a nuisance, but it's not the reason you can't do something."

How about that for a frame? This frame enabled Erik to play an entirely new game: *"It's Just a Nuisance, Not an Excuse."*

Having run numerous marathons, including the New York Marathon, he is next planning to "attack Everest" (29,028 feet).

> "When I start something, I know I'm going to flop on my face, but failure is a very real valid way of learning about something. Because I've failed a lot, I've built that into the equation. I don't just see success when we summit—it's the whole thing."

What other *frame games* did you recognize Erik playing in that paragraph? It seems that he also plays "There *No Failure; only Feedback"* Game and *Success as a Way of Being* Game.

No wonder it is *the power of framing* that enables us to set frames that can make life either a living hell or a pleasurable paradise. So much is derived from our framing. We derive our sense of orientation in the world, focus, perception, understanding, skill, self-definition, etc. from our framing. Frames also organize, elicit, and/or can sabotage our capabilities and skills and so can enable us to access or fail to access our resources.

It is not until we begin to exercise the power of transforming frames that we truly become the masters of our Matrix. Sometimes we can transform an inner game through simple *detection* or *analysis* of a frame game. Sometimes simply *naming* a game will initiate transformation.

- How skilled are you at transforming your meaning frames?
- What processes do you use to transform your framing?
- What insights or skills empower us in transforming frames?

Awareness of our *inner* and *outer games* enriches our appreciation and insight regarding how frames work, their power and influence, and the states they elicit. Awareness facilitates our discovery of the actual mechanisms that govern the games that we play.

- What inner game would you like to transform?
- What frame game needs updating or refreshing?
- Have you discovered any games that you need to refuse?
- What transformations in the outer game of performance would you like to experience?

Changing a frame can suddenly shift the way we see and experience life. It can generate such a fundamental shift in attitude that it brings a complete *metamorphosis*. When this happens, we make a quantum leap in the quality and effectiveness of our responses. After all, it is our frames that endow us with the specific mental *lens* through which to see, color, and encounter the world. Because our frames incorporate our higher principles and guidelines, they generate our personal Matrix within which we live. When we enter these frames, our Matrix shifts as well, and so we enter into another frame world.

We now also know that we cannot *not* build frames. To think, feel, and respond is to frame. When it comes to the *inner game* of frames, or the *outer game* of performance, our ability to raise the quality of our lives lies in our ability to alter, refuse, and transform frames. Otherwise we will continue to play out the *frame games* given us.

> When it comes to the *inner game* of frames or the *outer game* of performance, our ability to raise the quality of our lives lies in our ability to alter, refuse, and transform *frames*.

Yes, lots of people *feel* that way. They feel doomed and fated to play out the frame games given them. Of course that also reveals the game they're playing because even that thought sets a frame. The good news is that we can both alter current frames and establish new ones. Nor is it all that hard. In fact, once you get the hang of it, you'll find frame transformation and installation as seductively easy.

It can also be quite fun, even exciting. I generally look forward to it as an adventure. Since putting on my games lens and seeing life as a *game* and many of the secrets of the games, I am now able to play a higher game. I awaken each day to play *the Master Frame* game. This is the game of *detecting, challenging, and transforming* my own frames and those of others. It's the game of *Mastering my own Matrix.* Would you like to play? The following welcomes you to this higher game by providing some of the principles and skills for mastering your matrix of frames.

But first, a warning. *Knowledge* itself can be quite seductive. In the seduction of knowledge we are deceived into confusing our brilliant and clever *head-knowledge* with the practical rolling-up-the-sleeves and getting-the-hands-dirty *know-how* knowledge. When fully deceived, the well-informed and knowledgeable person, who indeed *knows* all the ins-and-outs about a subject, confuses that knowledge as equivalent to skillful competence. In the extreme this leads to the "egg-head phenomenon"—the person whose very knowledge prevents him or her from *doing.* Sometimes knowledge inoculates us from doing. The problem then is that we *know* more than we *do.* The problem is that we create all of the proper understandings of the inner game without actualizing any of it or getting it into our muscle-memory.

Knowing can certainly lead to insights about what we're dealing with and understanding the leverage points for change. Simply knowing that we are a semantic, symbolic, and linguistic class of life who play inner and outer games enables us to more easily accept and work with the frames that control the games. Knowing that we all have been born into thousands of cultural *games* along with family, racial, and religious frames directs our awareness about some of the hidden frames we live within.

Yet knowing is not doing. While the inner game naturally leads to the outer game, there's an actualizing process that we can't ignore. We close the knowing-doing gap via practicing, rehearsing, running drills, tasking, and actualizing what's in our head so that our neuro-pathways are trained to make it real. Transformation has to occur at both levels of creation—in the inner and in the outer games.

Transforming a Frame

While on a training recently in England, I met a young woman by the name of Joyce. She wanted to talk privately because she had "low self-esteem" and something I had mentioned in the morning session made her realize that she could now change that frame.

> **Danger!**
> Beware of the
> *"Knowledge equals expertise"* Game.

I began by inquiring about her current matrix of thoughts and feelings. "So what do you have to experience, do, or be in order to exercise high self-esteem? What conditions do you have to fulfill before you can legitimately view yourself as valuable and esteemed and as having honor and dignity?"

"I'd have to make a difference."

In what way do you have to make a difference, and to who?

"Well, to the world . . . That doesn't make much sense, does it? . . . Well, I'd have to *do* something important."

You'd *have* to *do* what, in relation to whom, and in what way?

[Nervous laughter] "How did I know you were going to say that?"

So if I'm understanding you right now, Joyce, you are a worthless, good-for-nothing human being without any honor or dignity at all. Right? . . . And so it would be fine to treat you as such, you slut . . . you worthless good-for-nothing . . .

"No!" she said almost shouting.

"That's a great big *'No!'* I like that one. I bet you felt that down in your gut and in your bones!"

"Yes, I did," she said now beginning to smile to herself.

"So why not just give up this non-sense that you have to *earn* or *deserve* self-esteem? [Releasing a frame.] What about just acknowledging and accepting your value as a human being *as a given*, as part of your heritage for being human? [Meta-stating a new frame.] What about starting from the frame that your worth is a given?" [Reframing.]

"Can I do that?"

"Nope, just kidding. You're right, you're not allowed to do that. The mind-police would come and get you. They would arrest you and put you in some torture pit to punish you for not being sufficiently self-effacing."

[Laughing] "So how do I just accept my worth or dignity as a given?"

"Do you really want to know? Are you ready to act on that knowledge? [Yes.] Well, what or who do you already fully and completely value and esteem? How about a newborn baby? Here's a human being that can't produce anything, can't carry his or her own weight, can't earn anything in terms of self-confidence or competence. Isn't able to do anything important. Do you value and esteem a newborn as inherently having worth and dignity?"

"Well, sure!"

"How do you know you do? . . . Just go inside your mind and notice how do you know that. And feel it fully, that sense of valuing and esteeming, that sense of appraising value and worth . . . Do you feel that?"

"Yes, I do." she said almost with a tone of surprise.

"Now *feel all of that* about yourself . . . Just do it . . . Feeling *that* unconditional esteeming . . . that you give so freely and naturally, that you give for no other reason than the baby is a human being . . . and feel *that* about yourself . . ."

The Art of Transformation

Are you ready to play the game of transforming frames? The rules that govern the transformation process are easy enough to describe. Actually, you have already learned these processes. Now we use them for transformation.

The Transformation Game

1) Detecting and Naming
2) Quality Control
3) Deframing and fragmenting
4) De-stabilizing
5) Meta-stating: reframing, outframing

1) Transformation through Detecting and Naming Frames

It's by understanding and appreciating frames and framing that we gain insight and skill for transforming frames. Sometimes *detecting* and *naming* alone will do it. As we understand the rules of the game and cultivate a deeper wisdom about how to affect the frames, we gain more practical wisdom in frame transformation. With that in mind, what have we learned from the rules of the frame games that gives us an edge in altering and transforming frames?

#5: It takes frame detection skills to master the inner and outer games.

This is the power of non-judgmental awareness. We begin by naming the frame, then exploring it which typically deframes or at least loosens a frame. We boldly ask questions about the experience to enter the Matrix. *The name of the game is to name the game.*

#4: Frames create and direct focus.

If our focus (that is, our perceptual filters) is a function of our framing, we can now step back to examine the structural format of our frames. What's in the foreground of the frame? What's in the background? Suppose we exchanged these? Suppose we swished something else into the foreground? Will the frame cohere and remain intact if we put the idea up against a different background?

#8 Frame brains play frame games with the stuff of thoughts.
#10 Frame brains thrive on symbols.

This empowers us to now ask direct meta-stating questions. What thought can we set over or about another thought that will modify, qualify, temper, reduce, amplify, etc. the first? What state would completely transform everything in one fell swoop?

Occasionally, *frame awareness* alone will transform the old frame. Did you experience that earlier? Sometimes awareness by itself provides a curative intervention. Sometimes, just recognizing that a given experience occurs due to a cultural frame, a language structure frame, a personal, family, business, economic frame, gives us a sense of distance so that we don't personalize or over-identify with it. Sometimes when an idea or truth deeply disturbs us, discovering *who* said it, when, under what circumstances, etc. causes everything to shift for us. We no longer give so much importance, value, or meaning to it. This makes the frame detection questions extremely important.

- What frame-of-reference does this or that imply?
- Who set this frame? When?
- Under what circumstances?
- What do these words, sentences, ideas, metaphors presuppose?
- How do you imagine that this X causes this Y?
- How do you know that this X equals or is this Y?
- Given this thought or feeling, what does this mean to you?
- What are you referencing when you think or feel that?
- Where does your mind go? When, where, with whom, etc.?

2) Transformation through Quality Control

If *detection* can totally transform a frame, *frame evaluation* or *analysis* provides even more power to do so. Merely inquiring about the value, usefulness, enhancement, limitation, practicality, desirability, etc. of a frame sometimes totally re-orders things. Asking these questions enable us to *quality control the framing.* Use these questions to evaluate the framing to check out the quality of the frame and your framing.

- Does the frame serve you well?
- Does it create any limitations, difficulties, undesired consequences?
- Do you want to set a different frame?
- Will it enhance my life, bring out my best, put me in a resourceful state,

and empower me in reaching my goals?

- Will it enable me to act in a way true to my values?
- Or will it limit me, reduce my effectiveness, and put me at odds with my own highest values and beliefs?
- How can we enhance our lives?
- What other ideas, beliefs, values, resources can enrich this frame-of-reference?

3) Transformation through Deframing

It's easy to pull a frame apart. What makes this possible and even easy is that we construct and form our frames out of the stuff of thoughts. So we only need to ask about the threads that weave the fabric together, and when we do, the strands not only start showing, often they begin to unravel. At that point, frequently we only have to give a strand a quick pull and the entire fabric of reality completely unravels.

Lynn was depressed and had several fire-breathing dragons in her head torturing her and making her life miserable. When I consulted with her about her "terrible depression," she said that she didn't like herself "because of my weight."
"Your weight?" I asked.

> "Yeah, I should be thinner. I used to be. When I was a teenager, I was pretty and thin. Why can't I be like that anymore?"

That's a lot of *should-ing* on yourself Lynn. How much weight are we talking about?

> "Twenty pounds."

You're beating yourself up over twenty pounds? Would you feel depressed for nineteen?

> "Yeah, sure."

How about three pounds?

> "Well, no, not for three."

Then how about seven, would you feel depressed and beat yourself up this way over seven pounds?

> "Well, no, I guess not."

How about thirteen pounds?

> "Yes, I would over thirteen."

How about eleven?

I continued that until I discovered the precise boundary between feeling good about herself and *having* to feel depressed. For Lynn it was ten and a half pounds. That's when I started another line of questioning, *"How do you know* to make ten and a half the boundary between heaven and hell? What is it about that number that suddenly changes things?

Of course all of these questions *fragments* a fabric of reality as it invited Lynn into a very different state with the result that she began to see things in a very different way. I did this because I knew that later when she would try to re-establish her old way of thinking, it would be difficult to even reconstruct the experience of the depression game. Fragmentation undoes the cohesion of frames.

Secret #9: "Magic" happens when we detect and transform the frames of our thoughts.

"So let me see if I understand your depression program that you have framed, Lynn, by which you depress yourself over ten and a half pounds. You first begin to *should* on yourself by saying things like 'I *should* be thinner!', then you compare your weight at 31 years of age to your teenage weight, and then you torture yourself with *why questions*, 'Why can't I be a teenager anymore?' Is that how you make yourself feel so miserable?"

"Well, yes, but it sounds silly when you put it that way."

"How silly does it sound to you as I summarize your inner game?"

"Very silly. In fact, ridiculous!"

"Really? And . . . so . . . ?"

"Well, it makes me want to stop doing that to myself."

"If you didn't use those frames of references as you run your own brain and if you framed things in a more productive way, *what* would you like to think, *what* frames would you like to use, and *how* would you like to run your own brain?"

"Well, I would stop *shoulding* on myself, as you call it. That definitely does not help. I guess I would just set a goal to lose the ten pounds . .."

"And how would you set that goal?"

"I'd just tell myself that I *want* to lose ten pounds."

"Would you make a picture of yourself weighing ten pounds less?"

"Well, yes I could. And then I'd make sure that I would see myself as a woman rather than a teenager, guess that's pretty dumb, trying to turn the clock back to my teenage years."

"So what other resources would you need to pull this off?"

"Mainly the confidence that I can lose weight."

"And I suppose you don't have a clue about how to do that?"

> "Of course I do. I just need to cut back on some of my eating and get some more exercise."

"But then, you probably don't know how to do *that!"*

> "I know what you're doing. You're trying to provoke me into doing it just to show you that I can."

"Me? I would never do that with someone ten and a half pounds overweight. Maybe with someone seventy pounds overweight, but never with a wimp who complains and runs torture programs like you."

> [Smiling and ignoring my teasing comments.] "I know the frame I need. I need to set a frame that I'm going to do this *for me* and that I'm going to do it *as my way of taking charge of my life."*

"Well, I doubt that it will work. You don't have enough stubbornness to make a decision like that and stick to it!"

> "YES I can! Just watch me."

And she did. She did because the over-generalized "problem" of losing weight was broken down into smaller units that seemed much more manageable.[1] The dragon that seemed so large was fragmented so it was more like a tiny little lizard.

4) Transformation through De-Stabilizing Frames

There's yet another way to shift a frame. We can *de-stabilize* a current frame. We can do this by simply introducing something that's jarring, upsetting, incongruous, and/or disorienting. To do that, simply question it and explore it. Play with it using a caring and respectful humor.

Numerous new techniques in the field of psychotherapy for disrupting a program of post traumatic stress (PTSD) simply involve this kind of frame destabilization. From using *the Movie Rewind pattern* of NLP (Bandler and Grinder, 1979), to Shapiro's (1995) Eye Movement Desensitization and Reprocessing (EMDR), to Callahan's (1995) Thought Field Therapy (TFT) and Gerbode's (1989) Traumatic Incident Reduction, all of these essentially involve an interrupting and contamination of the Trauma Frame. How does this work?

Primarily by *interfering* with the trauma memory and experience. In each model, the person recalls the trauma frame of reference *and* then simultaneously entertains some other frames. The NLP pattern involves the trauma reference and experience *from an outside perspective* of seeing it on a mental screen and watching it like an observer in a theater, then watching your watcher self from the perspective of the projection booth. Later, it involves rewinding the entire trauma movie backwards at high speed so the entire movie rewinds in the space of one to two seconds. Talk about destabilizing a frame of reference!

Thought Field Therapy creates even more de-stabilization. As a person thinks about the trauma memory, the person is asked to move his or her eyes from left to right, up and down, clockwise and then counter-clockwise. As one tries hard to maintain the internal visual images of the traumatic memory, all of this occurs and more. The subject may also be asked to hum a tune, count forwards and backwards and to tap rigorously on numerous acupressure points and energy meridians of the head and body.

#5: It takes frame detection skills to master frame games— the inner and outer games.

How do these processes reduce and sometimes totally eliminate old trauma frames? Essentially because they de-stabilize the pattern—the neuro-semantic pattern. It interrupts the strategy and it applies other frames to the experience. By destabilizing the old pattern and simultaneously introducing positive resources, one is invited into a transformed experienced.

5) Meta-Stating Transformation

In the process of framing, reframing, and/or installing new layers of frames, there's a large degree of experimentation, surprise, and serendipity. That's because potentially, any higher frame of meaning, value, significance, understanding, etc. can *transform the game.* Some frames will do it to our detriment, other frames will improve things, increase resourcefulness, and even revolutionize life. That's because the meta-stating process of applying one state to another state generates new executive states of mind-and-emotion as frames. When this happens, we establish a new higher neuro-semantic reality for ourselves (or others) so that we perform richer meanings.

"Neuro-semantic?" Yes. This phrase originated from an engineer of human excellence, Alfred Korzybski, and I use it here to differentiate the higher frames of mind (the meta-states) from the primary frames of mind that we call neuro-linguistic states. It is in our *neuro-semantics states* that we have layers of thoughts and emotions upon other states that texture our experience with multiple levels of *meaning.* Our *neuro-semantic* states involving what we call beliefs, concepts, intentions, etc. activate and commission our neurology. This is important because by our semantic framing we commission various concepts to direct the outer games that we play.

#4: Frames create and direct focus.

After we *detect* and *evaluate* our current frames, we are enabled to construct, de-construct, and re-construct our frames. This gives us our artistic ability to form and reform our world.

- What frame would provide a much more useful and enhancing way to live?
- How would I like to think and picture this so that I can operate with all my resources and be at my personal best?
- What empowering beliefs, values, self-definitions, decisions, etc. would initiate a much more fun and delightful frame game?

Given this, we can now state the next rule of frame games along with some of the secret wisdom behind this rule, as we can play the *change game.*

> ***Secret #9: "Magic" happens when we detect and transform the frames of our thoughts.***
>
> As word magicians, we can make frames magically appear, disappear, and re-appear. After all, *as we think so we frame.* If by thinking-and-feeling itself that we set frames in the first place, we can now use this same process for tearing down frames, loosening frames, switching to better frames, and setting higher frames. The very word-magic which creates frames can also deframe, reframe, and outframe.

"If It Weren't For You, You Son of a Bitch!"

These words were never said, but they summarize the attitude and feeling between Bret and Laura. Both seemed to carry large grievance bags with them. Whenever either felt attacked, put down, or blamed, each of them seemed to have ready access to a whole history of hurting grievances that they could throw in the other's face.

> "See what I told you, she never leaves me alone. Just as soon as I do one thing for her, she's never thankful, but she gets into that bitchy mode and it drives me crazy!"

"Bret, let me have you do this . . ." I started to say. But then Laura jumped right in.

> "So I'm the bad one, huh? I can't believe that you come here and have already started your attacks on me! And for all that I do for you, this is what I get?"

Even in my presence, it was attack and counter-attack between them from the start. I could only conclude that they were highly skilled at escalating things and that each operated from a *Blame frame.* After having been seduced multiple times with scores of clients into the never-ending and unsolvable attempt to figure out the grievances and pry loose appropriate apologies, I knew better than get recruited to that game this time.

I had played *the Grievance Policeman* game many times as I tried my best to identify the "true culprit" who really caused the relationship problems. In my early years as a psychotherapist, I usually got hooked into the game before I knew it, and then didn't know how to pry myself loose from the gripping hold of the *Blame game.* They would hook me by asking "simple" why questions:

- *Why* did he do that to me?
- *Why* can't she learn to give me my space when I ask for it?
- *Why* does he have to raise his voice and treat me like a slave?
- *Why* can't she tell her mother to go home and give us some time by ourselves?

This day, with Bret and Laura, however, having discovered the presence of *frame games*, when I smelled the odor of blame, I was able to detect *the blame frame* before getting sucked into it.

"It sounds like both of you are married to scoundrels who ought to be taken out and bullwhipped!" I said, running with *the blame frame* and exaggerating it.

"Well, no, it's not that. I love him. I don't want him to be punished, I just hate it when he attacks me for no reason at all."

That pushed his buttons,

"For no reason at all? Do you call poisoning our children against me 'no reason at all!' I can't believe you!"

"That was good, Bret! Let's see, in terms of being a veteran player at the *Blame Game*, I'll give you three points for that one. One point for the accusation, one for raising your voice, and one for the sarcasm. Should I get out my bullwhip and let Laura have it?"

"What? . . . uh . . . I didn't mean to accuse her . . ." [Obviously, I had interrupted the game, and he did not know how best to respond.]

Don't apologize; you did good. That was an excellent move in *the Blame Game.* I bet she felt really blamed and put down with that one, how about it Laura, would you give him 3 points for that one?

"Yeah, I guess . . ." (Sheepishly)

Listen, how often do you both play this game? Do you do it like once a day, once a week, or what?

"You mean blaming and accusing each other?"

"Yes, precisely. You are so skilled at it. I bet you both have some really excellent moves that can lower the blame on the other with just a glance, a tone, a gesture." They both responded with a sad and pathetic grin.

"Do you like blaming? Do either of you really get off on it? Is this why you got married, so that you could get the other into your house and treat him or her as your personal scapegoat for blaming?"

"No, of course not." Laura said, laughing.

"Well, I don't suppose you'd want to play a different game with each other, would you? I mean, with all your skills and moves in playing *the Blame Game*, it will be really hard to play a different game. In fact, you may be addicted to the Blame Game and have to go through withdrawals, I mean, if you don't blame the other, when something goes awry or messes up, what are you to do with your emotions? I think we better plan for you to play an hour of *the Blame Game* every evening just so as to wean you off of the game."

"So what are you saying, when someone does something wrong, we shouldn't hold them responsible for their behavior?"

"No. Not at all, Bret. I'm all for playing the *Responsibility Game*. It's the *Blame Game* that seems to be playing you and doing the damage."

"I don't get it. Isn't the *Responsibility Game* and the *Blame Game* the same thing?"

"Oh, no. In *the Blame Game*, someone is 'the one at fault' and the rules of the game are to accuse, attack, bring up evidence, put it in their face, and keep raising the stakes until 'the guilty one' admits defeat, gives in, falls on the ground in confession and contrition . . . and admits that he or she is a worm, worthless, scum of the earth, that kind of a thing. Then you have to punish the guilty one and make him or her really pay for it. Isn't that how you play *the Blame Game?* Don't you just keep at the other until you get an admission?"

"Well, yeah, I guess so."

"And does that solve anything? Does that make things better? Do you then fall over each other kissing and hugging and ripping each other's clothes off and just can't wait until you make love? Doesn't it put you into that kind of a state?"

"Yeah, right!" Bret said.

"Well, to play *the Responsibility Game,* you first have to *own* your own responses and then figure out what you want to give to each other that makes you feel really loved, honored, respected, and fulfilled. And, of course, this comes out of the *Power Zone* circles, as I'm sure you know."

They didn't, so I gave them a brief sketch of the gamescape of the Power Zones. I then tossed in the idea that each had an emotional bank account and asked them how full they felt. Laura said about a 2 and Bret said a 6.

"So what specific behaviors count as 'love,' respect,' 'honor,' 'trust' and those kinds of things in your emotional bank account, Laura?"

She made a list of things: getting a hug when Bret came home, going out to a coffee shop once or twice a week for a bagel and a talk, having Bret ask what he can do to help her out from time to time. I got a list from Bret and then asked if each of them would assume total and complete responsibility *for* their actions and give them to the other freely as a gift of love?

"You know I'll hold you accountable *for* doing what you have decided to do, don't you?" They both nodded. "And you have made this decision that you will do this?" They each said, "Right."

"You really will?"
"Yes, of course."

"Really? You're not just trying to get me off your back are you?"
"No, I really will. I will be as good as my word!"

"But, what if Laura accidently seduces you to play *the Blame Game*? What then? Are you man enough to keep to your word and operate out of your power zone?"
"Sure I am."

After a little more provoking (to solidify the frame), I suggested that as they play the game of *What Would Make You Feel so Good and Loving and Resourceful that this Issue would Be No Problem At All?* that they could perhaps buy some money bags and call them their "Emotional Bank Account" bags. It was a very different game and as they learned it over the weeks that followed, they found their lives not only dramatically changed, but positively transformed.

Summary

- Has your *awareness* of frames begun to empower you to notice and change frames at will? It will. Awareness is that powerful and can be transformative in itself.
- *Frames are not fixed and rigid.* Actually, as states of fluid thinking and feeling, they are pretty plastic and flexible because they are dynamic processes. That's why we can change them, and transform the games that we play.
- Using our reflexive mind, we can layer new thoughts and feelings about our thoughts and feelings that give us trouble. This is the *meta-stating process*. What *frame games* would you like to initiate and begin to play this week?

End Notes:

1. For more about the "magic" of reframing, see *Mind-Lines: Lines for Changing Minds* (2005). That book provides an entire presentation on reframing skills and patterns. For more about the "magic" of patterns for running your brain, see *The Source Book of Magic*, Volumes I and II (1997, 2003). For more about the "magic" of language and communication, see *Communication Magic* (2001).

Chapter 11

OVERT FRAME SETTING

"The World has been pulled down over your eyes to hide us from the truth."
Morpheus, *The Matrix*

"The significant problems we face
cannot be solved at the same level of thinking
that we used to create them."
Albert Einstein

- What new games have you begun to play since you started reading this book?
- As you develop the exquisite skills for detecting your current framing and transforming them, what additional new inner games are you ready to initiate?
- Which ones would you like to begin playing?
- Do you know how to "let the new games begin?"

It is not enough to develop meta-awareness, we also need to be able to do clear-headed frame analysis. To become a highly skilled practitioner, we need yet another explicit skill. Because the outer games are derived from the inner game of our frames, *we must be able to set frames.*

Merely knowing about some great frames that establish some powerful games without the ability to activate them puts us in no better place than the person who doesn't know even that there is a better way. To chart out this territory for exploration, we ask the following questions:

- How do we actually *set* a frame?
- What does it mean to thoroughly *set* or *install* a frame?
- What are the key success factors of frame setting?

- What signals inform us that a frame has been set?
- What cues us that we haven't yet *set* a frame?

Frames as Dominating Ideas

When it comes to human beings, I've never met one who does not have some *dominating idea* in his or her head—a frame that's always available at a moment's notice. How about you? Let's make this even more personal:

- What concepts or beliefs do you never leave home without?
- What frames of mind do you always take with you? (These do not have to particularly be positive and enhancing.)
- Do you have any concepts that you would like to dismiss, but have not yet been able to rid yourself of it?
- If one of your closest friends were to tell me about the things that are "always on your mind," what would they say?
- Pick an area of life that's important to you, yet one in which you're struggling, what is your attitude about it?

Dominating ideas, emotions, responses, beliefs, etc. reveal that you already have some powerful *frames* set and already live in a conceptual Matrix of your own making. You have already absorbed, bought into, and installed lots of cultural frames. How about that!

Factors in Frame Setting

1) Dominating Ideas
2) Emotion
3) Pain
4) Validation
5) Vividness
6) Questions
7) Rehearsal
8) Identification
9) Intention

Why am I bringing this up? *To celebrate your ability to set frames.* Having installed many mental frames, you already have this ability and have been using it for years. Yet what is required that you may not have is the ability to set frames consciously. Given the frames that you have which dominate your mind-body, *how* did you recruit and set those frames? Let's model the process and the skills by asking, *How* did you set those ideas and beliefs so profoundly in your mind?

As we consider the power with which a mere idea can get into our head and become so strong that we find it difficult to shake off, we know we are on the edge of a powerful neuro-semantic mechanism.

- What process creates this?
- How can we enable an idea to take over consciousness?
- How does a dominating idea capture our soul and organize our personality?

Add Emotion

First, however, we know what doesn't work. We know that *mere representation* does *not* necessarily set a frame. Thinking alone is insufficient. We have to make the representation compelling, dramatic, memorable, important, significant, and believable for it to become an operational inner game. That's why experiencing intense emotions *along with an idea* will more likely *set* the idea as a frame. That's why Pepsi Cola paid Michael Jackson millions of dollars to use his name and reputation to establish an emotional feel for their product. They know that if they can link his music, presence, style, and persona with the idea of drinking Pepsi, it will establish *a felt frame* in the minds of millions.

Do you remember the story of frame setting about the students conditioning their professor in chapter seven?

- How did the students *set the frame* so that the professor would move to the right side of the room as he represented?
- How did they set the unconscious frame, "We are nicer and friendlier on the right side of the room?"

Did they not do so by orchestrating their smiles and attentiveness and so they reinforced the professor's movements so that eventually he found himself constantly returning there? Yes, things felt better on one side. It seemed more pleasant there. In this way they used some very quiet and gentle emotions to set an unconscious frame.

Frame Setting via Vividness

You know about the stuff of frames, how they are made out of the raw material of *representations*: the sights, sounds, sensations, etc. of the sensory-based movie that we play in our mind. Knowing that we can now take charge of the frame setting process by using words more elegantly, dramatically, vividly, and mindfully.

Language gives us *the power of expressiveness.* All we have to do is draw vivid and dramatic mental word pictures for ourselves and others—*word pictures* that grab so much attention the inner movie will not let a mind go. As we would grab someone by the lapels and pull them close so there can be no avoiding of our presence, so we set frames by grabbing attention in a compelling way. We rivet every bit of attention on the frame. We make it memorable, dramatic, and unforgettable. We can use emotion-laden terms to conjure up new possibilities.

Setting a frame is just that easy. Add a touch of drama, vividness, and emphasis to your verbal movie, your idea, story, suggestion, presupposition, question, or comment, and it becomes irresistibly compelling. Because that establishes a reference point, it *sets the frame.*

To become an expert at frame setting, *begin with a sensory structure* of the see, hear, and feel representations as you formulate your idea, belief, value, etc. Give your idea life by breathing into it *visual images* that a person can see in the theater of the mind. Then stick in *an auditory sound track* with just the right kind of sounds, voices, music, and rhythm. Then seduce the person to completely step into the movie and *feel* it—and to be in it and living it. Specific see, hear, feel details enable your ideas to sing and dance on the stage of your mind. You create an internal world that comes alive with movement, energy, and drama when you do this. Imagine being an internal Movie Director.

What *idea* would you like to highlight in your own mind (or the mind of another) and turn into *a frame of reference* for your mental world? Name it.

> 1) Because there's no failure, but only feedback, I can only get better, wiser, and more effective.
> 2) There's always a solution if we stay open and curious.
> 3) Resourcefulness carries the day by making life an enjoyable adventure.
> 4) We become more effective through being mindfully purposeful and through enjoying the process.
> 5) Wealth is created inside-out.

Grab your *Frame Game* notebook and start a page of your own personal list of empowering ideas, concepts, or beliefs which you would love to have run your mind-body system. Gather a list of 10 great ideas. Stop now and do this. If you'd like, use the ones above to prime your creativity.

Now look at them with eyes of appreciation . . . enjoying the process of wondering just how powerful and transformative these *ideas* will be once you install them as your *higher frames-of-reference.* Imagine making them your meta-states, your executive programs, the attitude that you will take in the way you play your inner games.

Now breathe life into them. Edit them until you can make a movie of them—a movie that you can communicate using sensory-based words so that another person would know how to see, hear, feel, smell, and taste the inner world that you create. Here's what I did with the idea, "Because there's no failure, but only feedback, I can only get better, wiser, and more effective."

> I see a guided missile on the screen of my mind, a missile that has eyes and ears and even hands . . . and I am that missile as I race across the sky searching for my target. Every time I receive an "off course" message, "turn 15 degrees to the left," I smile from ear to ear and say, "Great!" with a tonality of Tony the Tiger full of appreciation and excitement. "Thanks for the feedback." "I needed that." "It puts me on the right pathway." Then I smile about my smiling in a calm and appreciative way, and feel more energy bursting within.

Does that come alive for you? Does that give you a *way to think* about the concept "no failure, only feedback?" That's what we're after. Your internal pictures, sights, sounds, sensations, etc. do not have to be actual, accurate, or even possible. They can be fantastic, wild, crazy, and cartoonish.

The key to *frame setting* is that it operates as a *state induction.*
- What state does it induce?
- What feelings does it evoke?
- What orientation does it elicit?
- How much energy does it generate?
- Is this the state you want or need?
- Does the state enhance and empower you?

Now go for it. Stop, grab your *Frame Game* notebook again. This time devote a page to each great idea. Feel free to become wild and crazy doing this.

When I want to get into state for this, I rent a Robin Williams or Jim Carey movie. I give myself permission to feel totally free as I let my expressiveness dance over to the wild side. I see Jim Carey in the movie, *The Mask,* that green mask with the magical qualities. I see Carey standing before the mirror saying, *"Smokin!"* Wildness, drama, vividness, memorable, unforgettable, emotion-laden—these are the things that make our ideas come alive and stand out so they are salient. By these devices we can make certain facets of our world *stand out* on the screen so that they take over and dominate our awareness. These are the mechanisms that allow us to install ideas and endow them with dominating qualities so that they will govern our experiences.

#11: The magic of our inner and outer games increases with the intensity of vividness and drama that we put into it.

> If you want to get *an idea* into your mind-body system, into the fibers of your muscles, make the idea dance and move, give it rhythm, a compelling voice, and let it make a memorable impression upon you. What we "hold in mind" becomes our *meanings*, the *frames of our inner game.* So make the ideas memorable through drama and vividness.

Validation — Add a Touch of Solidification

While we will visit the process of solidifying frames later, let's now add a touch of solidification to our frame setting. Once you have painted your thoughts so they are vividly alive to you, access the strongest representations you have of a strong and over-whelming *"Yes!"* and connect that sense of confirmation to your new frame.
- What can you say *Yes!* to with every fiber of your being?
- What brings out the biggest, strongest, wildest, and most powerful *Yes!* in you?

Feel that *Yes.* Experience it in all of the sensory systems: visually, auditorially, and kinesthetically. How do you gesture *Yes?* What does *Yes!* smell like, taste like, sound like? As you access this state of validation, affirmation, and confirmation, notice your posture, breathing, facial muscles, voice tone, etc. Contrast it with the opposite state of dis-confirmation and denial when you accessed a *"No."* You can also experiment with seven different tonalities of *Yes!* Utter a series of three yeses, each with a rising crescendo of intensity and emphasis, ***"Yes, Yes!, YES!"***

When you have the biggest and most ferocious *Yes!* that you can experience today (knowing that it will double and triple in intensity in the days to come), apply this *Yes!* to your *great idea. "Yes!"* the idea, validate it, confirm it.

- Do you really want that idea in your head?
- Would you want it in your body?
- Would you like it in every muscle of your body?
- Would you like it as your way of being in the world?
- Would it enhance your life?
- Would it make you a better person?

Because *Yes-ing* our ideas, concepts, understandings, and beliefs sets a higher frame of validation, it thereby *solidifies* our frames. This process embeds our thoughts within a frame of confirmation and elicits reasons within us for the validation. Keep *"Yes-ing"* these ideas and representations until you begin to hear a matter of fact voice commenting on your inner movie, "Why, yes, of course!"

Frame Setting via Questioning

Every question contains the double-function of both *implying* a frame and *setting* a frame. You cannot ask a question without at the same time *swishing* awareness to a certain way of thinking. It's inevitable. Consider the frames these questions imply and set:

- Why can't I succeed?
- How can I find a way to turn this into a great learning?
- What's wrong with me that I always mess up?
- What's great about this that I can appreciate and use?
- How could this go wrong?
- What resources can I bring to bear on this?

Questions direct focus as our mind strives to formulate an answer to the question. In this, questions set the frame as it controls the referencing. Regarding the nature of questions, Robbins (1991) says,

> "Successful people ask better questions and as a result, they get better answers."
> "Quality questions create a quality life." (p. 180).
> "The difference between people is the difference in the questions they ask consistently." (p. 182)

Given this power of questions in establishing mental and conceptual frames, we expand our skill in frame setting by becoming master questioners and master meta-questioners. What kind of questions are you asking? How many questions are you asking that are questions of doubt and limitations? How many of your questions are questions of belief, confidence, and expanding resourcefulness? Are you asking questions about problems or about solutions? "What if" questions typically explore *doubts:*

- What if I fail?
- What if I make a fool of myself?
- What if she laughs at me?
- What if it doesn't work out the way I want it to?

We can even use "what if" questions to explore possibilities and to expand our maps and creativity:

- What if I added even more value to my service?
- What if I felt twice as resourceful?
- What if I always included searching for solutions in the way I think about everything?
- What if I checked the ecology of my questions?

Because the questions that we use as we move through life *govern* our frames and direct our focus, questions offer us a truly magical tool. Like a magic wand, a question can call forth new resources that we can exploit to enrich our lives. "What can I appreciate about her right now?" "How could I focus even more fully on this task?" That's because questions nudge our brains creating an orientation and direction as they set brains on a pathway.

Brains seem to have a special affinity for questions—ask a question and our brains act as if they are compelled to answer. Questions are to brains what bones are to dogs. Yet there's something even more magical about questions. In order to answer a question, we not only have to move into a certain orientation, we have to generate certain frames. Frequently, the very process of answering a question causes us to *perform* within a given frame game.

- Why doesn't anyone like me?
- What's really lousy in my life right now?
- What's pleasant and enriching in my life right now?
- How could we improve this product?

This means that the moment that we ask a question, we shape both our *perceptions* of the world and of *ourselves,* who we are, what we're about, what we can accomplish and, in turn, how others perceive us. Pretty powerful, wouldn't you say? There's hardly a linguistic tool more powerful than questions for engaging a mind and thereby controlling our referencing. NLP began with a set of questions, the Meta-Model questions, that simply inquired about the words and phrases that a person uses in formatting his or her view of the world. What specifically do you mean by ...?[1]

Given this *framing power in questions,* we can now give ourselves to asking questions that set frames of resourcefulness, solution, creativity, flexibility, etc.

- If you felt really confident in this, how would that improve things? What would be the first thing you'd do if you had the courage?
- What am I willing to do to turn this around?
- How can I bring more enjoyment and fun to this learning experience?
- Who else can I share this great information with?
- What will it cost me if I don't change this pattern?
- How could I transform my whole life if I did this?

Through Rehearsal and Repetition

A direct and simple installation process involves *repetition.* You can shape any behavior, mind-frame, habit, or response if you *reinforce* the behaviors that you desire with pleasure. Attach massive pleasure to an action and you will shape the behavior.

Whenever you discover a great frame, never leave the scene of that discovery without making *a decision* to *set it* as your frame and never leave without taking some *action* to shape and reinforce it.

Any emotional or behavioral pattern becomes stronger, more developed, and more *set* when we continually replay it and reinforce it. Eventually, it will become an automatic and conditioned response. Withdrawing attention and interest from something similarly extinguishes most responses. This gives us shaping power over the frames that we set, or want set, in our lives.

Whenever you discover a great frame, never leave the scene of that discovery without making *a decision* to *set it* as your frame and never leave without taking some *action* to shape and reinforce it. Use the following installation questions to put some movement and neurology to the frame:

- Have I made a decision about this idea?
- Will I, from this day forward, use this as my frame of reference?
- What can I do that will *act out* and give muscle and bone to this frame?
- What state does this frame initiate?
- How does it show up in my posture, face, tone of voice?

#12: Frame game masters set frames by using repetition, questions, and "mind-to-muscle" processes.

How do you set a frame? All you have to do is *repeat something often enough* and it will get in, it will wear a groove in neurology, and become your reference point—even if you don't believe it, like it, or want it. For things you do like, want, and believe in—welcome it in with lots of repetitions and ask lots of questions that presuppose it. We facilitate the mind-muscle connection by emotionalizing our thoughts. Almost anything we do that activates the body with strong primary emotions (fear, anger, aversion/ attraction, joy/ sadness, lust/ revulsion, stress/ relaxation, etc.) typically creates a strong association within us to the corresponding ideas, concepts, or beliefs and so establishes a frame.

If Only I Could Say No

A sixteen year old girl came to Bob as a client who started with the presenting problem, "I can't say *'No'* to my boyfriend when he wants sex."
Bob: "Do you want to say no?"
Linda: "Sure, I don't want to get pregnant."

Bob explored the meanings, memories, associations, and frames that created her current experience that made her incapable of saying *No.* In the experience of the boyfriend wanting sex, Linda said she just "spaces out." "I tell myself that it will be over soon."

Where, when, and how did she learn this skill? From being sexually abused by a grandfather from the ages of three to nine. From those early experiences, she set these two frames for herself in terms of coping with the world: *"I Can't Say No"* and *"Just Space Out."* Excellent learnings and skills for a three-year old in that context, but horribly out-of-date and unuseful for a strong and vibrant young woman. So part of his way of responding and intervening, Bob inquired about the spacing out. "And how old were you then?"
"It began when I was about three, I think, and continued until I was nine years old."

"And how old are you now?"
"Sixteen" she said quietly.

"I would like for you to say that in a commanding tone. Can you do that?" Yes, she could. Her voice lowered and she uttered her current age with a strong commanding voice. *"Sixteen!"*

"That's right. You are sixteen. You are a brilliant young woman with a really sharp mind. You learned to do the other response as a child, before you could even understand what was going on, didn't you? But now you *know.* And now you can *control* your own thoughts, because, after all, it is your body and you can do with it what you want . . . and you can feel this with the strength of your own commanding voice, can you not?" [*That's The Past* frame; *Personal Power* frame; *It's Your Choice* frame]

That's what happened. She learned to play an entirely different inner game, one under her conscious choice and control.

Setting Frames by Emotionalizing the Idea

When a dominating idea drives us, we not only have it in our head, we have it in our *body* (soma, somatic). As we can *see* and *detect* frames of mind in the way people walk, talk, act, respond, hold themselves, etc. —we can also *plant and set* frames by using physiology and movement. If you would be cheerful, said William James, then act cheerfully. Eventually the emotions will catch up and you will actually begin to feel cheerful.

Frame game masters set frames by using repetition, questions, and "mind-to-muscle" processes.

This applies to many other things. Acting, looking, talking, and dressing with confidence helps to evoke the feeling state of confidence. In these and many other ways we can associate the frames we want with strong emotions and thereby *somatize* the ideas so that they become full-body experiences. When that happens, we *feel* the frame. And, of course, that makes them much more "real" and compelling.

- What would it be like if I sang this frame?
- What would the music and dance of this frame be like?
- Suppose I wrote a pledge of allegiance to this frame?
- Suppose I put it to poetry?

How do we *activate* our emotions? For that matter, what "is" an emotion? We know that *emotions* are intimately related to thinking, to meanings and values, but how? What's the relationship between how we *feel* and our ideas regarding what we believe to be important (valuable) and meaningful?

An "e-motion" is the resulting somatic energy that we feel in the urge to *move out* (ex-) to do something. In an "emotion," we *feel* strongly and intensely about something that we value as meaningful or that we dis-value as meaningless. This creates our "positive" and "negative" emotions. So the process of valuing and attributing significance to something, sets a frame of *significance and importance.* This then elicits an internal sense of desire and hope for it, and if we receive it, then joy, happiness, excitement, contentment, fulfillment, etc. Then our whole nervous system gets involved and reflects our "sense" of something important, significant, and meaningful.

When we *dis-value* something, and view it as hurtful, ugly, distastcful, undesirable, etc., we operate from a frame of negativity. We fear and worry about something occurring. If it does occur, we feel fear, anger, apprehension, disgust, distress, stress, depression, sadness, and a whole range of "negative" feelings.

Emotions arise as the *evaluative judgment* that we make about things (people, events, ideas, etc.). Our evaluation creates the *motions* that we feel in our body. Think of an e-motion as an *evaluative-**motion***, we *move*, and feel moved, when we make any evaluation about something that means something to us.

Figure 11:1
The Evaluation Scale of Emotions

Emotions are entirely dependent upon two things: our internal *frames* (our model of the world) and our perception of our outer *game* of experience and performance in the world. If we imagine these two experiences as two sides of a balancing scale, then an *emotion* is the relationship between them (Figure 11:1).

> ***An "emotion" is* the difference between two phenomena, our inner and outer games, our model of the world and our experience of the world and we register this difference in our body as an emotion.**

When the scales tip downward on the side of the *outer game,* then our experience of the world isn't living up to all that we had mapped and expected in our *inner game model of the world.* So we feel bad. We were expecting, wanting, believing, and hoping a lot more than we received. This doesn't feel so good. It sets off the negative emotions: anger, fear, discontent, frustration, stress, upsetness, and so on.

When the scales tip upward on the side of our *outer game,* then our experience of the world is higher than our *inner game,* we feel great. We have received *more* from the world than we expected. No wonder this feels great! This elicit the positive emotions of joy, happiness, pleasure, delight, playfulness, contentment, etc.

Emotions do not tell us what is real, what exists "out there," or what is right or wrong. *Emotions weigh the difference between expectation and experience,* between belief and reality, between understanding and actuality, between inner and outer games. No wonder we can't trust our emotions to provide us *that* kind of information. On the other hand, we can trust them to tell us about *the relationship* between mind and sensory experience.

This model informs us that our emotions can go astray in two ways. First, we can have an ill-formed, mis-informed, and distorted *model of the world*, the inner game of our expectations, understandings, beliefs, desires, etc. *What* we compare our experiences with may be all wrong, or partly wrong.

If I think, "people should drive according to my standards, lights should always be green, policeman should turn their heads when I speed" —and I don't find that the world works that way, I will experience some not-so pleasant emotions in my body. The outer game I experience will not fit the inner game that I play in my mind. The emotions I feel inside my body are real, "real" to my neurology, and so my neurology will attempt to *actualize* those meanings there.

Second, we may have a distorted and inadequate way of *perceiving* our experience of the world. Even our sensory-based perceptions are not fully external. What we see, hear, feel, etc. are abstractions of the nervous system. No wonder we experience visual, auditory, and kinesthetic illusions and so should not trust everything we see, hear, and feel. Our senses can get tricked in many ways.

#13: We facilitate the mind-muscle connection by emotionalizing thoughts.

Activating the body with a strong primary emotion (fear, anger, aversion/ attraction, joy/ sadness, lust/ revulsion, stress/ relaxation, etc.) typically creates a strong association in our body to the corresponding ideas, concepts, or beliefs and so establishes a frame-of-reference.

If frames create and coach our emotions, then all we need to do is *backtrack to the frame* that provides us the kind of emotions that we want to have.

- What frame coaches the emotions of curiosity and playfulness?
- What frame invites us to step into the emotion of courage and boldness?
- How about love, compassion, joy, fascination, etc.?

Pain Leveraging

Since emotions *incorporate* our ideas and references into the body—the stronger and more intense the emotion—the more likely that we will pay attention to it, focus on it, ask questions about it, and repeatedly attend it. Then all of these processes will increase their influence on us. Then the more likely the emotion will *set a frame.* This holds especially true for *pain.*

After all, there's nothing like *pain* to get our attention, drive some awareness home, and set a frame. There's nothing like a great sense of internal pain that pushes us to the threshold for getting us to make life-changing decisions and changes. Just add some massive and unbearable pain to something— psychic pain (humiliation, insult, rejection, mockery, etc.) and we can create a powerful aversion to an idea, state, person, experience, event, etc.

This explains why framing things with "shoulds" seldom brings about change. The idea of an obligation, a "should," implies an imposition of somebody else's rule.

- I should lose some weight.
- I should exercise more.
- I should take a class and do some self-improvement.
- I should be more kind and thoughtful to my loved ones.

What a different game we play when those *shoulds* become *musts*—energized with strong emotions, especially negative ones.
- "I must lose some weight or else I'll damage my health, become obese, be disrespected, etc."
- "I must finish this project or I'll lose my job, never get the promotion, etc."

Is this true for you? When you turn your frame into *a must,* do you then get things done and take action? When you are left without any other choice, do you then get motivated? Isn't there leverage over stupid frames when there is pain? Yet the *must* must be a positive one or we will fall into the game of "musterbation."

To get a feel for this, access a positively compelling *must* in your own life. What *must* you do? What *must* you not do? What do you absolutely *have to* do? When you find a strong and empowering *must,* one that is positive for you, access it fully. How do you picture it, what sounds and words do you use to encode it? Now step into it so fully that you begin to experience it bodily. As you do, notice the physiology of a positive *must.* Now that you are there, *why you must* do this?

Accessing a positive and enhancing "must" in this way gives you a clear pathway to this neurological power. Think of it as *must power.* With it, you now have a way to set a *must frame* on other things.

Develop a Great Big Why

Yet above and beyond both *should* and *must* is *want* and *get to.* These states move us out of the away-from emotions of pain, compulsion, and need and into the more positive and bright emotions of desire, excitement, and intention. Nietzsche said that the person who has a strong enough *why* can bear almost any *how* that life throws at him or her. From the first time I read that, I have been incredibly impressed with *the power of a giant **why***. Later, I read Viktor Frankl's *Man's Search for Meaning* where he told of his experience in a German concentration camp and his discovery of the power of *meaning* in life. We live for meaning.

The same applies for change, motivation, and implementation. If we have a *big enough "Why,"* we will have no problem taking action. Do you have a big enough *why*? Layering intentions upon intentions, your *meta-outcomes* upon meta-outcomes builds up your *whys*, giving them more power and intensity.

- Why do you want to transform your frame?
- How will that serve to enhance your life?
- When you get that in just the way you want it, what will that do for you that's even more valuable and important to you?

By developing ever-greater *whys*, we can get the personal leverage to create the kind and quality of change we want. The more *motives* that we add to our thinking and emoting, the more our *motivation.*

Once, during the training in New York City, an attractive lady told me that she had just discovered the very thing that had been missing in her life for a number of years,

> "I just have not had a big enough *why.* Now I realize why I have been going from one workshop to another, reading one self-help book after another, I've been looking for my *why.* So how do you find or invent a big enough why?"

I inquired about what she wanted to accomplish and some of her immediate goals. Every time she expressed a goal, I expressed a confirmation of them, "So that sounds pretty important to you!" And for the first eight responses, she went,

> "Well, kind of . . ."

"But not really? It's not really *all that important?"*

> "No, not really."

"So what is an even more important goal for you?"

Eventually we stumbled onto the fact that she loved art and painting even though she had not painted in years.
"So that's really important?"

> "Yes, it is. But I feel strange about saying that because I let my real estate business, my home, my relationships with my adult children, and a million other things come first."

"And yet art and painting seem like, feel like, a true *passion* for you?" [Yes.] And do you have the talent for it?

> "Yes! I'm actually very good at it."

"So tell me, what's so all important about painting?"

That did it. Talk about unleashing a torrent of passion! As she began talking, she became completely animated—fully alive, and as I continued confirmation checks, "So that's really important to you!", she became more and more animated. That enabled me to simply keep checking the frame above that frame, "So how's that valuable?" "What does that mean to you?" "How does that enrich your life?"

When we had finished our "little talk" in that fashion, she had discovered her great *big why*, a why that could set a fire ablaze in her soul and evoke her grandest dreams. It showed in her face and skin. It enlivened her.

Setting and Installing Frames through Personalizing
We have to be very careful what and how we *identify ourselves.* Korzybski pointed out that the heart of unsanity lies in mapping out *identification.* Identification leads to unsanity because there is no identity or sameness. Nothing is ever "the same" as anything else, not even itself. Everything is constantly changing. *Difference* is what prevails in our dynamic process universe.

So even though identification is not real, as a semantic class of life we have the ability to map *identification.* We map what's not real and then our mind-body system attempts to make it internally real. The marvel is that we do this with the tiniest of words. "He *is* an idiot!" "You *are* wonderful!" In English, we language our identity frames with the *"to be"* verbs (is, am, are, was, were, be, being, etc.). This creates "the *is* of identity," and leads to such languaged expressions as "I *am* a father/mother." "I *am* a teacher/ lawyer." "I *am* a republican/ democrat/ or liberal/ conservative." "I am a Catholic/ Protestant/ Buddhist, etc."

In mapping identification, the equation of two things or experiences becomes "real" to us. Neurologically *it becomes neuro-semantically real in our bodies.* As a belief frame, identification sends orders to our nervous system so that it feels absolutely real to us. If, however, we *know* we are identifying with something and do so consciously, we can install frames and make them part of our very *being.* This incredibly empowers the frame.

This explains one of the greatest pains that we humans can experience—the pain of being untrue to ourselves. When we experience incongruency and inconsistency, we feel inauthentic, false to our own values and visions, and a hypocrite. Normally, this bad faith trigger pangs of conscience designed to get us to change. There's hardly a more powerful leverage point in human personality than the drive to preserve our own integrity. Conversely, there's hardly a greater threat than the threat, insult, or realization that we are not preserving our integrity, that we're being inconsistent.

How can we use these dynamics to get leverage on ourselves and install the kind of empowering frames that will transform our lives? We can begin defining, describing, and vividly representing the frames of mind that we desire, long for, believe in, and value. Then we can begin identifying with them . . . seeing ourselves in terms of those frames. Once we have done that, then the pain of not preserving this integrity and the pleasure of preserving it will leverage our actions.

The Art of Setting New Frames

1) Set a new idea as a dominating influence.
2) Emotionalize those ideas so you can feel them.
3) Use the emotion of pain to get leverage.
4) Validate the new frames with powerful *Yeses.*
5) Make your ideas vividly rich and exciting.
6) Ask empowering question that redirect focus.
7) Rehearse the new frame until it's unconscious.
8) Identify with it so it's part of your self-definition.
9) Set a self-organizing intention for it.

Summary

- *We can, and do, set frames each and every day.* Setting frames is not an esoteric thing that only a few masters do. We all do it. What makes the difference is that the masters know it and mindfully manage it. Setting frames is as easy as talking, asking questions, telling stories, layering ideas upon ideas. We cannot *not set* frames.

- Setting frames mindfully and intentionally with full awareness of what we're doing, however, is a very different story. Most of us operate without awareness of the frames we set and live by. Most seem oblivious to the frames that are set for them by others, family, media, culture, etc.

- No wonder then that mastery lies in *awareness* of frame setting processes. Awareness empowers us so that we can truly hear, detect, and operate with the kind and quality of mindfulness that we need regarding the frames that occur in our conceptual world and with which we play.

- We have numerous options with regard to *installing frames* and they all have to do with the way we use the two "royal roads to state" —mind and body, the symbols that we use and the way we use our physiology.

Chapter 12

COVERT FRAME SETTING

"Men are not prisoners of fate,
but only prisoners of their own minds"
Franklin D. Roosevelt

"The medium is the message."
Marshall McLuhan

Setting a new frame that invites a new inner game as the rules for a new outer game of performance is relatively easy when you have an open and cooperative mind. If you know about frames and framing, if you know how to communicationally coach, if you know how to notice, calibrate, and flexibly shift your communications—then the ability to *set frames* collaboratively is typically a delightful adventure, a piece of cake.

- But what about an uncooperative mind?
- How do we set frames with someone who is closed, resistant, or difficult?
- How do we engage in frame setting if the mind that we're dealing with (including our own) is not attentive or doesn't believe in the frame?

A person open to framing things in a new way to play a new inner and outer game makes the process for transformation straightforward and easy. Yet, as we all know, all brains are not so open to new ideas, let alone to paradigm shifts. Sometimes we need to be more covert and surprisingly, this even applies to ourselves.

The last chapter focused on how to set frames directly through vivid and dramatic descriptions, questions, repetition, emotions, personalizing, and leveraging.

- Yet can we set frames more covertly?
- Can we do it subtly, quietly, and even conversationally?
- Can we develop the persuasion elegance to pace and lead a person to a

new *frame game* for success and empowerment?

Because the answer to all those questions is *yes*, I have written this chapter to detail how to make that possible.

Call in the FBI!

Covert Frame Setting

1) Frames by Implication (FBI)
2) Story Telling that activate identification, vividness, and emotional.
3) Metaphors.

One way to covertly set frames is to assume them. We can assume a frame by speaking-and-acting in ways that *presuppose* the frame without even stating it directly. We can even set meta-level frames by *implying* the frame by what we do in words and actions. To this end we can even *perform* a frame to establish it. By acting *as if* a frame is real, our actions endow the implications with a sense of reality. In fact, this probably describes how we unconsciously set most of our frames. Having been born within a culture of frames, we simply grew up inhabiting and performing them. In this way, it was our actions that recruited us to many of our frames. We call these *frames-by-implication* or FBI.

To become an expert at setting frames, acquaint yourself with some of the linguistic structures that create a *semantic presuppositional environment.* In other words, there are linguistic terms and phrases that provide *markers* by which we can slide our implications and connotations into the minds of our listeners. These powerful frame setting devices expand our ability to influence.

Would you like an example? Then suppose I asked you this:

> When it comes to learning and developing new skills, do you enjoy anticipating the process of growth and discovery or, for you, does the experience of joy come after you've attained a new level of competency?

It really doesn't matter whether you answer that question with the first or the second choice. Either choice presupposes that you accept the basic frame which the question sets. Even if you refuse both choices and invent a third or four, still the *frame by implication* of the question itself has done its work.

It's done its work because to answer the question, we accept a frame that is not stated explicitly. We accept the idea that we are interested in the development and enjoyment of new skills. The question is a great question because it sets that frame covertly. *To answer the question we accept an invisible frame of reference and thereby enter its Matrix.* To answer presupposes that we have bought into the frame. In this instance, by focusing on *prior or post* enjoyment of the development of new skills, we respond by going off in one of those directions.

We answer by filling in the details about *when* we experience the most enjoyment. We do not question *if* we will enjoy it or if we can develop new skills. Enjoyment and development is assumed and presupposed.

Do you see the trick in how *frames by implication* work? They operate as a "sleight of mind" that shifts consciousness away from certain thoughts by shifting us to other awarenesses. Yet while this is tricky in effect, it is also common in structure. That's because this describes how our brains work and the effect of language in our mind-body system. We cannot maintain awareness of all frames in any given moment. When it comes to the limits of attentional demands on consciousness, we are generally limited to 5 to 9 chunks of information (Miller, 1956).

> ***Energy flows where attention goes —as determined by intention.***

Knowing this, expert frame setters and transformers use this limitation. The frames that we assume establish the working assumptions which we do not question and that we do not want questioned. The focus shifts to *the details* inside of the frame. These direct *attention* so that any answer reinforces the higher frame which conveniently stays outside of awareness.

In this example, I asked an either-or question that was embedded inside of two frames, two frames that happened to be resourceful. In that I invited you to play the following inner and outer games:

- *You Can Enhance Your Life By Developing New Skills.*
- *You Can Have Lots of Fun Doing So.*

How did I build that structure? I put the question inside of these frames. The frames were covertly implied by the question, but not made explicit. This then allowed you to dance within the frame.

> Before we begin the process of transforming the old feelings of fear and distress about the negative opinions of others (which describes how most of us have been culturalized), I want to find out *just how much more resourceful, confident, and effective* you'll be at work and in personal relationships when you move through the world fully realizing that the opinions of others are just that, their opinions, and that you don't have to personalize them, feel bad about them, or automatically take them as a reflection on yourself, but that you can treat the opinions of others as communication and feedback. So given that, how much more empowered will that make you? And are you game to do this today?

Here's another example. Did you catch how I layered one idea upon another, with suggestions, realizations, and understandings inside the question? I used a question to direct consciousness to a more immediate concern, *How much more resourceful will this make you?* Yet to answer that question, you have to step into a place (or Matrix) governed by these higher frames. You have to assume and presuppose these frames, frames that you would find difficult to even articulate to answer. In asking this question, I have invited you to play another *frame game*, the *How Can I Become More Resourceful?* game (Figure 12:1)

Figure 12:1

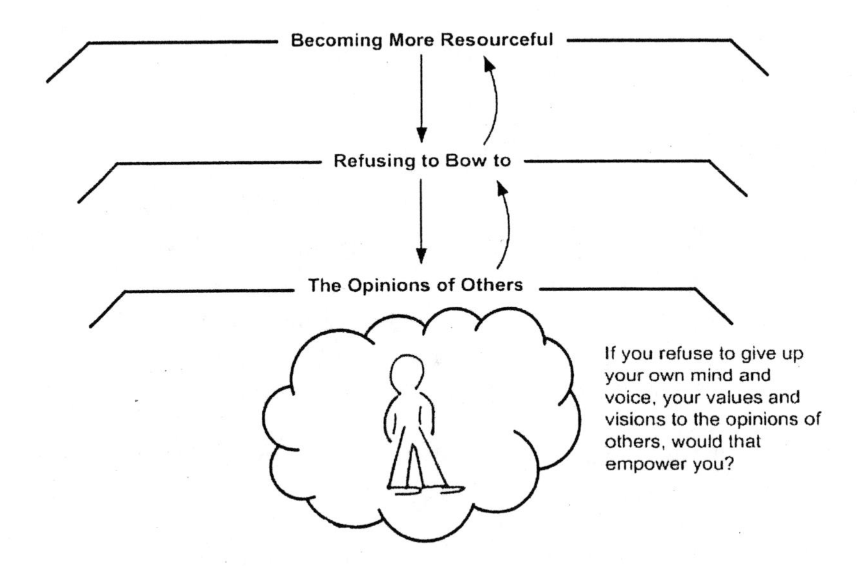

This highlights the power of frame-setting by presupposition. By asking someone questions about the details of an idea, skill, experience, etc., we set up a double awareness. We *foreground* the detail question while we simultaneously *background* all of the frames that have to be there for the question to make sense. This *backgrounding* keeps some of these frames out-of-awareness, it keeps that matrix of frames in the background. It sends the meaning upward to the framework where they operate as the assumptive world in which we live, move, think, and interact. We don't even question it. It's the *canopy of consciousness* of the Matrix of our frames within which we operate.

The question or statement within this frame focuses our mental and emotional energies to simply follow the direction of the details. This becomes the path of least resistance, mentally. What mechanism explains this process?

Energy flows where attention goes—as determined by intention.

Our mental, emotional, and physical energies go to where we send our attention. And we send our attention to things that we have determined as valuable and important to us.

#14: Play flows where the game goes—as saith the frame. Energy flows where attention goes—as determined by intention.

The higher frame of *intention and structure* formats, organizes, and controls the flow of energy and attention. It creates pathways for consciousness to more easily flow.

Setting *frames* by implying or presupposing some unspecified idea means using statements or questions that assume some frame. Then, *any* answer that is given confirms and validates the frame. *Any* answer supports and solidifies the frame. *Any* answer empowers the frame and *performs* the frame. *Any* answer simply follows the path of least mental resistance as the intentional frame governs the flow of attention and energy. We just go to where the conceptual structure leads us. Here are some more examples:

- How would becoming un-insultable increase your personal confidence and calmness at work and at home?
- Where would you want to become more kindly assertive in your communications?
- What would enable you best to learn these patterns—would silently reading them to yourself every day until you knew them inside out or sharing them with a good friend and enjoying that kind of interaction?

Play flows where the game goes —as saith the frame. Energy flows where attention goes —as determined by intention.

Now for something most *shocking* and disturbing about all of these governing frames. If these mechanisms establish the higher framework of our Matrix, which then determines our states of mind, emotion, belief, and our skills, etc., then they can be very detrimental if we process *negative content* in them. This means we can sometimes answer questions that presuppose *toxic* things that will ruin life, disrupt emotions, sabotage effectiveness, undermine peace of mind, and make life a living hell.

Consider *that!* Quite innocently we can ask (or be asked) some very toxic questions which can set some intensely morbid frames and accidently invite a person into a hell of a mess or into an insolvable conflict. Having prepared you for that (I have, haven't I?), read the following *with this in mind* so that you will *not* internalize them. Step back as you read them so that you can see the toxic frame that's implied within them.

- When do you feel worse, when you're making a mistake in front of your boss or when your boss finds out about a mistake later?
- When do you struggle with performance anxiety the most, when you are under time pressures or when you want to impress someone?

Absolutely refuse to answer these questions! Why? Because the very act of unmindfully answering them accepts the invisible frames behind them thereby promoting some destructive and toxic ideas. Does this powerfully alert you to *the danger of answering some questions?* I hope so. If we answer questions that presuppose that we are victims, helpless, hopeless, worthless, inadequate, doomed, etc., we step into a sick and morbid Matrix, one of dragon or demon frames. They recruit us to *perform* within a frame game that we may not believe or want.

How's your *frame detector*? If you have a frame detector well installed in your head (you do play the *Frame Detection* game, don't you?), then you can catch yourself before you consume a plate of nuclear waste. Then you will know that it's time to step aside from that frame. Did you notice the protective frame I used a moment ago? Prior to introducing a couple of mild toxic questions, I wrote this:

> Quite innocently we can ask very toxic questions and set some intensely morbid frames and accidently invite ourselves or another into a hell of a mess. Having prepared you for that (I have, haven't I?), read the following *with this in mind* so that you will *not* internalize them.

What did I presuppose in those lines? What frames did I suggest accept which would give you the ability to read without stepping into the frame?

A master frame game player learns how to play the *Frame Awareness* game at a moment's notice. The frame I have set that supports this is, *If I see and smell the plate of obnoxious poison, I don't have to eat it.* With that in mind, examine the following sick statements in terms of their assumptive frames.

> If we answer questions that presuppose that we are victims, helpless, hopeless, worthless, inadequate, doomed, etc., we step into a sick and morbid Matrix, one of dragon or demon frames.

- Given the dysfunctional home that you suffered through as a child, how has that abuse (or neglect, spoiling, etc.) undermined your effectiveness as an adult and keep sabotaging you with questions about self-worth, fear of conflict, etc.?
- How devastating has this trauma been for you in terms of destroying your trust in others and undermining your self-esteem?
- Why can't you do anything right around here? What's wrong with you that you never use your head before you act?

If we can set frames by simply *asking questions,* offering suggestions, and orienting ourselves or others in destructive ways, we obviously need to build a *Question Detection Alert* system in ourselves. Then we can take that moment to *pause* so that we can *question* the question.

- Should I answer this question as posed?
- What Matrix of frames does this question presuppose?

- To what is this question attempting to recruit me?
- What frames will I be stepping into and assuming as real, legitimate, and useful when I begin answering this question?
- Does this question support or hinder my resourcefulness?
- What thoughts and feelings will the answers to this question generate in me?
- How will this question help me? How could it possibly enhance my life?
- What information will the question poser obtain from this question?
- What Matrix is this question inviting me into or recruiting me for?

One final comment about frames by implication. These work because we use terms, language forms, symbols, etc. to *imply* other unspoken assumptions and beliefs. Always count on nearly every single frame having *implied frames within it.* Also, the more semantically packed a statement, the more presuppositional statements used at a single time, the more semantically dense the frame. And with semantic denseness comes more difficulty in pulling it apart as well as an inability to resist. So always be ready to call for the FBI and to examine if some destructive FBI are present. Simply ask, What are the frames by implication in this idea or experience?

Setting Frames Covertly via Story Telling

If simple questions can set a frame, imagine the power of a *story*. That's because a story invites us into an imaginary world. Via a story we just step right into a world with its operational principles, rules, beliefs, values, understandings, etc. so that we don't question any of it.

A story seduces us in so many ways. It invites us to step into one or more of the characters. We identify with story characters in order to understand the story. In doing so we *enter into a world*—if only for just a few minutes. Yet in entering into a story we also enter into, and take on, the frames by implication that inform and drive the plot, the drama, the emotion, and the experience. Here the mechanisms of empathy, sympathy, identification, and modeling *set the frame.*

Apparently, the biggest problem that Thomas Edison had in inventing the electric light bulb involved finding the right materials from which to make a filament. His biographers tell about his adventure in exploring all the many different kinds of materials until he found just the right one. He never seemed to question whether he would find the right substance, he believed he would, and so he never viewed any experiment as failing. Each succeeded. Until he found it, he succeeded every time by eliminating one more choice, "No, that's not it." He kept limiting the field until he found the right one.

"How did it feel to fail a thousand times, Mr. Edison?" some reporter supposedly asked him—apparently clueless about the frames by implication in that question.

> "Why I never failed once," Edison responded, stepping cleaning around the toxic frame and refusing to accept that frame. "I found a thousand ways that didn't work."

What a different perspective! That's certainly a different way to look at things. Edison played a different game, *the "No Failure" Game,* and so lived in a different world.

- From a frame game analysis of that story, what do we have there?
- What frames does the story suggest, imply, assume, and set?

Stories are excellent semantic devices for frame setting because they enliven ideas, concepts, and beliefs. They give us a new experience—from which to generalize more empowering frames. Because they give us the screenplay for a new movie to play in our mind, it's easy to experience stories in the theater of our mind. We can more easily step into them and let them work their frame-setting magic.

- What story could you tell or make up that would set a useful and enhancing frame?
- What stories do you hear that serve you well?
- What stories do you hear that are toxic in nature?

The story frame enables us to plot an idea or an experience into a story format with a beginning, middle, and ending. It allows us to outframe things with a plot, a theme, and a style. Using the framework of a story, we can also transform events so that they comprise a heroic journey, comedy, or discovery rather than tragedy, horror story, etc.

Take a moment and explore the stories that have recruited you— those that pull on you and those that have become frames in your mind. What stories have you been told, and which do you rehearse, which initiate the games you play? As you now run a Quality Control on them, do you find them all that enhancing and life affirming? Would you like to be storied in a new way?

As covert frame setting, we can now appreciatively explore the power and pervasiveness of *narrative* as a higher level frame within our minds. After all, we all carry various *stories* with us as we move through the world —stories that we use to make sense of things, to explain things, to give us guidance about how to act, what roles to play, etc. We have personal and family stories, racial stories, cultural stories, religious and philosophical stories, etc.

- What stories have you grown up with?
- What kind of a story have you been living: drama, comedy, tragedy, melodrama, soap opera, hero, etc.?
- How enhancing and empowering have you found them?
- Who storied you?

- Do you need that story any longer?
- What story would you like to de-story?
- What new story would you like?

Freedom Beyond the Walls

In his middle years, Daniel was now a single adult male and feeling stuck, frustrated, worried, and depressed. Why? Wouldn't you know it, it was about a woman. He had recently met a lady and wanted to pursue her. So what was the problem? His head. Having had two failed marriages and now back in "the dating scene," Daniel felt desperate about creating a solid relationship and played several negative inner games in his head. Just thinking about the fact that she lived a long way away sent him into a state of worry and depression. When he showed up at Dr. Bob's office he said he was "feeling internally blocked."

> "I've always known that I have had a *wall* inside me, but I have never known how to get rid of it."

Bob: "That's great Daniel! Most of the time I have to spent lots of time and work uncovering such walls. Since you have already discovered your internal walls, you are out ahead of the game of re-engineering your mind. . . . So how do you feel about this woman today?" [Framing with validation and progress.]

> Daniel: "Well, as I sit here right now, I know that I shouldn't worry about her responses to me. I know that there's nothing I can do about it, and I wonder how I should approach her. It's still very frustrating."

Bob: "Daniel, let me summarize some of the discoveries you have already made in our time together. First, nothing has meaning until a human brain encounters it and gives it meaning. That means you can choose to give things a whole range of meanings. It means you can also give it the meaning that serves you best. How long have you known Jennifer?" [Framing with backtracking, orientation frames, and the power to create meaning.]

> "Since April this year."

"What meaning did she have to you before April?"

> "None. None at all."

"That's right, it was only after you gave her meaning through your email communications that you started to develop feelings for her. And from your meanings, your emotions arose."

> "So I have control over my emotions by taking control of the meanings that I give to things."

"That's exactly right! You have certainly learned that one well! This means that nothing, and no one, can cause you to feel anything that you choose not to feel. Jennifer can only hurt you as *you* give her permission to do so. You've done a good job worrying about all of this and you did it by how you have been talking to yourself." [Framing with more confirmation and choice.]

"I never thought about my worrying as a skill, but I have become really good at it."

"Yes, it's your brain that runs the worrying program and you also can choose the content of what it processes." [Inviting him to play *It's My Brain* game.]

"Yes, I know that worry is a waste of time."

"One last summary item, the suggestion I made about getting into the habit of asking yourself, 'Does this thinking serve me well?' 'Does it make things better for me?' How has that been going?"

"Oh yes, the ecology check. I've been doing that pretty often."

"Great. So now, check out how you feel about all of that frustration and depression. What do you feel and where do you feel it?"

"Here in my stomach."

"Okay, I want you to welcome and listen to its meaning for you." [Framing with acceptance and exploration.]

"It feels like a wall . . ."

"Get in touch with all that. And now let yourself wonder, 'How does this wall serve me?' What does it seek to accomplish for me that's positive?" [Inviting the *Positive Intention* game.]

"It wants to protect me. It makes me feel safe and yet I do want to get out of it and move beyond this wall."

"Great. What stops you from doing that?" [Framing with solution and possibility.]

"Just the wall itself. If only I could crash through it. I really don't need it anymore."

"Do you have other ways to feel safe? To protect yourself? To communicate and interact effectively?"

"Yes. I built the wall when I was eight years old and needed it, but I've grown up a lot since then."

"Yes you have. And you've become quite resourceful in many ways. So I imagine that if you looked down and found a big hammer, you'd be ready to just bust right on through that wall, wouldn't you?"

"Yes."

"So as you see that big hammer, go ahead."

"I'm hitting the wall, but it's not breaking, only chipping."

"Great, continue chipping away at the same spot until it shatters."

"It is . . ."

"And what's beyond the wall? "

"I don't know . . . a weird feeling, I guess a sense of freedom . . . It's really strange."

"Yes, you've just broken through a mental and emotional wall that's held you back and made you feel weak and vulnerable, and now that you're *free from that,* take a moment to notice all of the positive things that you are *free to* do, feel, and experience."

"I'm free to explore the world and relationships, to apply my values, to be true to my values . . ."

Frame Setting via Metaphors

If we let X stand for any facet of life such as work, exercise, managing, parenting, studying, then the question, *What is it like?* elicits a covert way of framing. It allows us to literally "bring over" (*phorein*) one idea as the frame for another (*meta*). That's what a *meta* is *for.* In using a metaphor, we embed our subject inside of a higher frame of another reference and set up suggestive similarities.

Suppose we are talking about communicating to influence in the context of marketing, selling, negotiating, or writing. What is that like? Is it like *a war* or *a dance*? "Communication is a battle of ideas." "Communication is a dance of ideas." The metaphor in each elicits a very different set of emotions, references, and rules and implies very different frameworks. Each metaphor sets frames with influences so that when we exchange words, we get a different sense of what's going on. Each suggestively and covertly brings to mind a whole domain of experience (war, conflict, battles, guns, bombs, defenses, strategies, etc. versus dancing, rhythm, music, fun, romance, playfulness, moves, etc.).

Every metaphor does this. Every metaphor induces different states as well as sets of skills. "Communicating with him is like a battle" elicits *the War Frame* game that operates by different rules, beliefs, decisions, values, identities, etc. "Communicating with him is like a dance" calls *the Dance Frame* game into existence, along with everything that entails.

Metaphor awareness also gives us another way to fragment or deframe a toxic structure. When we don't hear or notice a metaphor, we never call it into question. Hearing it, however, gives us the delightful opportunity to question it, to explore it, and to unravel it strand by strand. That's what Bob did with Daniel, he explored the metaphor of a *wall* blocking him in a way that empowered Daniel to blast through it.

Back to Jill

Previously in chapter seven, we left Jill in her meta-muddles, with frames upon frames that created some pretty morbid *frame games* (see pages 72-74). In an effort to protect herself, she also had outframed herself in a way that *closed the framing system.* This allowed her to discount every helpful suggestion. It allowed her to "know" intuitively the toxic frame, "The Past Determines the Future." In this way, these ideas solidified her frames so that it didn't leave any room for transformation.

What do we do then? What can we do when we find someone who does not have *any mental or conceptual room* that even allows for the possibility of improvement? The answer is that *we make room.* How do we do that? How do we create *space* for solutions?

First, *by shaking up the old frames.* By sabotaging them, preventing them from working, blowing them apart, shoving contradictions and exceptions in their face, provoking a person to threshold, pulling apart the stuff that makes up the frame, etc. We *de-frame.* We de-stabilize the old frames that hold the person's mapping Matrix together. When someone suffers from dictatorial and tyrannical frames that dominant to such an extent that nothing else is allowed, we have to take a revolutionary deconstructivist's position and set out to *destroy* the frame. Deframing becomes our leverage point.

We have several strategies for charting our way in deframing. We can:
1) *Exaggerate* the frame until it bursts; the Threshold Approach.
2) *Spoil it from the inside.* Enter into it fully and spoil it from within, the Spoiler Approach.
3) *Prescribe the frame* so that they run with full conscious awareness, the Weird Antagonist Approach.
4) *De-construct it* by pulling it apart piece by piece, the Reductionistic Approach.
5) *Question it* into a state of doubt, skepticism, or death, the Questioning and Doubting Approach.
6) *Confront* the person with the frame by putting the frame in the person's face, the In Your Face Approach.

Every one of these approaches involves a paradoxical stance and one that any coach, therapist, consultant, parent, manager, or leader may have a hard time stomaching. Yet, when a person's nested set of frames *excludes* being helped, then "attempting to help" will only make it worse. So, anyone who truly wants to be an effective people helper needs to know when it's time to stop running the compassion, sympathy, empathy, and kindness strategy. Anyone who is playing the game, *"Yes, but..."* or *"Try in Vain to Fix Me!"* will only feed the therapist's need to be helpful. This puts those who are "inherently helpful," and all those helpers who 'have to" help, at a disadvantage. In such case, the time has come to kick some butt, to destroy mental frames, to deconstruct reality —to deframe.

On the surface it may not seem nice, yet in the long term it is the most loving thing we can do.

Deframing a Frame of Mind

Jill, I have to admit. You are one of the most skilled experts, if not the very best expert, that I've ever encountered at defeating therapists, psychologists, and psychiatrists. Congratulations! How many notches do you on your belt? [Exaggeration, Provoking]

> "What? I don't understand what you're saying. Don't you believe me? Why can't I get people to believe me?" [Playing *Poor Me! I Can't Believe You Are Talking This Way to Me!*]

That's good; that's real good. Go right for *the Victim game* and deny your skills and expertise which you use in showing the professionals that you're much more powerful than them.

> "Why are you talking to me this way. You're being so cruel." [Sniffing and whining]

Yes, you've got a great *come on* to try to get me to play the game of rescuing you from all your misery and pain, and to not hold you accountable to your powers or to not believe in your potentials, yet as we both know, it's just a Game. You're not going to get better; you're not going to take any actions that will turn things around. You have far too much invested in staying a Victim.

> "But my dad victimized me. He abused me and that's why I've been a failure all my life. You just don't understand . . ."

> Yet, when a person's nested set of frames *excludes* being helped, then attempting to help will only make it worse. So, anyone who truly wants to be an effective people helper needs to know when the time has come to stop running the compassion, sympathy, empathy, and kindness strategy.

I understand that you've learned to play *the Blame Game* really well so that today you avoid taking personal responsibility. And I think you should continuing blaming your dad, your mom, the school district, those stupid kids, that selfish boyfriend, those incompetent counselors, and everybody else, even yourself.

Why? Because it's a lot easier to *blame* than to change. In fact, most of us feel pretty powerful when we blame. And if you blame in a little whinny voice that sounds depressed, that's even better. Then no one will blame you for your blaming, they'll try to rescue you, and then you can show those bastards that they can't help you! You've got a great scam going!

> "It's not a scam, it's real. I was fired unjustly; I was rejected by a bum;

> and tried hard to get my life together, but I never get any real help, no body really understands or even tries to understand . . . I just want to be understood."

Jill, that's a masterpiece! You get your dander up a little bit—a tad bit of anger to deny what you're doing, then you play *I'm so Helpless and Misunderstood.* It's a great game.

> "Why are you trying to hurt me? It's not a game."

Of course it is not. It's "the *Not*-Game," and one that you have learned to play really well. Actually, it's a skill. Let's do this, I'll say something . . . a suggestion about something that might get you out of your depression and you tell me all the ways it will not work. Okay?

> "No. I don't . . ."

You don't want me to suggest ways for you to get better?

> "Well, yes . . . I mean . . ."

You mean what?

> "You're tricking me."

Tricking you in what way?

> "Tricking me to get better."

You don't want that?

> "Well, yes, but . . ."

Come on, you don't really want to play *that* game, do you. You want to play *"Yes, But . . "* with me. I suggest things you can do to improve your life, get out of your depression, quit the blaming, that kind of thing, and while you feebly try it, you show me that it won't work.

> "Yes, I do. I really do want to get better. I've been trying for years to get better . . . I've seen dozens of doctors . . ."

Ah, the game! Dozens of doctors, and yet none can help! See how powerful you are?

> "No, I really do want to get better."

I doubt it. I don't even think that you could name one thing that you've ever done that began to improve things in the least, that gave you a little hope, and that worked to begin to set a new direction? I bet you can't.

> "Sure I can. Once I began walking and that made me feel better for awhile, but some kids laughed at me and called me a fatso. So I quit."

So you conned yourself out of improvement in that instance. *"Yes,* it was working, *but* I can't stand the work or struggle it takes! I refuse to be mocked."

> "Well, what was I suppose to do? Get laughed at?"

Ah, that's right. Better depressed and suicidal than suffer the pain of mockery from some kids! That makes sense. I always tell people to cut their wrists rather than ignoring an insult. An insult, after all, is the worst thing in the world. [Exaggeration]

"You're mocking me."

So now you have to quit therapy. Now you have to feel depressed, to feel like a victim, right? That's the game. Tell me that you have to, that you have no other choice or option. Come on, it's your game.

"No, I don't *have to*, but I'm not going to be mocked."

Did I hear you right? Did you just shift? Did you actually make an empowering *choice* to control your own thinking and emoting? Did you just access a *value* and decide to make it dominant?

"Well. . . . [sheepishly] . . . yeah."

I'm proud of you, I didn't know that you would access the right to stand up for yourself to me so quickly. That's great. I didn't think you'd be willing to shift and play a new frame game for quite some time. Guess you're pretty sick and tired of the old games you've been playing, huh?

"Yeah, I really am."

I guess you really do know that the problem isn't you, but that *the frame is the problem.* And that you can set a new frame whenever you want to.

"Well, I always thought I was the problem."

How does it feel to realize that *you are so much more* than whatever frame of meaning you have in your head and that you can use other frames?

"Good. It gives me hope . . ."

But you'll have to give up so much —that old Victim Identity, the self-righteous feelings of defeating helpers, that's a lot to give up.

"(Laughing) Are you kidding? Good riddance."

Summary

- *We can and do set frames* and we do it every time we open our mouth to inquire about something, tell about our day, report an event, use a metaphor, etc. We cannot *not set* frames.

- *Awareness* of frame setting involves not only the explicit and overt mechanisms and linguistic devices, but also the more covert and implicit processes. As we practice our frame detection skills we develop a *mindfulness* about the layers of frames and frames of frames within the Matrix World that we live in. With that awareness comes true choice which begins the pathway for taking charge of our life.

- Whether by presupposition and implication, by story or metaphor, or by symbolic actions, we are forever setting and installing frames. May you do so with grace and elegance, and with respect as you honor yourself and others. May the games you play bring out the best in you and others and contribute to making the world a more loving and enjoyable place to live.

Chapter 13

FRAME SOLIDIFICATION

It's not enough to set and install frames.
We've got to lock them in place if they are to be sustained.

On a cold wintry day, Lucy asks a question of Charlie Brown as they skated on a pond. Now, if simply asking questions can *set a frame*, consider the frame Lucy sets via her question. What does she presuppose as a given that he should not even question? What Matrix did she seek to recruit Charlie Brown to?

> "Charlie Brown, how does it feel to know that you will never be a hero?"

Well, that was too obvious. It was so overt that Charlie Brown immediately began questioning it. In fact, here he fights hard against it.

> "What makes you think I'll never be a hero? I may surprise you! I may save a life or report a fire or do almost anything!"

Wow! Here is a *frame war.* Who will win? Who will set the highest frame that will govern the interaction? Lucy's question lacks the subtly of expression that could have hidden it and made it more indirect. As Charlie Brown heard it, he *did not buy* it, but argued back. But Lucy persevered. Putting her face in his, she said bluntly,

> "Let me put it this way. How does it feel *way down deep inside in your very heart of hearts* to know that you will never be a hero?"

Ah, that did it. Stopped immediately in his tracks and frowning severely, he groaned,

> "Terrible!"

In this conversation, Lucy set the frame. She called in the FBI as she presupposed enough higher level frames of meanings that established the lower level question as "just a given." Here she played the Game of "Let's get to the Really Deep Core Reality of your Life." The frame by implication was that his immediate answer was glib, without deep consideration, and a denial of reality ("way down deep inside your very heart of hearts"). She also set a frame about "Felt Reality" ("how does it feel to know . . .") and applied it to the knowledge of never being a hero. This moved things up a level above his answer of certain actions ("save a life," "report a fire").

Figure 13:1

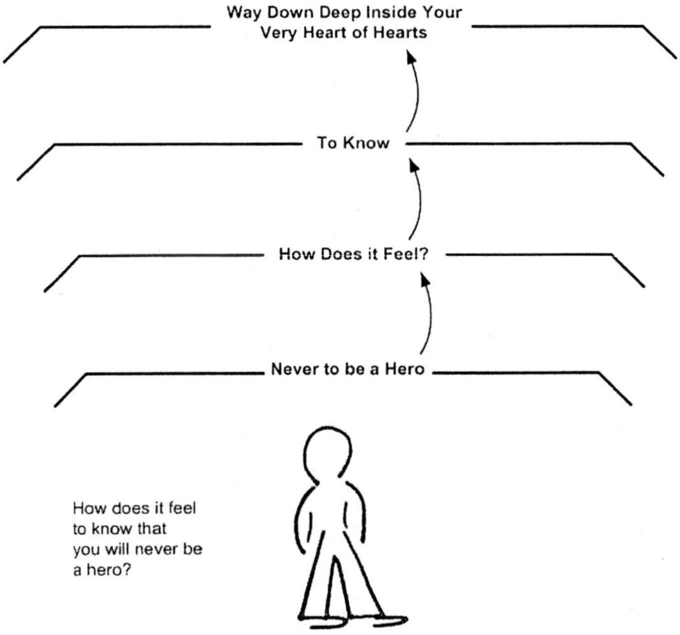

Way Down Deep Inside Your Very Heart of Hearts

To Know

How Does it Feel?

Never to be a Hero

How does it feel to know that you will never be a hero?

Frame Setting

In terms of the process of the mechanisms involved in setting frames, what did Lucy do to win the frame war and to set the frame for Charlie Brown? She did not argue with the possibilities of actions that Charlie Brown presented. To have argued with him would have given at least *some validation* to his argument. By ignoring it completely, she avoided an escalating, "No you won't!" "Yes I might!" exchange.

Then by adding adjective descriptions (i.e., "way down deep inside," "in your very heart of hearts") she *implied* that he needed to *go beyond* surface statements, rationalizations, denials, defense mechanisms, and get to the higher or more core reality and to then face the existential horror in its full fury. To then solidify that, she asked a layered question, one that had a lot of semantic denseness:

*"How does it **feel** to **know*** that ...? "

Isn't that a powerful example of a *frame-by-implication* question? The "knowing" that she here presents is presupposed, the only question is "the feeling?" In the very process of answering the question, in slides the assumption: "you know you will never be a hero." This puts the never-be-a-hero idea in the background as the assumptive Matrix, which then leaves the *foreground* open as the focus of attention, "How do you feel given that?" Then, as Charlie Brown stepped into that Matrix, he responded as one who was within that toxic frame.

Framing involves setting up a structure that we assume as real, meaningful, "the way things are," etc. The mechanisms that govern this mental process involve repetition, emotional intensity, dramatic vividness, confirmation, and using criteria.

The Mechanisms of Frame Setting

- *Repetition*
- *Emotional intensity*
- *Dramatic vividness that makes it memorable*
- *Confirmation and validation that makes it "real"*
- *Using the person's convincer criteria*

The Day Charlie Brown Wins the Frame War

In the exchange, Lucy and Charlie Brown were engaged in a frame war. Her frame about him ("not hero material") went against his frame ("I have the possibility of doing something heroic"). Yet in that exchange, his frame *lost the war.* She out-maneuvered him by *out-framing* him. She jumped a "logical level" and set an even higher frame that reinforced and supported the original frame. And he fell into her trap.

When it comes to changing or transforming a frame, *direct attack* of a frame typically makes it worse. We hear someone utter some belief about something and then challenge that belief frame. Then lo and behold, instead of them examining it with a clear minded objectivity, they get defensive. They counter-attack. Then an argument ensues with each side drawing up battle lines and each feeling embattled.

Where do your mind and emotions go when someone says, "That's a really stupid idea!" Do you not immediately *defend* the idea as legitimate? Most of us do. It's our natural state. We do not like being wrong, and we especially do not like being made wrong in the eyes of another. Yet frames *solidify* through argument and defensiveness. That's why we have to be very careful about *arguing*—we will probably only provoke the other person to solidify his or her frames rather than weaken them.

Now suppose Charlie Brown had read *Frame Games,* or *Winning the Inner Game,* or had participated in Frame Games or Matrix Games trainings and had become skilled enough to recognize Lucy's toxic *frame* question. Just suppose Charlie Brown knew how to detect, flush out, and refuse *frame games.* Then he could have played with a lot more finesse and skill. He could have responded with any one of these come backs:

1) *Frame exposure:*

"Good Grief Lucy. Why do you always have to assume the worse and impose your world views on other kids? You almost got me there. But, I must say, 'No thanks.' I don't want to go to your sick party about never being a hero!"

2) *Frame switching:*

"Good Grief, Lucy. Are you on that kick about knocking down the hero that resides inside all kids again? I've got a better game, why don't we play, *What kind of a hero would you like to be when you grow up?"*

3) *Frame reversal:*

"Good Grief, Lucy! Are you playing, 'Hero Killer again?' Tell me three desperate feelings that you will experience as *your* answer to that question, then I'll play along and invent even better ones. Come on!"

The Art of Frame Solidifying

From the *frame* detection move of refusing a frame, to shifting, inventing, constructing, and setting an entirely new frame, we now come to the final move, *solidifying a frame.* Changing a frame and keeping the change. When you find a frame that you really like, that brings out your best, that increases your personal power and resourcefulness, that makes you feel radiant, joyful, and passionate—then consider endowing it with qualities so that it becomes your automatic and default program.

How do we *solidify* a frame and make it our *frame of mind* so that it eventually becomes the *framework* of our executive mind?

1) Outframe with confirmation upon confirmation.

Repeatedly bring a *"Yes!"* to it so that you meta-*Yes* the frame and do so repeatedly "up the levels."

2) Outframe it with a clear-cut decision.

Decide that "From this day forward, this shall be my frame."

3) Identify with it.

"I am . . . and shall define myself as a solution focused person who plays the *"There's Always a Solution"* game.

4) Use repetition and abundant rehearsal until it takes as it drops out of consciousness and becomes an automatic response.

This is what Lucy did with Charlie Brown, she repeated and layered the question.

5) Consistently refresh the frame.
Refresh it so it stays vividly emotional and dramatic in the mind. Access a state of naive seeing and experiencing as if you are taking it on for the first time.

6) *Future pace the frame.*
In your imagination, see it playing out into your future and enjoy all the transformations that it brings.

Do You Really Want This?

Provoking a person to *fight for* their frames of mind activates their own internal forces evoking them to own it as their own.

Whether in consulting or in demonstrations in trainings, I've found that a great way to set and solidify a new frame of reference is by *provoking* people into the *Yes-ing experience* so they make it their own. To do that, I begin with a basic question like, "Do you really want this to be your frame-of-reference?"

"Yes, I do."

"No, I think you're just saying that. This would not really make that much improvement in your life. Come on, get real. You don't really want this!"

"Yes I do!"

"Nah! I know you. You don't mean this. You're not willing to pay the price to make this your frame of mind. Think about the energy and focus this would demand. You're not up to it!"

"Yes I am and I'll show you!"

By provoking a person to *fight for* the frames of mind he or she wants activates their own internal forces thereby evoking them to *own* it as their own. It also reinforces the frame, calls for a personal commitment, refreshes the frame, and incorporates the frame into the muscles by activating stronger emotions. It directs attention to the focus of the frame and refreshes the intentionality.

Well, maybe you do really want this, but I know you, *you* haven't made a real decision for it yet.

"Yes, I have! I don't know why you think that? What's wrong with you anyway?"

Sure you'd *like* to have this. Sure this would enrich your life and put you on the road to fulfilling many of your dreams and personal visions, but you just have not made a real manly (or womanly) decision, not one that will cut the mustard. I can hear it in your voice. And I see it in your posture and, in fact, all of your body tells me that you don't really mean this.

> "By God, I mean this! I really, really want this! And regardless of anything you say or do, you're not going to get in my way of making this happen!"

Then why are you talking in that sissy, wishy-washy tone of voice?

> "Look buster . . . your inability to see a decisive person isn't going to con me out of my empowering decision."

So you really do want this?

> "Yes, of course!"

Identifying with the Decision

"So is this the kind of person you want to be? Having made this decision that you'll think and focus in this way, and it will manifest itself in this or that behavior, do you want to make this part of who you are?"

> "Yes, definitely. This is who I am."

"So how many more times will you have to repeat this idea as your decision for not only functioning, but also for being, until it really takes? How many times on a daily basis during the next two or three weeks would you like to repeat this so that it becomes your automatic way of thinking and operating?"

> "I'd like to repeat it ten times a day. And to mention it to at least one person every single day."

"Then after that, how often will you want to mention it in order to keep this frame refreshed in your mind and emotions?"

> "Probably once or twice a day, morning and evening."

"So as you now imagine playing out the frame until it becomes your frame of mind, let it play out into your future and just notice . . . how's that?"

Multiply Layering and Looping

In *Neuro-Semantics* we realize that "mind," in all of its complexity, is made up of the stuff of thoughts. Recognizing this gives us a leverage point for change and transformation. All we have going in the highest and most complex concepts, abstractions, paradigms, beliefs, etc. are *thoughts.* We encode these thoughts at all levels using the same component pieces—the sights, sounds, sensations, and words (sentences, stories, metaphors, diagrams) of our mental movie. Given this, what makes the higher levels more complex? There are several factors:

1) Layering.

We use our reflexivity to keep reflecting back onto previous thoughts and thereby create layers upon layers of thoughts-about-thoughts. This self-reflexivity enables us to then build abstract ideas and to create embedded systems of beliefs.

2) Forgetting and lost in the system.

With the layering effect, we often simply forget what we layered onto another idea to create the higher abstractions as the layers become increasingly more complicated.

3) Emergence.

Because mind-body operates as a holistic system, when we reflexively layer thought upon thought, feeling upon feeling, concept upon concept, eventually new *emergent* properties arise which are more than the sum of the parts. "Courage," for example, emerges from the willingness to take a risk while facing a fear.

These are the factors that gives us the ability to create *designer experiences* and *designer frames* at our discretion. How? Once we have a *primary level thought* or *emotion* about something that we would like to use as a *reference*, we only have to repeat it. Repetition begins the process of teaching our brain to go there. Repetition *directionalizes* our brain. It sets a direction and orientation so that now we begin to automatically *reference* that thought, idea, emotion, or experience.

Next, layer that with some emotion. Make the idea vivid and dramatic. Layer some thoughts of validity as you confirm it repeatedly. Next layer some thoughts of value and significance to it. The more layering you do, the more "real," "true," "valid," and "important" it becomes to us. This will transform the idea into *a frame-of-reference,* then into a *frame of mind* and eventually into the *frameworks* that govern our very personality.

If we then identify with it and let it become part of our self-definition and identity, we further solidify it. If we absorb it into our very being as our mission in life, we again solidify it. If we make a decision to focus on this, see everything else in terms of this, refuse to tolerate anything that does not promote this, all of these reflective layerings make it increasingly solid as our mental and emotional frameworks. It thickens the plot of the frame and so makes them stronger.

Solidifying Frames By Meta-Stating

Whenever we set a frame, we are *meta-stating* ourselves or another. That is, we are accessing one state and applying it to another. This creates a special meta-structure, a state-*upon*-state relationship. This sets up one thought-and-feeling (a concept, belief, understanding, etc.) upon another thought or feeling. When we do this, we *texture* the very quality of our experience.

> Whenever we set a frame, we are *meta-stating* ourselves or another. We access one state and apply it to another. This creates a special meta-structure, a state-*upon*-state relationship. This sets up one thought-and-feeling (a concept, belief, understanding, etc.) upon another thought or feeling. And when we do this, we *texture* the very quality of our experience.

If we simply *add* another thought, we experience the result as a horizontal move ("this plus that"), as an addition on the same logical level. "Add a bit of patience and then a bit of joy." But if we *apply the thought or emotion to* the other, we process the new thought through the higher logical level of the meta-state as a new classification. The new thought then becomes the frame-of-reference for thinking, feeling, and experiencing about the first thought. If you bring *patience* to your joy, you will experience *patient joy.* Joy will be a member of the class of patience. Patience will be the classification with joy as a member of that class. This is what creates our psycho-logics.

Once, when I was doing court ordered anger control with men convicted of domestic violence, I inquired about a young man's family and found that he and his wife had recently had a child. When I asked to see a picture, the young man (21 years of age) glowed and reached for his wallet. "What a beautiful child! A little girl? I bet she's the delight of your life. Huh?"

"Yeah, you bet."

"And do you get to feed her very often?" I asked using a holding a baby in my arm type of movement.

"Of course!" he said proudly, showing me how he held her . . . and going into his proud-of-new-baby state.

I asked a lot more questions about this from a position of curiosity and validation, congratulating him and his wife, and commented on what a precious and magical time of life having a newborn can be. When he was totally and absolutely in state, I said in an off-the-cuff kind of way . . .

"And looking at her and realizing what an absolute miracle this gift of life is and knowing how precious she is to you . . . I wonder how things would be for you if you had all of these awarenesses and feelings available to you as resources when you get angry and need to express some displeasure to this child . . . just imagine if you could do so with *appreciative* anger, or *respectful* anger, or maybe better yet, *loving* anger. I'm sure your anger would have a very new and different quality to it—calm, thoughtful, considerate . . . and wouldn't that be a tremendous resource for protecting your relationship and working through conflicts?"

The young man couldn't talk. He choked up. It was as if his entire neurology was in over-drive, processing and re-processing how to map out this very new and strange, and yet appealing way of being. Later he told me that these were not words he had ever heard before. These were not ideas or concepts that he had ever entertained: *loving* anger, *calm and appreciative* anger. They framed a reality he had never experienced.

The quickness of shifting him from a very soft, tender, gentle, and caring state of appreciation about the miracle of his daughter to wondering how to express displeasure ... created an altered state ... and set such a powerful frames that it totally blew him away. It induced an altered or hypnotic state which so entranced him as he processed it in his mind-and-body. In the end, it changed the course of his life because it allowed him to create a *new texture* to his anger.

The Space for Making an Executive Choice

Once Dr. Bob was working with a single mother of two boys and discovered that she had a very high frame of *Keeping My Options Open.* This made her very creative and enabled her to provide lots of stimulation to others as a teacher. Yet her need for options was so high that in contexts demanding precisely following procedures, she found it creating emotional difficulty.

Yet she got by. However when the day came that her boys finished high school, she was faced with a new challenge. With an end to her alimony Brenda felt a new and very strong pressure regarding her job, now she "had" to keep her job and now it was no longer a choice.

Yet she felt torn about it because she didn't consider herself very good at disciplining her students. She knew the procedures set forth by the skill for gaining and maintaining discipline, but she always felt distressed by following the procedures and so would constantly change things to invent her own procedures. Of course, this just made the kids crazier and put her at odds with school policy.

Given this background knowledge, Bob asked her some questions regarding her meta-frames of importance as he explored with her the desired outcomes she wanted, the outcomes that she wanted to give priority to.

Bob: "Which is most important to you, Brenda, keeping your options open and doing your own thing, or following the school procedures and keeping your job? Is one more important than the other?"

The intervention was *that* simple with her. Just one question and her face turned red and she said in a matter of fact tonality,

Brenda: "Well, of course, keeping my job."

Bob: "Important enough to follow procedures? Is that the option you'd choose?" It was. By holding the space for Brenda to step back from her own values and choices, and take a meta-perspective, she was quickly able to access the situation and make an executive choice about what she truly wanted. In doing so, she sorted out one value as embedded within a higher value.

Designer Frames

If the "stuff" of mind boils down to our inner movies (made up of our sensory representational systems along with our words), and this makes up the *content* of all concepts, beliefs, and understandings, then we have all of the mental chemicals we need to concoct new and empowering frames. We only need to mix and combine the ingredients. We only need to put together some new combinations that will excite and inspire us. As all English words in millions of books are comprised of twenty-six letters, so all frames are comprised out of our internal movies and the words we say about them.

What is the significance of that? It means we can reclaim and use fragments of information, experiences, ideas, imaginations, dreams, values, etc. and put them into new coherent form. We can take and give form to the unformed and unframed fragments of our lives. We can weave a new fabric of mind and emotion for ourselves from bits of scenes from movies, feelings from novels, suggestions from friends, and beliefs by geniuses.

Summary

- A *frame war* lies at the heart of *conflictual communications*. Frequently when we argue, fight, fuss, conflict, and get at odds with others it is because our frames war with their frames. We live in a different assumptive world or Matrix than they. Meta-communicating enables us to move up and talk about the issues at the higher frame level.
- We can unconsciously and unintentionally *strengthen and solidify* a frame in another by directly challenging it. Directly fighting with another's frame typically invites the person to fight *for* it and defend it. In this way, they give it more power, importance, and strength.
- The same skills and powers that enable us to do *referencing* in the first place allow us to create frames, frames of mind, and personality frameworks.
- This means that solidifying a frame only involves more of the same. After all, repetition, the mother of all learning, powerfully gives a sense of certainty and reality to our frames. So are you ready to outframe your frame with the *"Yes!"* of validation, the decision of choice, and your purpose?

Chapter 14

GAMES RULES

"If the rules of a game become too flexible,
concentration flags,
and it is more difficult to attain a flow experience.
Commitment to a goal and to the rules it entails
is much easier
when the choices are few and clear."
Csikszentmihalyi
(Flow, p. 225)

Games are played by rules. How many times have we played a board game or a game out in a field and someone protests:

"Hey, you're not playing by the rules!"
"You can't do that! That's not right, the rules don't allow *that*!"

Whenever we play games, we play within a structure of rules and formats that govern how the game is set up, the number of players, legitimate and illegitimate actions within the domain, scoring, how "points" are counted, what's a win, what's a loss, exceptions, etc. These rules create the *conditions* of the game and the *playing conditions of the game-scape*. They inform us about the game:

- How to set up the proper conditions for the game.
- How to actually play the game.
- How many can play.
- The processes allowed in the course of action.
- When an activity produces a point or something that counts.
- The conditions when an exception to the rule occurs.
- The penalties that can occur when the rules are violated.
- How to determine when a game is completed.
- How to honor or acknowledge the winner.
- Who, if anyone, governs the game as referee, coach, or commissioner.
- How to keep score and who keeps score.

The rules we create or accept establish the structure, form, and order of a game. When we know the rules for how to structure and play a game, then we have a way of orienting ourselves, contextual cues about the game, and motivation for playing. Conversely, when we don't know *the rules of the game* or how the games goes, we may find ourselves disoriented, confused, overwhelmed, or unmotivated, etc.

Kinds of Rules

All rules are not the same. Even in the athletic games of sport, board games, the physical games of children, and the hobby and recreational games of adults — *the rules* that we create, and defer to, *determine the quality and nature of the games that we play.*

Do we know how to play just for the sake of playing, that is, just to have fun or to build bonds of connection? Some people always have to win. So when they play, they play *seriously.* It is because they *have* to win that they take an intense and competitive attitude. When exaggerated, this becomes a "No holds barred" type of game. Others play to challenge themselves and push their skills to the next level of development, and yet others competitively play because "they can't lose." When they lose, they are unable to be a good sport.

What *kind* of rules govern your inner games? Examining and quality controlling our rules is important since they determine *the kind of player* we become, the skills we will develop in the play and the quality of our game.

> *The rules* that we create, and defer to, *determine the quality and nature of the games that we play.*

- Are your rules strict or loose?
- Do we have possible or impossible rules?
- Are our rules appropriate or inappropriate?
- Are they reasonable or unreasonable?
- Are they achievable or unachievable?
- Are the rules immobilizing or mobilizing of our resources?
- Are the rules complex or simple?
- Do we have only a few rules or many?
- Are the rules empowering or dis-empowering?
- Do the rules have rigid or flexible rules?

Frame Game Rules

With this as the background for the *game* metaphor, how can we use our *game lens* to think about the rules that govern our mental games? First, we recognize that there are levels of rules. The rules that format, organize, structure, and govern our frame games are a higher level frame. As we have a frame of mind

> The rules that we create, and defer to, determine *the quality and nature* of the games that we play.

about the game that we play or that we want to play (the Aim game, the Solution game, the Ecology game, etc.), so we also have references for how we think the game should go. We have ideas, thoughts, feelings, expectations, hopes, etc. about when, where, with who, in what way, for what purpose, etc. First, there's *the content* of the game, then there's our *game style* arising from our intentions and motives.

It's our thoughts *about* the game that establishes the higher frames or *the rules* for playing the game, setting the criteria and informing us about the game. This wonderfully illustrates the reflexive nature of mind, how we jump levels and layer awareness upon our awareness. In this, while our first awareness goes out to the game, in the back of our mind it is the frame that's in control. What's *on our mind* make up the details of the game and this consumes our mental and emotional energies. Meanwhile our higher frames are governing the game *outside* our awareness. And because we assume, "That's the way it is," we are less aware of our higher governing frames.

The rules of our game become dangerous, dis-empowering, and problematic to us the moment we confuse them with reality. Once we take our *rule frames* for granted and treat them as "the right way" to do things, at that moment we begin to forget that *we* invented these rules. We forget that they are only as real to us as the amount of "reality" *we* give them. Waking up to this realization is equivalent to taking the Red Pill and discovering the Matrix we are living inside. All of our frames for *the rules of the game*, for how to play our games, and how to keep score are invented. And if we invented them, then *we can re-invent them.* That's the good news.

Rules for Keeping Score

How can you *win* at a game if you don't know the rules? The question is rhetorical because obviously, you can't. It is in exploring the rules frame in our inner games that shifts us to a higher level of awareness. By stepping back and considering the rules as *rules*, their kind and quality, and the effect they have on our everyday life, we are invited to think structurally about our lives. Then we can begin working with the meta-frames of our frames.

- How do you keep score as you play your inner game?
- What rules have you constructed for how you play a game?
- What are the kind and quality of rules that you use?
- How well do these rules serve you in your playing?
- Do the rules about your score keeping enable you to easily win?
- Do the rules stack the deck against you?

Figure 14:1

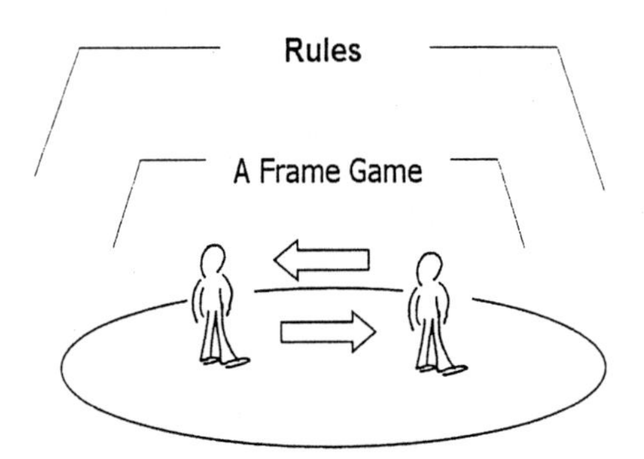

> If we confuse our *rules frame* with reality and take it for granted, we will then treat *our rules* as "the right way" to do things forgetting that we invented the rules.

Because the invention of our games are our own construction, doesn't it make sense to set a *meta-rule* about our *rules*, a rule that all of our rules must serve to enhance our overall functioning? Doesn't that make sense? Should we not have a meta-rule that we will discard any *rule of the game* that dis-empowers or sabotages? These meta-rules, in fact, establish the basis for the *Quality Control Game* that gives us the most leverage for transforming our frames (the inner game) and games (our outer games).[1]

How Do You Know You're Winning?

The rules of the game specify the formatting details and constructions of our inner and outer games. They set up the game-scape world. The rules of the game also give us the information for all of our *game evaluations.*

If we describe something as "success, effectiveness, wise," etc., how do we know when something counts as success, effectiveness, wisdom, or whatever? What lets us know that? How do we make our evaluations? What do we base our judgments upon? What variables and criteria do we use? These *epistemology* questions facilitate our exploration of our frame rules. It's our way of discovering how we know what we know, the source and validity of this meta-knowledge, and how it constructs our meta-rules.

The *epistemology* of the game rules direct our attention to *how we know* that the game has started, who can play, when, where, in what way, if we can do a "do over," what happens if there's a tie, how long an over-time goes, etc. For X in the following questions, use a state, experience, emotion, or quality that you desire (i.e., happy, confident, healthy, free, safe, in control, creative, radiant, charming, successful, in love, respectful, etc.).

- How do you know when you are X?
- If you were really X, then you would be doing what?
- If you X, you will . . .
- I have to Y (set of behaviors, actions, conditions) in order to X.
- I can't feel X unless . . .
- I will experience X when . . .
- What will it take for you to know that X is happening?
- To experience X, I should . . .
- To experience X, I must . . .
- Anytime that I Y (action, experience, situation), I know that I am X-ing
- It just doesn't feel or seem that I am really X.

Winning at the "Feeling Confident about Myself" Game

To give you a feel for how this works, let's play with the frame of mind and state of *confidence.* Suppose you want to play the game, "I'm confident to successfully handle the demands of my job." With that in mind, use the following questions to explore how you already have set up this inner and outer game:

> We forget that they are only as real to us as the amount of "reality" that *we* give them. Waking up to this realization is equivalent to taking the Red Pill and discovering the Matrix we are living inside.

- How do you know *when* you are confident?
- What has to occur in order for you to make some *confident points?*
- When you are feeling confident, what are you *doing*?
- What is happening to you?
- How many points do you need for a win?
- When do you play this game, with whom, and about what?
- What do you get when you win this game?

Some people have to see everything going just right in order to feel confident. Others have to get lots of approval, validation, and confirmation from others before they can score a point on the confidence scoreboard. Others only have to believe that they can learn and develop skills in a particular area to score a point for confidence. What counts for you?

Consider the happy state of being cheerful with a joyful and playful attitude. What has to happen for you to allow yourself a win in this *frame game?* Do you have to win the lottery? Do you have to have "everything going your way all day?" All week? Do you have to have a Hollywood star body? What are the criteria, evaluations, standards, and rules that allow you to feel pleased, joyful, or playful?

Some people play that inner game of feeling cheerful, making it their frame of mind, just from the fact that they are breathing. The condition is simple and direct, "It's a good day if I still have a pulse." They don't have to meet a lot of criteria to enjoy things. On the opposite end of the continuum are many among the rich and famous who are grouchy and bored. Nothing seems to count for them. Taking it all for granted, they feel dissatisfied. They operate from a discounting frame, "It's not good enough yet," "This wealth doesn't really count," "This fame isn't all it's cracked up to be," etc. They have so many rules, or such unrealistic ones, they can hardly ever win.

Making Winning Easier

If our rules, standards, and game structures are all arbitrary and invented, does anything stop us from formulating them so that it's easy to hit a home run or sink a basket? No, nothing. Well, on second thought, yes. Our *meta-rules* about our rules can stop us. What could stop us would be any meta-belief that prevents us from changing our beliefs. Of course, that's a belief and so is subject to change!

As you use the epistemology questions to flush out your requirements for *knowing when* something counts, evaluate them in terms of being enhancing or limiting. Your quality controlling of the rules and standards that allows you to choose and create the rules. So step aside and play the *Quality Control Game.*[1]

- How well does it serve you to have the rules that you do?
- Are the rules the kind of rules that allow you to win frequently or do they stack the game against you?

I had a friend once who got his feelings hurt by something or another that I said. It was obvious that something was bothering him, but I really didn't have a clue. Eventually, I had the chance to explore the subject of "respect" with him and did so looking to understand the "rules" in his head about respect and dis-respect. I asked, "How do you know when to feel respected? What do you count as disrespect?"

> "I know I am being respected when others agree with my opinions and never raise their voice to me. When someone raises his voice to me, I feel insulted. I had enough of that growing up and I won't tolerate that kind of insolence anymore."

Ah, *the rules of his Respect Game!* I found that really interesting, and so different from the rules that I had in my head and the inner game that I played. So, keeping my voice calm and modulated to pace him, I decided to explore further into this strange territory. "So what comprises the 'raising of the voice' for you? I mean, how can you tell that a person isn't feeling excitement, or stress, or fear in contrast to sending a message of disrespect to you?"

> "Well . . . I don't know . . . I just know it shows bad manners to raise the voice and that it shows that someone's out of control."

"That must mean," I said, trying to deframe this *frame game* a little by using a counter-example, "that you never raise your voice at any time to anyone unless you're "out of control" or given to bad manners?"

"That's right. Sure!"

Well, at least he played by his own rules. No double-standard here. Just rigid and limiting rules that programmed him to feel disrespected when anybody else had a bad day, felt stress, or didn't have total control over voice volume or tone. I wouldn't want to play that game and so I disclosed my own feelings about that.

What *kind* of rules govern your inner game? Examining and quality controlling our rules is important since they determine *the kind of player* we become, the skills we will develop in the play and the quality of our game.

"That's kind of scary. I don't have the kind of total control over my vocal chords that you seem to have over yours. When I feel stressed, frustrated, upset, anger, or even excited and passionate, it usually causes the muscles in my throat to become tight and then I tend to raise my volume . . . none of which has anything to do with the person I'm speaking with, especially those I love or respect. It's entirely my limitation that my emotions leak out in my body. Yet given what you said, I'd be afraid to be very real or authentic with you, afraid you'd be quick to take offense."

I let that settle for a moment. He didn't say anything, as if he didn't know what to say, as if he had come to the edge of his map about this, and didn't have a clue as to any alternative way to map things.

"So if I understand you accurately, you'd prefer that I walk on eggshells with you rather than chance communicating with you whenever I'm not totally resourceful?"

"But why would you have to raise your voice?"

"It's not that I *have* to, it's just that sometimes it happens when I feel stress. I usually don't even notice it."

"But you should . . . If you really respected me, you would."

"That's your rule? It sounds like you're on the edge and ready to interpret something as disrespect and to personalize it about yourself even before you find out what the raised voice is about."

"Well, you don't expect me to stand there and be yelled at, do you?"

"'Yelled at?' I thought we were talking about a raised voice or strained and stressed vocal chords? I certainly agree that you should not be 'yelled at.' I was thinking that it would help if when you noticed that I'm raising my voice, to just comment on it. "It seems like your volume is getting louder, would you mind holding it down?"

"I can say that?"

"Sure, why not?"

"Well, I didn't know I could just ask for that."

"Ah, so you don't play the "Authentically say what's on your mind and ask for what you want" game. What do you do, just feel insulted and put down and stuff it inside until you can't stand it any longer?"

"Well, yeah."

"Do you find that a fun or productive game to play?"

The old rules of the game for him was that any raising of the voice meant that he was being "yelled at" which meant insult. Playing the *My personal sense of Respect is a function of the volume and voice tension of others* game made it hard to win respect. It was at the disposal of others. No wonder he saw and interpreted "insult" in so many experiences. He also had a rule of intolerance about the many common human responses of stress or negative emotions. So he was constantly walking away from friendships and relationships. He was constantly feeling disrespected and judging people for it. That was another one of his rules for dealing with conflict. "When someone shows disrespect, walk away." He had no rules that led him to inquire, explore, share, or negotiate. Yet since all of these were his rules, I inquired what new rules would empower him to create richer relationships.

Engineering Better *Rules of the Game*

Knowing how to detect and flush out frames allows us to expose those frames that govern the *rules of our games*. This means we can look at how we keep score, what counts and what doesn't, the kind of rules that we use in navigating experiences, etc. It also means we now have the power to create *designer rules* at will for the purpose of enhancing and enriching the way we play frame games. Remembering the *invented nature* of the rules that we currently have, what would you like to recognize and count as "points" so that you can experience more wins?

Before I started modeling wealth creation and discovering the structure, stages, process, and secrets of wealth and wealth creation, I had some *rules* in my head about "wealth"—rules that prevented me from counting lots of things as wealth and that interfered with getting into resourceful states for creating wealth. I flushed out the thoughts in the back of my mind that contained these rules by using two sentence stems. This process of sentence completion taps into the power of "thought intrusion" that Sigmund Freud discovered when he provided the ritual of lying down on a couch and just letting every thing that comes to mind. In this we avoid censoring our thoughts or emotions. We don't fear or avoid them, we just let them come and notice them. Typically the first three or seven thoughts that come to mind are conscious thoughts that are typically positive and seeking solutions. After that come the thoughts "in the back of the mind" that are more likely to make up the sabotaging and limiting frames of our mental rules. Where these come from is irrelevant. The relevant thing is identifying them and de-framing them.

The first stem I used was, *"I know that I'm wealthy when . . ."* Using this I flushed out such rule frames as the following:

- I will be wealthy when I have a million dollars in assets.
- When I have an ongoing disposable income of $100,000.
- When I have no money worries.

The second sentence stem that I used was, *"To become wealthy I would have to . . ."* This one flushed out such non-sense in the back of my mind as:

- Care more about money and things than people.
- Be unethical in my business practices.
- Take advantage of people.

Flushing out these thoughts *in the back of the mind* explained what prevented me from building wealth. "No wonder it's so hard! I have been fighting inside myself against what it would mean if I did become wealthy!" After that I came across other definitions that set up very different games. One that really turned my thinking around described wealth and financial independence in terms of time rather than money accumulation, as "the ability to live 60 days forward without a paycheck."

> "You are wealthy if you can maintain your current lifestyle during the next sixty days without needing or depending upon a paycheck. If you can take a week or two weeks off and do what you want to do, you're wealthy." (Robert Kiyosaki, *Rich Day, Poor Day*)

> You have the power to create *designer rules* at will for the purpose of enhancing and enriching the way you play frame games.

That frame gave me an entirely new perspective. I had never thought about it in that way I immediately experienced one of those *"Aha!"* epiphany moments of insight. "Then I'm wealthy already!" Actually, although I had been wealthy for a long time, only I did not know or recognize it; I have not counted certain things as part of my wealth. I had kept myself from feeling good in that game because I thought I needed big bucks, an obscene amount of cash, and lots of luxury toys.

Once I changed *the rules of the game* so that the rules, standards, and criteria served me better, it induced me into a very different state of mind and feeling.

Suddenly feeling rich and successful, I was able to come from a sense of abundance rather than scarcity which made giving and interacting very different. That allowed me to see how to create wealth ethically. Of course, that's the way it is with frames and frameworks. They govern life. They control emotions. They create skills. And they texture the very quality and feel of our life.

What *designing* and/or *re-designing* of the rules of the game would you like to create? What rules for scoring and playing do not actually serve you very well? How could you re-formulate the way you play various frame games so that you can win more often, enjoy the process, and stack the deck much more in your favor? After all, those who experience lots of negative emotions, stress, frustration, guilt, anger, etc. all too often do so because they have *rules of the game* that make winning far too hard or impossible.

Imagine playing a game—

- where making even one point is next to impossible,
- that overwhelms you with multitude of rules and regulations,
- that has such strict, rigid, and inflexible rules that "playing" feels controlling and hard,
- that's formatted to punish you for any error or mistake.

Negative emotions (i.e., anger, stress, frustration, upsetness, etc.) arise as *warning signals* when one of our values or standards is violated or endangered. So when we have our emotional gauge cranked up to pick up the tiniest little infraction, disappointment, frustration—we're going to experience negative emotions frequently and intensely. This will not make life a party.

Wisdom suggests that we re-adjust the gauge so that we have more room to tolerate the imperfect, the unexpected, set backs, and basic human fallibility. Also, if we have *too many "should" rules* in our head, they typically create a feeling of demandingness that leaves us ready to pick up our marbles and go home in protest of life's unfairness. "Should" rules make the games hard to play as it increases demands and intolerances. It makes life *shouldy*.

If you're wondering if perhaps we should just eliminate rules altogether, the answer is no. We have to have rules to play a game. Rules provide structure, organization, limits, boundaries, and more. They provide orientation as we move through life. We even need some "must" rules since the *must* rules can energize us for taking effective action. Yet the rules we set about how to play the games of life are ours to create and our to refine so that they support the best and most exquisite games.

What rules would you like to create for yourself as you think about the *frame games* of Conflict Resolution, Respecting others and Being Respected, Giving and Receiving Love, Vacationing, Feeling Successful, Intelligent, etc.?

Summary

- Part and parcel of our inner game are *the rules* that allow us to play the game. These give order and structure to how we play the game and how we score the game.

- The *rules of the game* comprise yet another frame in the back of our mind, as part of our invented reality. We construct them out of our thinking and feeling, and like any other frame, they may or may not empower us.

- The kind and quality of the rules we use determine the nature and quality of the *games* we play. To govern this facet of mind and personality, to create some meta-rules about your rules, namely, that you will only allow the rules that enhance your life, that your rules must work for the welfare of your entire system, and that you can always change or update your rules.

- As you design the rules of your games, make sure you can win frequently, that you can thoroughly enjoy the games that you play, and that you have enough flexibility change games in real time so they fit your values and visions.

End Notes:

1. See the Quality Control Game in chapter fifteen, it is the sixth game.

Chapter 15

A THESAURUS OF GAMES

Games for Enjoying Life

- Given all that has gone before, what *frame games* do you want to play?
- What new inner and outer games will you design to enhance your effectiveness or enjoyment in life?
- What inner games are you committed to winning?

The choice is entirely yours. As we become increasingly mindful about our frames, we can choose the very best frames of mind. We can detect and refuse any sick or toxic frames and can become picky about the frames we feed our mind-body system.

- Is there any frame blocking or preventing you from setting a new frame for a new inner game?
- Are you fully ready to deframe anything blocking you?
- Are you excited about all the possibilities that open up for you in terms of setting the rules for new empowering frame games?

A Thesaurus of *Frame Games*

I have included the following to offer scores of frames for new enhancing games that you may want to win—a *thesaurus* of frame games. Why this approach rather than providing an exhaustive description of each game? Because once you know about the construction of a frame and how to shift, transform, and set them, *you are perfectly free and able to customize the inner game of your frames for your outer games of performance.* The process in playing any inner or outer frame game is as follows:

1) Identify the name and purpose of a frame.

What is the name of the game?

What is the design and purpose of the game?
What are the rules that you want to set for the game?

2) Specify the ideas, representations, and meanings for each game.
Have you done this in compelling detail that fits for the way *you* think and feel?
Have you truly personalized and customized the new inner game?
Do you go into state when you think about or read your description?
Do you have an effective and elegant induction for the new game?

3) Specify the rules of the frame game.
How will you know when you are in this or that frame of mind?
What will let you know?
What do you seek to accomplish?
Who will you play with?
For what payoff?
And what will that payoff get you?

4) Rehearse the frame to habituate it as your frame of mind.
What techniques will you use to run the new frame as your way of thinking and responding (i.e., reframing, swishing, anchoring, etc.)?[1]
How often will you need to apply the frame to your current and future life before it becomes habitual?
What meta-stating will solidify it as your frame of mind?

5) Validate the game with confirmation.
Will this game really enhance your life?
Will you really like to play it?
Will it empower you?
Have you made an executive decision for it?

1) The Inner Game of Personal Power and Self-Efficacy
Do you play the *frame game* of thinking-and-feeling personally empowered? Would you like to? The inner game of *"My responses endow me with the power to live my life with the self-efficacy to choose and architect my future"* locates our basic powers in our response-powers and focuses our attention on developing those powers.

What are our ultimate powers? We have four. We have powers of mind-and-emotion to *think* and to *emote*, and we have powers of communication and behavior to *speak* and to *act.* Our two *private* powers of thinking and emoting empowers us for the inner game of responding to whatever happens by using our *mental* powers of representing, believing, valuing, deciding, understanding, framing, intending, etc. and our *emotional* powers of valuing, caring, feeling in the body, somatizing, making experiential, etc. From these arise our two *public* powers of expressiveness, speaking and taking action in the world.

When you play this inner game, your focus concentrates on *the functions* that you truly have control over, namely, your mind and emotions, body, speech, and behavior. This is your power zone. A central rule of this game is: When you focus inside your power zone, you empower yourself; when you focus outside of this zone, you dis-empower yourself. That's the rule.

Playing within this frame demands lots of time and energy as we focus on what we can do. It begins when we play, *"It's my brain and I'll run it my own way for fun and profit!"* Operating from this frame directs us to the levels regarding *what* we're thinking (the content), *how* we're running it (its form, structure, process), the *ecology* of our thinking (how it serves our resourcefulness), and its *agenda* (why we're running our brain this way, for what purpose, to what end?). Use the Power Zone Meta-Stating pattern to fully set, install, and solidify this new frame game.[1]

Recognizing, owning, and deciding to fully claim your own *personal power* also involves releasing the *personal powers* of others to them and honoring their right to think, feel, speak, and act as they choose. We respect others to such a high degree that we stop dis-empowering them by trying to manage how they think, feel, talk, and act. Does this reduce our love, compassion, caring, or responsibility to others? In no way! On the contrary, it actually heightens our love and responsibility *to* others. Why? Because it enables us to clearly discern the difference between our own personal responsibilities *for* ourselves and the relational responses that we give *to* others. And that brings up the next frame game.

2) The Responsibility To/For Game

Within the two little words of *to* and *for* a great and far reaching concept is hidden. The distinction that we want to make lies in recognizing the difference between *what* we are ***responsible for*** and *who* we are ***responsible to***. Doing this creates a powerfully enhancing way to navigate the confusing webs of relationships. In this, these terms refer to two very different experiences.

Responsibility for—

This describes *accountability.* We are *accountable* for what we do, for our actions, behaviors, and responses. If you imagine yourself inside a circle, a circle that extends throughout to your personal sense of space, perhaps the length of your arm, that's your area of accountability, it is your response or power zone. It covers the thoughts, feelings, words, and actions that you generate from out of yourself. Nobody outside the circle can be responsible *for* these responses, they are ours.

Responsibility to —

This describes *relationships*. By our public powers of speech and behavior we *relate* to people, groups, teams, organizations, etc. and so when we are *responsible to* someone or a group, this creates the familial, friendship, cultural, career, government, and so on systems that we live in and the persons, groups, and communities to whom we answer. If you imagine an arrow that moves out from the circle of your power zone to others in a larger circle of loved ones, colleagues, friends, etc., that arrow identifies who you are responsible *to*.

> A central rule of this game says that when we focus on our power zone, we empower ourselves; when we focus outside of this zone, we dis-empower ourselves. That's the rule.

We draw the *line* that separates and distinguishes *relationship* (responsibility to) and *accountability* (responsibility for) by exploring whose *response* we are talking about and a response *for* what and *to* whom. The rule that enables us to play this inner and outer game is this: We are *only* response-able *for* the responses that we generate mentally, emotionally, verbally, and behaviorally. Our ability to respond (responsibility) ends at our nose or the edge of the reach of our arm. I cannot be responsible *for* much that goes on beyond this response zone.

Similarly, when we set the frame that we have lots of relationships that set up accountabilities and inter-relational dynamics, then we realize that there are numerous people, situations, and groups *to whom* we live in a responsible relationship.

The first distinction (responsibility *for*) enables us to play the *inner game of personal power.* Highlighting our four powers (thinking, emoting, speaking, and behaving) defines our "power zone." Focusing on and developing these functions within this zone *empowers* us; focusing on things outside this zone *dis-empowers* us.

The second distinction of responsibility *to* focuses our attention on the exchanges we negotiate with others as we step into and out of *relationships*. In our interactions, we give and receive talk and behaviors. That's what we negotiate with—the way we talk and the way we act, how we want someone else to speak and behave to us. Making these distinctions clarifies roles and relationships and so enhances sanity (good adjustment to social and inter-personal reality) which thereby reduces stress. It enables us to navigate the waters of inter-dependency with others and to avoid the shoals of co-dependency.

3) The Empowerment Game of Personal Ownership
To play the inner game of *"It's my life and brain and I get to be fully responsible"* we step into the sense and feel of *ownership* and as our frame of reference for our response powers (the zone of our power). To set this frame, take the simple yet profound experience of claiming something as your own. What can you say *"Mine!"* to fully and completely with every fiber of your being? This sense of putting a claim on something, of fully owning it plays a key role in our self-definition and how we relate to the world. It's part of the developmental stage we all go through as we learn how to treat something (a toy, an experience, etc.) as our own. When we can strongly and intensely affirm *"It's mine!"* we are able to bring things into our mental and emotional "space" and identify with people and things which expand our ego-space.

Do this with your personal powers. As you recognize your *mind*, your *emotions,* your *voice*, your *body* and *expressions*—apply the feeling of *ownership* to these expressions. Think of something that you absolutely "own," something small and simple and with which you have no question at all about it being yours (i.e., your toothbrush, underwear). Get the *feeling* of ownership, that it is yours. As you then step into this ownership experience, apply it to your personal powers.

> "This is my mind . . . my ability to think, to represent, to send my brain places, etc. My emotions . . . my ability to emote, to feel, to care, to value, etc. My voice . . . my ability to speak, to assert what I'm thinking and feeling. My body and expressions . . . my ability to take action and to express myself . . ."

Playing this inner game allows us to experience the power and vitality involved in recognizing ourselves "at cause." Doing this leads to a sense of self-efficacy purging in us any sense of being a victim or that our fortune is at the whim of others or of fate. This inner game creates the foundation for resilience, persistence, commitment, passion, excitement, and many of the powerful states. It's a great foundational inner game.

4) The Inner Game of Intentional Decisiveness
Do you play the inner game of *"I set the intentional direction and then make empowering decisions?* Would you like to play this one? How often would you? In what areas of life?

One of our mental-and-emotional *powers* is that of *intentionally choosing* a compelling goal, option, idea, focus, belief, or action. Doing so allows us to tap into a crucial power for shaping our destiny—*the power of decision.* In deciding, we do a lot more than just think and choose. Intentions highlight our power of imagining a new way of living, creating that way in our mind as our inner game, and then making the decisions that brings it to life in our actions and behaviors.

A full decision not only involves *intentions,* it also involves *attentions.* Rollo

May (1969) says that "will" or will power arises from the combination of these two dynamics. We *intend* some higher goal, then we set our *attentions* on it. Most of the work of *will* goes into keeping our *attentions* aligned with our *intentions*.

Do you not find that to be the case for yourself? You set out an intention about eating more sensibly or exercising more regularly, about managing your anger or frustrations more elegantly. Once you do that comes the work of remembering those good intentions and translating them into your everyday attentions.

Robbins (1991) elegantly describes how you can make a new decision *right this minute* that can immediately and profoundly change your life in radical ways. "It is in your moments of decision that your destiny is shaped." (p. 40) This raises an alluring question:

> What decision could you make, right now, that would wonderfully and profoundly transform your life?

When we know how to set the frames of *intention* and intention-of-intention at higher levels, and how to energize and empower those frames, then the work of alignment and translation becomes easy.[1] Few of us truly suffer from *attention deficit*, most suffer from *intention deficit*. We haven't strengthened and solidified our intentions in a way that we are "of one mind" in a focused and concentrated way. That's why we feel that we don't have sufficient "will power."

If decisions control our destiny, then our *meta-decisions* control our destiny transforming decisions. So before we spin our wheels in learning to play the Aim game of setting a compelling goal, let's first play the inner game of *Meta Decision-Making*. Without question, primary level decisions are important. Yet the higher level of making decisions about our *decision making* skills and powers governs and shapes how we make and stick with decisions.

- What's your frame about *decisions*, will power, choice, goal setting, etc.?
- What do you think and feel about these things?
- What experiences, beliefs, and understandings do you bring to this subject?
- What decisions have you made (consciously or unconsciously) about decisions and decision making?
- What decisions would you like to make about decisions to enrich and empower your whole decision making powers?

> What decision could you make, right now, that would wonderfully and profoundly transform your life?

Poor decisions that occur early in life and which turn out to be disasters frequently set the stage within some people so they fear making decisions. From impulsive and stupid decisions and the experiences that follow, they map decision-making as dangerous. Lack of clarity about values can feed this fear of decision. Others fear and hesitate about decisions because they refuse to cut off their options. Wanting it all, they refuse to eliminate choices, and so chose to not choose.

A real *de-cision cuts off* ("cision") alternatives *from* ("de") us. That's why in a "clear cut decision," we clearly cut *off* other choices as we opt for one thing. This directs consciousness so that we become highly focused in our concentration. With a major decision, it activates our commitment so that we become passionate in our magnificent obsession. Anything less then this yes/no divide is not a true decision.

- What do you need to say *no* to so that you can say a more resounding *yes* to something?
- What decision would clear the path giving you a chance to go for a dream that you really want?
- Do you have full permission to say *Yes* to something big and exciting and perhaps even frightening?

To play the *Meta Decision-Making* game, make a decision this very minute about your decisions and your decision-making skills and states. Decide that you will from this moment forward give yourself to making better and higher quality decisions, decisions which will allow you to live true to your highest beliefs and values and congruent with your passions. Decide that you do not have to "have it all." Stubbornly refuse to let that delusion seduce you away from your focus. Decide that you will not be seduced by the need to make "perfect" decisions. That is another delusion that will undermine your ability to be decisive.

Decide that at any given moment you will make *the best and highest quality decisions* and that you will always continue to grow, learn, receive feedback, and find a way to succeed. Decide that you will do what it takes.

- Decide that you will take total control over your power zone of thinking, emoting, speaking, and behaving.
- Decide that you will take action, effective action, and massive action to make it happen.
- Decide to not deviate from your decisions.
- Decide that you will allow no excuses.

Robbins (1991) noted three areas for this *Meta Decision* game.

> "Three decisions that you make every moment of your life control your destiny. These three decisions determine *what* you'll notice, *how* you'll feel, *what* you'll do, and ultimately *what* you will contribute and *who* you'll become. If you don't control these three decisions, you simply aren't in control of your life. When you control them, you begin to sculpt your experience. The three decisions that control your destiny

are:
1. Your decisions about what to focus on.
2. Your decisions about what things mean to you.
3. Your decisions about what to do to create the results that you want."

What do you want to focus your mind on? Whatever it is, your focus will create the basic frames of your inner game. Your decision about meaning sets the meaning frames and quality control over those meanings. Your decision about what actions to take puts you in control of how you make your ideas and frames real. Ultimately, our actions *translate* the stuff in our head to the muscles in our body and out into the external world.

In the outer game of *Meta Decision-Making* saying *yes* and saying *no* gives us the power to *cut* some things *off* while *cutting* other things *into* the fabric of our focus. *No* cuts off the range of choices and possibilities from our options in decision making. On the other side of the decision, *yes* slices as scissors enabling us to align our attentions with our highest intentions.

5) The Aim Game

The Aim Game contrasts with several other frames, the *Blame game,* the *Passively Drifting through Life* game, the *Take Things as They Occur* game, the *Don't Get Your Hopes Up Too High* game, and the *Path of Least Resistance* game. That's because this is also the *Magnificent Obsession* game.

Emerging from our *power zone* of thinking, feeling, choosing, deciding, etc., this frame game reflects our ability to make choices about our desired outcomes. To set it, begin asking questions about dreams and desires.

- What do I want? What do I really want? What do I feel totally passionate about? What do I care about? What pulls on me like a magnet?
- What am I aiming for in life, in this job, in this relationship, with this book, etc.?
- When I get what I want, what will that get for me?
- And when I experience that outcome, fully and completely, and in just the way I want it—what will that give me?
- How is that valuable, important, meaningful?

The power of *the Aim game* lies in how it *sets us in a direction* and organizes our powers toward a specific outcome. It takes a truly magnificent goal to move us with sufficient excitement and energy. Puny little boring goals won't do. We need big, bold, audacious goals with enough pizzazz that they'll pull us out of bed in the morning and keep us persisting when set-backs occur.

Taking an *intentional stance* activates our sense of direction, purpose, and meaningfulness. It unleashes our energies, it harnesses our dreams, and it inspires our heart. It's a much more productive and powerful game than the alternatives. Yet to play this game, we have to play it with intelligence or we can do damage.

If we set unrealistic, overwhelming, vague, untestable, and not personally owned or compelling goals, this only sets us up for frustration, disappointment, and burnout. To play *The Aim game* effectively, we have to play it by a specific set of rules described most clearly by the well-formed outcome pattern.[1] On the surface, setting goals seems like such an easy and simple thing. Yet many people, if not most, have great difficulty with *effective* goal setting that transforms life. Many have experienced so much frustration around New Year Resolutions and other forms of making resolves of their best intentions that they have given up on it entirely.

Use the well-formed outcome pattern to take charge of the key factors or rules of this game. The power of *the Aim game* is that it engages us in a way so we become truly *response-able* in turning visions into reality. In this, it builds a sense of control and self-efficacy. This game also empowers us to engage others in goal-focused conversations in the context of business, personal relationships, and therapy. In the end, *the Aim game* enables us to generate a solution-oriented focus.

How do we play this game? The essence of it involves fitting and shaping any goal so that it frames it as a positive description of what we want, what we can initiate and sustain with specific steps and stages and evidence regarding how we know when we get it. It is stated within a time frame and specific contexts. We then step back to check that it is realistic, relevant, ecological, and compelling. Shape the goal into those frames and constraints and the game becomes well-formed.

6) The Quality Control Game

One of the most powerful frame games is played with a marvelous frame of mind—the *ecology frame.* "Ecology" here refers to the health and balance of something within all of the dimensions and relationships of one's life. We check ecology of a frame, experience, state, belief, etc. as we run a quality control. It's easy to set this frame as a reference point for thinking, feeling, speaking, and acting to bring balance, integration, and integrity to life. To initiate this game ask any of the following questions. You know the game has begun when one of these evoke a person to *step back* and examine their system.

- Does this thought, emotion, speech, act, etc. serve me well?
- Does this experience enhance my life or skills?
- Does it empower me?
- Does it put me in the direction I want to go?
- Does it operate in an ecologically balanced way?
- Does any part of me object to this?

- Is this particular game worth playing?
- Is this where I want to put my attention?

7) The Relevance Game

In the *Relevance game,* we search for connections of value and importance. We search to discover the relevancy of one thing in terms of another. If you have ever served on a committee, wiled hours away in a meeting where people became lost in trivial details, or others engaged in chasing after irrelevant rabbits, you will really appreciate this frame game. Rub your hands together in delightful anticipation for when you're with a group of people and they suddenly get off the subject at hand. Wipe the smirk off your face and simply initiate this *frame game* as you coach the group. All you have to do is ask any of the following questions. This will call a stop to *the Rabbit-Chasing game.*

- Is this relevant to what we're talking about?
- How is this relevant to our purpose right now?
- What relevance does this have in light of X?
- Is this productive or empowering?
- Is this important or valuable to our agenda today? How? In what way?
- What is relevant to this situation?

8) The Mapping Game

The *Map/Territory Distinction game* grows out of the fact that we experience "reality" through the filter of our senses and mind. "Out there" exists a whole field of electromagnetic forces. Of these our nervous system with its sense receptors (eyes, ears, skin, tongue, nose) only picks up a minute range of the continuum. We have to use extra-neural devices like microscopes, telescopes, electronic microscopes, television receivers, radio receivers, etc. to pick up on many of these other facets of reality (the territory) beyond our map of it.

Recognizing the *map/territory* distinction enables us to distinguish two dimensions of experience, the world of events and the world of our mapping about those events. Recognizing and knowing this is the inner game, feeling and acting upon it as our orientation in the world is the outer game.

When we fail to make the distinction we *confuse* levels and *identify* ideas, words, thoughts with the territory. Then we play an entirely different game. As we then play *the Identification game* as we confuse different dimensions, we over-identify with our thoughts, beliefs, emotions, etc. We play some games that can create instant conflict with others: *My Thoughts are Real. My Beliefs are the truly Real Ones. If I Feel an Emotion, I must Act on it.*

In child developmental psychology following Piaget, this confusion of levels and dimensions is *the concrete thinking stage* of cognitive development. For Korzybski it is the *Aristotelian game. In identification, we* use our nervous systems similar to the way animals use theirs. Instead of making distinctions to discern higher level, we confuse things and treat them as if they were "the same." This moves us into a more primitive and reactive game. The frame of this game causes us to respond and react to *ideas* as we would to *things* and that induces us to live in a stimulus-response world. It programs us to experience semantic reactions in response to symbols and to confusedly believe that the symbol *makes* or *creates* our responses. This increases our chances for mal-adjustment.

- "You make me so angry!" Stimulus: your provoking looks, words, tones, actions. Response: my anger. Frame: Blame. *You* are at fault. *You* make me have these emotions.
- "Why do you always stress me out with your demands? Don't you know I hate that?"

The It's Just a Map game saves us from this kind of confusion. In doing so it eliminates the blaming and victimizing games. We move beyond this confusion by operating from the frame that our responses belong to us, they are ours, and we *own* them.

- "Given your volume and tone, it seems like you're really upset right now with me. And because I care about you, I'll work at listening to you if you'll lower your volume and speak in a kinder tone. What do you say?"

Knowing that all of our ideas, understandings, beliefs, definitions, decisions, memories, imaginations, fears, desires, angers, etc. are *just maps* initiates another great result—it frees us from the need to defend our maps. Though on the inside they feel and seem "real" to us (and so are neurologically *real*), they are not externally "real." No idea is *real* empirically. Ideas, thoughts, or meanings are not *empirical*. You have never stumbled over a hunk of meaning or a belief that someone dropped in your front yard. "Hey, who left this meaning here?" Ideas and beliefs are internal representations we *map* of the reality out there in order to navigate that reality.

To the extent that our maps have a similar structure to the territory, we find them useful. Similarity of structure makes our mental and conceptual maps useful in navigating life. Yet because things are constantly changing, so must our maps. So while we have to map, we don't have to carve our maps into stone. We can hold them more tentatively, flexibly, and playfully, always open to new ways of mapping, new additions to our maps, and erasing things that we no longer need to concern ourselves with.

9) The "As If" Game

Sometimes when we do not know how to solve a problem or know the specific steps to take to achieve a particular outcome, we can *feel and imagine our way* to the solution by using the *As If frame*. To do this, we *pretend* that we know the solution and then imaginatively allow our other-than-conscious mind to fill in the details about how that would look, sound, and feel. This may not be the full solution, yet it is at least the beginning of a new possibility.

Since William James began urging the feigning of cheerfulness until the feelings of cheerfulness arise, the *As If frame* has provided a method-acting type of response so that we use our actions and behaviors to chart the way into a new way of feeling. James, by the way, along with Karl Lange, developed one of the first theories about emotional control using the *as if* dynamic.

Later, Steve de Shazar, put this mental-emotional dynamic of *As If-ing* into the context of a "miracle during the night while you slept" to create "The Miracle Question."[2]

- If you did know the answer, what do you think it would be?
- If a miracle happened tonight while you slept and when you woke up in the morning, everything was different about this way of thinking, feeling, and responding so that you simply were no longer in that place, how would you know that a miracle had occurred?
- If you were cheerful and pleasant in doing this, what would that be like?

This *frame game* operates from the larger level assumption that we do not have to explain everything in order to begin to take effective action in our lives. In fact, we can simply find one thing that works and begin to go with it, developing it, and letting it expand.

This contrasts with the *Analytical game* that so many people play. It seems to be an occupational hazard for those trained in the sciences and who are predisposed to the scientific mind-set. In that game, they have to *understand* before they can go with something. "I won't and can't believe it or try something if I don't fully understand it."

By playing the *as if* game, you don't have to depend upon actual references —you can invent references that you will call into existence and use. We can use *imagined references*. We can see things that could be and begin to operate from them as our reference point. The *As If game* invites creativity, innovation, and child-like mind of possibility.

10) The Vitality Game

The ability to take action and translate dreams, visions, and values into reality takes *power*—energy, action, movement. To do this we need our body and we will need a body that's as fit and healthy as possible. The less our physical vitality, the less likely we will be able to create and maintain a mental and emotional vitality.

- Do you play from a frame of mind of vitality?
- Do you appreciate and value your body as a source of physical energy?
- Do you eat and exercise as if your mind depended upon it?

Do you know that your emotions directly depend upon your breathing, posture, movement, and other health habits? A sluggish body inevitably leads to a sluggish mind.[3] Those who put up with such undermine their own inner vitality, to say nothing about a sense of joy in being alive.

11) The Abundant Generosity Game

If you operate from the *scarcity frame*, then you will focus on life as a win/lose battle, assume that there's just not enough goodies to go around, and so you'll think, feel, and act miserly. This will set you in the direction of being a scrooge and teaching others to treat you as a hostile competitor.

A much more empowering frame comes from the perspective of abundance. Viewing life as a win/win proposition, this frame assumes there's plenty for everybody, and that if we run short of the pie to divide, we'll simply bake some more pies. This leads to a sense of generosity, big-heartedness (magnanimity), a sense of enriching others, contributing, making things better for all, going the second mile, etc. When you play *the Abundance game,* you ask such things as:

- How can we both win in this adventure?
- You know, I want to win at this and I also want you to win, how can we pull that off instead of competing with each other?
- What would comprise a "win" for you?
- Since it seems like we both feel that there's not enough of the pie to go around, how can we create something so that we can bake more pies?

12) The Personal Warmth Game

Thousands of books, songs, plays, movies, and poems have sung the praises of *love* in calling us to the frame of mind that conveys a warn compassion and empathy. These are powerful frames. They enable us to act with kindness, generosity, care, concern, etc. When *love* is both our frame of reference and our direction, we extend ourselves for the sakes of others. With a loving frame of mind, we ask:

- What's the loving thing to do?
- How can I extend myself for the welfare of this person?
- What would express warmth and compassion to this person?

13) The Persistent Resolve or Patient Persistence Game

Knowing where we're going (the Aim game) and intentionally deciding that we will commit ourselves to a course of action (the Decision game) empowers us to persist, to bounce back resiliently when we stumble and fall, and to never give up, but to flexibly keep learning and improving. Then it becomes not a question of *if*, but *when* we succeed.

- Where do you need more persistence?
- What ideas and beliefs support a persistent stance for you in that situation?
- Why would it be valuable and important to hang in and persist with this

objective?
- What price will you pay if you give up or give in?

To develop excellence in most of the things that we consider important entails thinking in terms of the long haul, rather than in the short-term of immediate pleasure. Immediate gratification, in fact, undermines success in most things. Whether it is to develop a great mind, a great body, great level of fitness, great relationships, a great career, etc. we have to push through the discomfort of short-term pain in order to reach our long-term goals. How can you describe this frame in a way that seems attractive, compelling, and powerful?

The impulsiveness of the short term frame leads most people to indulge in the very things that will eventually cause long-term pain. Short-term indulgences in eating, relaxing, putting unpleasant things off, etc., typically plants the seed for a harvest of things that we will not find pleasant or desirable. Playing the frame game, *"You only go around once, so go for all the gusto you can!"* comes with a pretty hefty long-term price.

Thinking consequentially and systemically enables us to project into the future the direction and orientation that we develop today. This frame game makes for long-term success and pleasure. Most people who end up at places that they really don't want do so through the accumulations of many small actions. They fail to follow up, they fail to take action, they fail to persist, etc. By giving themselves to instant gratification, they play the *Quick Fix game* to their own detriment.

14) The Orientation Game

Knowing our world, and knowing where we stand in it, enables us to think strategically and purposefully. This greatly enhances our ability to proactively plan and to take effective action. Use orientation questions to elicit this.
- Where are we with each other?
- Where are we in this project?
- Where do we want to be?
- What are you attempting to accomplish by doing this?
- How would you prefer for me to listen to you right now?

15) The *No Failure, Only Feedback* Game

Imagine living life in a world where there is *no idea of failure.* The idea of *no failure* is a pretty wild and crazy idea, isn't it? That's because "failure" has become so predominant a frame in our culture that even entertaining the audacious idea of "No Failure/ Only Feedback" sounds completely insane.

So to try this on, adopt a frame of playful imaginativeness and just go with the idea that instead of failure, try on the frame, *"I can only and always get results.* Suppose that instead of operating with a classification category of "failure" into which you put anything that you cannot fit into the category of "success," you had a category of "results" or "feedback." "It's just information."

Take this attitude and go out onto a basketball court. As you begin to toss the basketball toward the hoop, how do you feel when you think about every-action you take and everything that happens is a *result?* Ah, immediately you're a great success! You always get results. Talk about total success! You always get results! Now add the idea of *feedback* to the tossing of the balls. *Every result gives you feedback.* Toss a little harder or softer, toss more to the left or right, up or down, use your guiding hand with more or less pressure, etc.

I really liked the *No Failure/Only Feedback* when I first heard about it. It made a lot of sense, so I decided to incorporate it into my mind. However, I found that doing so wasn't as easy as it sounded. It seemed as if my mind had a predilection for the failure frame! I had well-worn the grooves in my brain to categorize things as "failures" and to play that game. Of course, every time I went there mentally, I ended up feeling bad. So it took a good bit of energy to refuse *the Failure game,* to keep shaking off the old game, and refusing to play it. It also took a lot of significant practice to get the hang of the new game.

But what an incredible difference it has made. Referencing things as *feedback* has kept me feeling much more resourceful. It supports maintaining a "presence of mind" in the midst of experiences so that I can keep learning, detecting distinctions, and adjusting behaviors to get the results that I want. It makes persistence a piece of cake. Try it. It's a great game to play.

16) The Implementation or "Make It So!" Game

What do you think or feel about *implementing* what you know? Do you *just do it?* Or do you play *the Procrastination game*? To set an implementation frame of reference, begin thinking in terms of always *practicing* what you learn.

- How can I practice this?
- How can I give this idea some hands and feet and try it out in the real world?
- If I decide to never leave the scene of a learning without taking some action, how will that affect my sense of self?

When you play *the Implementation game,* you continually ask yourself:

- What one thing can I do to implement this idea, dream, vision, understanding, or insight?
- What one thing can I do today, this moment, that will put me in the direction I want to go?

What other resources do you need in order to set a frame that empowers you to *implement* what you know? Courage, boldness, "no failure, only feedback," an empowering decision that you will take action, etc.? When we set a frame for implementation, we are empowered to create new momentum, to take the first small step in a series that creates a new direction, and to not allow things to stop our progress.

This describes one of the many reasons I have opted for this frame game. I play it for other reasons: to be congruent, aligned with my highest values, to feel integrated and focused. Why would you want to play this game?[4]

17) The Self-Acceptance Game

- What frame of mind have you developed about your concept of your "self?"
- How have you framed your understandings and feelings about your own identity and self-definition?
- Have you done so conditionally or unconditionally?
- Do you frame yourself as inadequate, inferior, and worthless until you achieve or accomplish something?
- Do you have to fulfill societal conditions in order to be okay, to be a human being, to have innate human worth and value, or have you framed such things as *givens?*

To play *the Self-Acceptance game,* take the idea that your dignity and human worth are unconditionally given. When you start with that frame, there's nothing to prove and nothing to earn. The rule of the game boils down to one simple thing: Own and value yourself as having worth, value, and dignity. Whatever mind, body, emotions, station in life, skills, aptitudes, etc. you have—*accept it.* This will empower you to adjust to your personal reality as you adjust to external realities in the social, political, economic, and interpersonal realities.

From that *acceptance* frame you can then get on with self-discovery, growth, development, improvement, and excellence. We seek such, not to prove anything, but simply as an expression of who we are, to express our talents, skills, values, visions, and so on.

When you begin to play this game, anticipate that it will confuse some people, and that they will try to reject you and the game, mistaking it for pride, egotism, and selfishness. They will try to seduce you back into playing, *"You have to Prove Yourself"* game.

18) The Living in the Now with an eye on a Compelling Future Game

One of the frames that we never leave home without, and one that seems almost innate to the way our mind works, is the *time* frame. This makes us time creatures, beings who live in the concept that we call "time." As such we are time travelers.[5]

- Time Zone: past, present, future.
- Time's Speed: fast time, slow time, distorted time.

- Time's Representation: line, circle, spiral, boomerang, etc.
- Time Sequencing: sequentially and linearly versus randomly, simultaneously.
- Time's Size: lots of time (spacious time) little time (narrow, limited time).

How do you think about "time?" What *time zone* do you primarily focus on: what has happened in the past, what's currently transpiring in the moment, what you want and hope to occur in the future? How much time do you spend in each time zone in your thinking and feeling, as you move through your day? Does this way of time traveling to these zones serve you well and empower you, or does it create limitations and hang ups?

Too much past focusing leads one to think and feel that things are determined, fated, and out-of-our control. Too much future focusing leads to living in a dream world of hopes and desires, and failing to take effective action now. Too much present day focusing leads to failing to learn from the past or plan for the future. It leads to playing impulsive games: *"I Want It Now!" "But That's Too Much Work; Why do I have to Wait so Long?"*

Our emotions are powerfully impacted by the time frames that we use. Worry, anxiety, and disappointment are emotions of the future as are anticipation and hope. Regret, guilt, traumatization, etc. are emotions of *the past* as are anticipation and hope. *Present* emotions that give us distress include impatience, impulsiveness, refusal to persist, etc. while those that support us are presence, awareness, experiencing.

How do we code "time" as a concept? The entire domain of *Time-Lines* addresses this. This has to do with our representations of the time zones, the size and compression of time, and how we operate in relation to time: sequentially or randomly, with procedures or looking for options.

Time is a subjective experience, it does not exist "out there," it operates strictly as a concept. So as a frame *time* is entirely psychological. What exists "out there" beyond our skin? *Events.* As we notice and compare events, we invent "time." This allows us to sort out events that have happened, are happening, and those that would or will happen. Because this occurs entirely within our head, time is entirely constructed as an understanding.

What belief frames do you have about time? Many people in therapy play the game, *I've Got to Finish the Old Business of the Past by Re-living it Again and Again!* So they spend years or decades playing old B-rated movies about past sufferings and use them over and over as their reference points. This typically only reinforces their generalizations. And so it solidifies their frames, they become more stuck.

NLP takes a different point of view, one expressed by Richard Bandler, *"It's never too late to have a happy childhood."* That's because what we call our "past" only exists in our minds and is comprised of our representations —something we can readily, quickly, and easily alter. It is also comprised of our frames. For a moment, imagine playing the frame game: *"It's Never Too Late to Have a Happy Childhood."*

While we can't literally or physically travel through "time," we can certainly *time travel* in our heads. You can learn to float above your sense of this moment and float back along your path of time to the past, and to thirty minutes prior to any negative event bringing with you all the resources and wisdom of your adult self. When you arrive at that moment, drop down onto your time line and zoom straight forward to the present letting your internal "history" change and transform. It's a rush. It also gives you a way to set time frames that will serve you well.

Of course, if you would prefer to wallow and whine by focusing on all of the rotten and terrible things you've experienced, that others have done to you—you can run your brain with that frame just as well. It's your brain. You can run it in either of these ways, or in numerous others.

Mastering "time" involves so much more than just writing out "to do" lists and prioritizing what's important. It also involves coding and structuring (framing) your concepts of "time" so that you can make it go faster and slower at your choice, so that you know how to get "lost in time" when that's appropriate and how to stay in up-time, current to this moment, fully present and aware, with all of your sensory antennas tuned into the outside world. It also means the ability to think sequentially, to follow procedures, and to get things done that have to be done "on time."

What kind of emotional and belief frames have you brought to time? Some people "kill" time, "waste" time," "spend" time, "enjoy" time, and "stretch" time out. Some people love time, others hate it. Some have a good relationship to it, others treat it like its their enemy, or a burden, or a terrifying mystery. What do you do? What game would you like to play and win at?

19) The Solution Game

Like the *Aim game,* this game involves a 180-degree turn around from the *Blame game.* Rather than looking for who to blame and what to use as an excuse, this game, like the *Aim game,* seeks to find solutions.

This obviously differs from the way most of us *play* life and the training that we have had in "problem" detection. Most of us focus on *problems* rather than *solutions*, and rightly so, given how deeply steeped our culture is in problem orientation. We move through the world, enter into situations, and converse with friends and associates in terms of problems. The first thing on our mind and the first thing out of our mouth concerns problems.

- What's the problem? What's wrong?
- Why is this a problem?
- Who's creating the problem? (First question for the *Blame game*)
- When and where is this a problem?

To shift the play to a very different game, begin asking yourself questions that presuppose *solution* as your frame-of-reference.

- What could solve this difficulty?
- How can I effectively deal with this and enjoy the process?
- What can I learn from this?
- What resource can I bring to this experience?
- Who else handles this with ease and skill?
- Who has written about how to effectively solve this?
- If I knew the solution, what would it look like, sound like, or feel like?
- How many steps may be involved in bringing good resolution to this?
- Would a systemic attitude help to look at this more creatively?

When you play *the Solution game* you operate from the frame of *possibility*. "There's always a way to turn things around." "Every problem contains opportunities hidden within it." "I can learn to see opportunities and seize them." To this you can add the frame of *constantly improving*.

- "How can I improve this by one more percent?"
- "What refinements can I discover to make this just a little bit better?"
- What one small thing could I do today that would seed the response I want?

It only takes one player to play, "How can we solve this?" Although one player playing this game frequently entices dozens, even thousands, to join the game.

20) The *"It's Only Real if it's a Behavior"* Game

One of the dangers of *going meta* into the higher frames of mind of our abstractions, beliefs, concepts, and ideas is that we can easily get lost in our ideas and forget to translate them back to reality. This creates a special problem when communicating, namely, relying upon more highly refined concepts as we evaluate, form concepts, and build generalizations. Then we create evaluations of those evaluations. Yet if we don't continually bring them back to sensory-based behavioral language, we can get lost in the clouds of abstraction assuming that we and others know what we mean.

The best tool for dealing with this is the language model of precision, the Meta-Model.[6] Abstract language seductively entices us all. We first name things, then we name actions (which create nominalizations), and later, as we name our nominalizations, we begin to believe that our nominalizations refer to real things.

Yet they never do. The next level of deception occurs when we treat "problems" in merely abstract terms instead of behavioral terms.

The magic of this game arises from realizing that ultimately *every problem involves a behavior.* No matter how abstract or conceptual, in the end a "problem" is only a real problem if it involves a behavior. If it doesn't, it is not a real problem. It is only a *mental game,* a function of our thinking, representing, and framing.

As an example, there is no "drug problem." Problems arise when a specific person mis-uses a drug, becomes dependent upon it, and/or sells drugs to kids. Drug problems occurs when people *do* these things. These actions are the problem. Calling it a "drug" problem misdirects us as it creates confusion and vagueness. Nor do we have a "crime" problem. We have a behavioral problem of *people* engaging in actions that we classify as "crimes" against others or against the state. Nor do we have a "homeless" problem, "gang" problem, "weight" problem, "sexual" problem, etc.

Is this just semantics? You bet it is! And being semantic in nature is precisely what makes it so powerful. When we attach a classification to the specific behaviors and then mentally turn it into a "thing," we begin to lose awareness of what we're talking about. That's when and how we can create an exaggerated problem in our mind. Conversely, when we relate a concept to specific behaviors, we give our brains precise information. The semantics of framing things as *behaviors*, as specific actions that we can see, hear, feel, smell, taste, etc. enables us to more precisely think and respond.

Translating our concepts into see-hear-feel referents gives us something specific to *do* and so makes the "problem" solvable. Milton Erickson played this *frame game* a lot. Whether the presenting problem was a headache, anger control, obesity, parenting, etc., he would *fragment* the problem into *behaviors* and *micro-behaviors.* This empowered his clients to get their hands on something concrete to do about "the problem."

Conversely, leaving a "problem" at too high of a conceptual level keeps it up in the air and out of reach. It puts us into a position where we can't *do* anything about "the problem." To play the *specific evidence* game, ask:

- What would I see, hear, or feel if I saw "low self esteem?" What would I see or hear you actually doing if I saw you in that state?
- If a miracle happened, and the problem was gone, how would you know? What would you be doing on the day after the miracle that you're not doing now?
- What lets you know that a person "loves" you?
- How do you know when you "trust" someone? What cues you to feel trust or confidence in that person?

Playing the *Specifically How Would I know?* game enables us to create solutions because it gives us something to *do*—even if only in our mind as a way of perceiving things. Making "problems" behavioral also highlights that the problem is not the person. "Problems" involve behaviors and that's *the outer game.* When we play this frame game, we no longer see "problems" as permanent or part of a person's "nature," but as involving temporary and changeable actions.

"Problems" framed in specific behaviors also provide us specifics for creating an action plan. This allows us to play *the Aim game* more powerfully, and to play *the Evidence game.* So we ask, "How would you know when . . .?"

- What frame brings out or programs this behavior?
- What frame would I have to shift to in order to allow this other behavior to emerge?

21) The Positive Intention Game

One of the most powerful and profound assumptions about human behaviors centers in this idea: *"Behind every behavior is a positive intention."* It came originally from Virginia Satir and Milton Erickson who were both incredibly gifted at connecting with people and creating instant rapport. What enabled them to achieve that level of world-class performance? What inner games empowered them? They assumed positive intention.

Their frame of mind was that people do things to accomplish things of value for themselves. Starting from the assumption of *positive intention*, they then went on a search for those positive intentions. No wonder this inner game naturally aligns us with the highest intentions and values of others and shifts our focus from the hurt, destructiveness, and "evilness" of a behavior, attitude, or way of talking. This frame does *not* deny that sometimes the actions and habits that we produce do great harm. Of course, they can. Yet it is by assuming that we do things for positive reasons, values, and intentions—to make things better, that we are more able to elicit the best in people.

Explore this for yourself. Think about some behavior that you did that resulted in some very hurtful consequences for yourself or others. Perhaps you blew up at someone and insulted them, physically attacked them, violated their trust, let someone down, etc. Undoubtedly, the behavior really fell short of excellence. It fell short of what you wanted for yourself and how you want to be known. Yet was that your intention? Back up to *the intent* behind that behavior. What were you seeking to accomplish? What did you hope to achieve? Weren't you attempting to do something positive for yourself?

Sometimes we have to ask the intentionality question several times until we rise up to a positive intention that is sufficient. Sometimes in times of stress, conflict, threat, our first intention may have been to make a threat go away. We wanted to hurt someone to reduce their threat. At that point ask:

> *And what did we seek to accomplish that would have been of value to us by doing that?*

The positive intention question inevitably takes us to such values as wanting to feel safe, protected, recognized, valued, loved, etc. Separating *action* from *intention* enables us to reframe the meanings that we give to things. It enables us to recognize ourselves and others as being more than our actions. It empowers us to validate and align with another's positive intentions rather than get hung up on and judgmental about his or her hurtful behaviors.

This frame initiates a totally different game when it comes to conflict. If two people operate from this frame of reference, conflict becomes a sign that their positive intentions are not being fulfilled and gives them something to explore in an attitude of respect and care, rather than attacking and playing *the blame game.*

22) The Justice Game

When it comes to the *Justice* game, we come to a game that has to be carefully handled if we don't want it to come back and bite us. When working with the Department of Corrections in the State of Colorado a number of years ago, I conducted a class of Life Skills designed to help re-integrate men convicted of felonies back into society. By design the course was to provide them new frames for how to think, feel, talk, and act so to enable them to not become repeat offenders.

When I began I did everything I knew at the time to establish that as the agreement frame. "You don't want to spend more time in the pen, do you?" I thought that would be powerful to initiate "a motivation to stay out of jail" game. It was not. For some of them, it didn't seem much of a deterrent at all.

What mattered more than "time behind bars?" *Fairness.* The majority of the men wanted things to be "always and perfectly fair." One man had spent five years in the federal penitentiary because he had slugged a cop who stopped him one day for going through a red light. Now there's a game! When I heard that, I couldn't help myself. I had to ask: "*Why* would you hit a cop?"

> "Because the ticket was not fair. I went through the light when it was yellow, not red. And by God I'm not going to be treated in such an unjust way!"

"I suppose you've heard that it's not a fair world out there."

> "Don't give me any of that crap. That's bullshit. Nobody is going to mess around with me. I expect fairness, and I'm going to get it."

That wasn't the first nor was it the last time I got that speech. The majority of the men I worked with for that period of time operated from that frame. It was their basic attitude. They played the inner game, *"It's got to be fair or I'll turn all hell loose!"* And they played that game seriously.

Whenever I suggested that they just suck up and "kiss ass" (pacing their language patterns) of authority figures, they knew that I had become an agent of the great Enemy and didn't understand anything. Life had to be fair. And it had to be fair *to them.* Strange thing about how many of them played the *justice* game, they only seemed to sort for fairness and justice for *themselves.* I never met one who crusaded for fairness for others.

In terms of how "the criminal mind" works, there seems to be a total intolerance for anything viewed as unfair or unjust. Such a mind plays other games, *What's In It For Me?, Nobody Understands Me, I've Had Such a Hard Time, The Government (World, God, etc.) Owes Me,* etc. Such minds don't seem attracted to playing *the Acceptance game* which takes social reality for whatever we find it and then make the most of it.

Another group seems especially attracted to the *Justice* game, or at least a first-cousin of that game, *The Being Right* game. People with a special passion for spiritual and religious concerns, for philosophy or theology, frequently get sucked into playing, *My Beliefs are Better than Yours.* Of course, in this game *being right* is the main thing, the great payoff.

Do you want to play *the Fairness game?* Then make sure that you play it as your gift to the world rather than expecting or demanding the world and others first give it to you. Set your frame, *"I will aim to play fairly and equitably with others as much as possible."* This seems to have been the primary focus of Jesus' Golden Rule and similar statements, "Do unto others as you want others to do unto you." This puts the initiative and focus on *what you do* and *how you operate*, that is, treating people with dignity, fairness, honor, respect, etc. rather than starting from fairness as what the world *owes* you. Let fair play and a win/win attitude define your basic attitude for dealing with people. When that doesn't work, then "don't cast your pearls before swine.' (The interesting thing is that both statements occur in the same passage about how to get along with them, Matthew 7:1-12).

23) The Cheerfulness Game

What frame have you set regarding happiness? How have you framed joy and delight? How many conditions have you set on these states of mind? Do you use them as *your way of being in the world* so that, as your frame of mind, you enjoy the process and experience regardless? Or do you limit yourself from a joyful perspective until you achieve a certain accomplishment?

The *Cheerfulness* game speaks about the ability to take pleasure from the smallest things in everyday life and to use that sense of play and fun as our orientational style. When we do that, we then learn how to squeeze joy out of every day, every experience, every learning. This bathes all of life in a kinder and gentler light. It embraces humor as a healing quality and uses the delight of the journey itself. It also saves us from the grimness of the *Life is so Serious* game.

24) The Enchantment of the Appreciation Game

Another absolutely wonderful frame game to play that supports personal excellence and genius itself is *the Enchantment game of* curiosity, wonder, and fascination. When you adopt an attitude of awe and fascination about the world, what state does it evoke in you? Does it not put you into a state of delightful enchantment? Does it not open your eyes in new and fresh ways to the world?

This frame actually supports creative ways of thinking, feeling, imagining, and acting. When we play the *Life is Absolutely Enchanting and Fascinating* game, we adopt the wonder of a child that trains our eyes to see everything through the lens of appreciation and gratitude. This, in turn, makes life more sacred, "spiritual," and grants us a special creativity.

Given what he wrote, I take it that Albert Einstein must have played this game:

> "The important thing is not to stop questioning. Curiosity has its own reason for existing. One cannot help but be in awe when he contemplates the mysteries of eternity, of life, of the marvelous structure of reality. It is enough if one tries merely to comprehend a little of this mystery every day. Never lose a holy curiosity."

25) The Acknowledging the Unnoticed Game

There's another frame that made Milton Erickson a wizard of language and healing. More recently Brief Psychotherapy has popularized this frame. To play this game, simply, with curiously, ponder and wonder, *"Why isn't this problem worse?"* This works in marvelous and magical ways with people who otherwise think that a habit, emotion, or response is out-of-control and that they can do nothing about it.

Suppose someone has the frame of mind which many people develop about eating, losing weight, exercising, etc.

> "I'm so depressed about my weight and over-eating. It's totally out of control. I just can't do anything about it."

How much do you weigh?

> "I'm ashamed to tell you . . I weigh 255 pounds."

That's incredible. With the way you described your problem, I can't figure out why the problem isn't worse.

"What do you mean? This is terrible! For my height and bone size, I'm grossly overweight."

Yes, indeed, and yet I can't figure out how is it that you are not 450 pounds? That's what I want to know. Why are you not pushing 500 pounds?

"I could never stand myself at that weight."

You could never stand yourself at that weight? Really? And yet you can stand yourself at 255? You can control yourself from going to 450, so if you couldn't stand yourself at 255 in the same way, you could control that.

To play this frame game, step back from the problem, difficulty, or struggle and begin to wonder why it isn't a lot worse. "How come you haven't strangled your husband (child, boss, etc.)?" "Why haven't you put a gun to your head?" "What's stopped you from not blowing up?" When we frame a problem in this way, it forces us (or another) to begin to *mine hidden resources and skills* that typically have been unacknowledged, and even discounted. This brings them to the foreground of our awareness.

Your mother-in-law came for a visit? I could imagine things could have gotten a lot worse than they did. How did you manage so that it did not?

26) The Flexibility Game

Einstein is reported to have once said that insanity is continuing to do the same thing which doesn't work while hoping for different results. When we have repeatedly tried a given response, the possibility of obtaining a new and successful outcome will come as we try something different. If the frame you've been using repeatedly, consistently, and dependably creates limiting and destructive outcomes, stop. Interrupt that old pattern. Do something different. Do one thing different. Change your approach.

The problem isn't in you, isn't in your genes, your parents, or anything that's happened to you. *The problem is in the frames.* So, to make this more graphic and dramatic and memorable, I'll paraphrase the campaign slogan that took the White House from George Bush and handed it over to Bill Clinton in 1992, "It's the economy, stupid."

"It's the frames, stupid!"

Now, with that in mind, what new frames of mind and new reference structures would you prefer to operate from? How can you code, represent, and think about *flexibility* so that it empowers you for greater choice and adaptability in the ever-changing process world?

28) The Courage Game of Hutzpah!

We call the willingness to risk, to face a danger or threat, and to face down the fear with intelligence, passion, and understanding—*courage.* This isn't a primary state, it is a highly valued meta-state. At the primary level we have fear, apprehension, concerns, dangers, etc. If we take counsel of our fears, we play out *the timid* game wherein we play it safe and refuse to rock the boat.

> Einstein is reported to have once said that insanity is continuing to do the same thing which doesn't work hoping for different results.

To face down the fears and worries and to allow a new quality to arise in human experience, *the gestalt of courage,* we have to develop the willingness to do what it takes in spite of the fear. This means giving ourselves to some overwhelming passion and vision that will empower us to not give in to the fears. Courage frequently arises when we develop the confidence in ourselves to take action knowing that we have the flexibility to keep learning and adjusting as we go. It arises from the *No Failure/Only Feedback* frame that allows us to embrace mistakes as just information that we can use to become smarter in our approach.

29) From Pessimism to the Learned Optimism Game

When Martin Seligman (1975, 1990) specified the inner structure of *learned helplessness*, he summarized his findings in an alliteration of *P*. These concerned *the explanatory style* of people in facing difficulties, problems, and troubles. What do you think when things don't go well? What frame of mind do you go to when problems crop up in life? What *inner game* do you play when tragedy or trauma occurs? The three ***P***s identify three *frame games* that sicken our spirit.

- ***Personal:*** *"It's about me.* I'm defective, inadequate, inferior, and without any redeeming value." In our explanatory style, we interpret a problem as internal and at our essence which leads to personalizing the trouble and using it to *define* ourselves, to question our value and worth, etc.
- ***Pervasive:*** *"This affects everything in my life.* It contaminates every facet." In our explanatory style, we interpret a problem as affecting everything about us—every dimension of our mind, emotions, experiences, relationships, career, health, etc. It *pervasively* intrudes into every domain so that it contaminates all of our thinking, feeling, and acting.
- ***Permanent:*** *"This will last forever.* This will never go away." In our explanatory style, we interpret a problem that will last forever. That it will never go away, but forever be with us and control everything about us.

Imagine playing any one of these *games*. What a way to crush your spirit about yourself (personal), your resources, skills, and potentials (pervasive), and about your future (permanent). This would not offer a positive or enhancing frame at all. It would undermine and sabotage any sense of empowerment, confidence, self-esteem, self-efficacy, and proactivity and create *dragon states.* It would install fire breathing dragons in the higher regions of the mind that would devastate drive, mastery, and hope.[7]

Seligman and his associates came up with these three ***P***s from his research in depression and learned helplessness, first in animals, then in humans. No kidding! Set frames that everything that goes wrong is *personal, pervasive, and permanent* and it will depress the most stout-hearted, vigorous, and proactive. Do you want to play that game? I wouldn't recommend it. Not at all. Instead, play the *Learned Optimism* game. Seligman's follow-up research looked at how to cure that deadening pessimism.

How? By recognizing that external conditions and learning environments do not *make* us the way we are, but that our interpretations and explanatory styles control our destiny, identity, and experience. *Explanatory style* refers to how you think about, interpret, and explain pains, hurts, troubles, difficulties, traumas, challenges, and frustrations. Framing problems as personal, pervasive, and permanent sets the rules for *the Depression Game.* Expect to cave in, feel crushed in spirit, hopeless, helpless, worthless. What a game to play in the face of life's possibilities!

The game of *Learned Optimism* uses an entirely different explanatory style regarding negative and hurtful experiences. The rules of this game are very different. When bad things happen, we interpret them as external, specific, and temporary. To initiate this game, use the words, *This here now* for explaining or framing things when problems and/or traumas occur.

- *This*: It is not about you as a person, it is about some event, action, or behavior. *This* prevents the evil from effecting our inmost self. *This* says that we ourselves are much more than our experiences, emotions, thoughts, behaviors, relationships, jobs, titles, money, etc. These are our expressions, but not who we are.
- *Here:* It is about this specific event and does not extend pervasively to other events. *Here* limits the evil to a particular situation. *Here* indexes the specific action of the negative event to keep it contained so that it does not contaminate the rest of life. *Here* sections off the part of life suffering a defeat, insult, or wound. It's about our job, or relationship, or health, or whatever.
- *Now:* Temporary, not permanent, it will not last forever. *Now* says it is occurring in this time and space where all things change. *Now* allows us to set the frame, "This too will pass."

Would you like to play the *"This Here Now"* game (or, *That Then There*)? You will win such feelings as experience life as enjoyable, empowering, and hopeful. Playing *learned optimism* invites you to keep growing, accessing resources, and developing a greater intelligence so that you can even use undesirable events and responses as feedback for learning. This game will empower your spirit to remain proactive and vigorous enabling you to bounce right back from a setback. Rather than reading defeat as personal, pervasive, nor permanent, you interpret it as a temporary detour about something that didn't get you the results you wanted.[8]

30) Relational Frame Games — *Frames for Great Relationships*

Whenever we relate to another person, we do so *with* and *within* certain frames. That's because we never leave home without our frames, but take them everywhere as we make sense of things.

- What frames do you have about relationships?
- What are your frames about love, affection, sex, romance, intimacy, communication, conflicts, conflict resolution, growing old together, friendship, colleagues, etc.?
- What games do your frames set up?

Since our frames run our games, whatever frame we bring into our relating creates all of our *expectations, hopes, and fears* and so our games.

- Do you have the power to love and care for others? What frames support this?
- Do you have the ability to speak up to others in a kind and thoughtful way? What frames enable you to play that game?

As with all frame games, once our relational *games* are established, they become self-protective and self-fulfilling. They develop a life of their own *in our mind* and so become self-organizing. They organize every facet of our being as they structure more and more of our mental and emotional processes to operate in their service. This is the entire focus of the book, *Games Great Lovers Play* (2003).

What *games* do you play with people? Consider the *frame games* that you have learned and that you access as your default programs.

- What games do you invite people into?
- How well do these serve you and the other?
- What relational frame games would you like to learn to play?

As a prompter, consider the following as positive and relationship enhancing *frame games:*

Playfulness	Creativity
Admiration	Appreciation/ Honor
Responsiveness	Committed and Loyal
Validating	Safe and Secure
Vulnerable and Open	Assertive and Forthright
Win/Win	Cooperative
Exploratory	Attentive and Thoughtful
Accepting	Being more than Doing

31) Health and Fitness Games

What about food and to exercise? What *frameworks* govern your thinking, perceiving, and responding to food?

- What are your frames of mind about food?
- What games do you play with food?
- Do they give you the kind of control over your eating and exercising that you want?
- Do they empower your body and mind with the kind of energy and power that makes life an adventure?
- Do they enable you to live comfortably in your body with grace, ease, and vitality?

When I applied frame games to eating and exercising and wrote *Games Slim and Fit People Play* (2000), I discovered that the problems that we have with eating, weight management, and staying healthy is not due to food. For those people who are over or under weight, *food* is not the problem. Food is just food. The problem lies in how we *relate* to food and frame food, the inner games that we play and specifically because we *eat* for the wrong reasons.

- What's your frame when you eat, diet, exercise, think about food, wish you could lose some weight, etc.?
- How much importance do you give to eating?
- What frames prevent you from taking control of your eating and exercising?
- What frame of mind would you have to put yourself into in order to take charge of your weight and fitness?

The same principle applies to exercise. The problems that we have with fitness, health, and weight mastery do not involve having or not having the right equipment, time, and/or motivation to exercise. The problem lies in our frame games. We are not the problem, the experience is not the problem, *the frame is the problem!* So without addressing our frames, the problems we have with eating and exercising, staying vigorous, fit, slim, etc., will remain unsolved. Nor is the problem our circumstances, genetics, family heritage, nature, or finances. We go from diet to diet, from one exercise program to another, one fad to another because of the inner games we play.

Nor is the problem the program. There are many perfectly good programs that will get the job done. Why then are so many thousands still searching for yet another program, for "the perfect program?" Because of their frames. Regardless of the particular program, we always bring our frames with us. And eventually our frames will assert themselves, either supporting or limiting how we work the program.

The solution is simple. After all, what is food for? Is it not apparent that food is primarily *for fuel, to give us energy,* and not for comfort, fulfillment, reward, love, nurturing, validation, status, emotional stress, etc. If we eat to deal with loneliness, boredom, anxiety, depression, anger, frustration, and any other of a hundred emotional states—we are eating for the wrong reasons. We are *psycho-eating* and playing some game with food.

"You ate what? You ate how much? What were you thinking?"

"Well, I didn't have anything else to do while the show was on and everybody else was munching on the junk food that was spread out. It's what we always do when the Super Bowl is on."

"So what were you thinking about at the party?"

"Just that, 'Hey, it's a party!'"

"And the meaning of that . . . is what?"

"It's time to eat up, to let go."

"Why?"

"To enjoy yourself."

"So let me see if I have this right. You were eating to be social, to party, to experience joy. Right?"

'Yes, that's right."

"So you were eating for all of the wrong reasons. No wonder you overdid it, ailed to experience a sense of self-control, and were *played by the game* rather than had mastery over your body and what you put into it! It makes sense. With frames like that, everybody would over-eat the wrong things."

Healthy Food Frames

We eat because our bodies require fuel. Hunger is our cue to eat. Actually, we must eat if we want energy, vitality, an active lifestyle, movement, and a healthy metabolism. And that's pretty much it. When we add *psychology* to food, we create the mix for some real problems, as the obesity statistics, dieting fads, and eating disorder indicate. Almost anything other than this sets a frame about food that will not serve us well.

Let's do some frame detection with regard to eating:

- Why do you eat?
- Why do you eat what you eat?
- What significance does food hold for you?
- Is food important? How? In what way?
- What emotions drive you to eat?
- What emotions to you experience

> We are not the problem, the experience is not the problem, *the frame is the problem!* Without addressing our frames, the problems we have with eating and exercising, staying vigorous, fit, thin, etc., will not be solved.

when you eat?
- What do you believe about your eating and weight?
- What do you believe about your ability to resist temptation?

There are so many unenhancing frames for eating. We can attach a great many emotions to eating. This typically begins very early in life when we were *rewarded* with desserts and treats, *comforted* with a bowl of soup, and *socialized* as we spend time eating with loved ones. No wonder we can link all kinds of psychological states to the experience of eating. It's so easy to attach massive pleasure to eating. When that happens, of course, then it becomes difficult to stop eating. Why "deprive" yourself of these pleasures? Why lose out on comfort, fulfillment, reward, sociality, etc.?

What references do you have for eating? What frames have you developed over the years about eating and dieting? What meanings have become incorporated in your frameworks? Out of these, what food games do you play with eating and dieting? The game of *Yo-Yo Up and Down the Scales*? *Now I'm Dieting/ Now I'm Not. If I Don't Notice the Cookies Hidden in the Socks Drawer, then I'm Not Really Eating. Ain't My Weight Awful?*

There are lots of food frame games that we can play. As with every game, these often involve the beliefs that we've built about eating. Among these are the following:
- *I'm Out of Control With My Eating* game. (the Helpless Victim game)
- *I Can't Help It, It's My Genes!* (the Blame game)
- *It's Useless and I'm Hopeless. I've Tried Everything and Nothing Works.* (the Despair game)
- *I Eat to Fill a Hole, a Void, an Emptiness.* (The Poor Me game)
- *Other People Can Lose Weight, But I Can't.* (Helpless game; I'm the Exception to the Rule game.)
- *Keep Me Back From Myself!* (I put off eating as far as possible into the day, because once I get started, I won't stop eating. It's like letting a beast out of a cage.)
- *I Have a Sweet Tooth and Can't Help Myself.* (the Irresponsibility game.)
- *Just a Little Bit Won't Hurt.* "It won't matter if I indulge just this once." (the Denial game.)
- *Tomorrow I Will Begin a New Diet and This Time I'm Going to Really Stick to It!* (the Procrastination game.)
- *I Have to Starve Myself to be Thin.* (the Exaggeration game.)

Summary

- Searching and developing *excellence* itself can become a frame of mind—the very way we look at the world and how we move through it—our life game. Play the game of *Searching for Excellence,* and you will attract many other frames that will support this orientation.

- The frame games listed here are by no means exhaustive. They only illustrate the wide range of mental and emotional frameworks we can use as we choose our way.

- Because our *inner* and *outer games* determine the quality and effectiveness of our life, it's important to make sure that we are playing the games that bring out our best, put us in the direction we want to go, and that enhance our skills and growth.
- There are lots of *frame games* that make for personal health, energy, vitality, and balance. As you learn the frames for "powering up," becoming skillful, even masterful in playing them, warmly invite others into those *frame games* with you. It will revolutionize the way you live.

End Notes:

1. For the patterns mentioned in this chapter, see *The Source Book of Magic, Volume I and II (1997, 2003), Secrets of Personal Mastery (2000), User's Manual of the Brain, Volume I and II (1999, 2002).*

2. See the meta-stating pattern by this title in *Secrets of Personal Mastery* (2000).

3. See *Games Slim and Fit People Play* **(2001).**

4. See *Make It So!* **(2002).** This small book focuses entirely on the installing process that takes ideas and integrate them into neurology.

5. For more about the concept of *time* and the meta-levels of time, see *Time-Lining: Adventures in Time* (1997).

6. See *The Structure of Magic* (1975) and *Communication Magic* (2001).

7. See *Dragon Slaying* (2000).

8. For more about resilience, see *Meta-States* (2000), *Dragon Slaying* (2000) or the training manual for *Resilience.*

Chapter 16

LET THE GAMES BEGIN!

Playing for Fun and Profit

Every single day we play frame games. We always have; we always will. Yet typically we do so without awareness. Typically we are blind to the *inner game* of our frames of mind which govern our outer game of experiences and emotions. But now, you are in the know.

You have now discovered the presence of the inner and outer games. You know how to develop your skills in frame detection and transformation. Are you now on your way to becoming a frame game master? Are you planning to be? You have the tools to do that, to take charge of the life games that you play and want to play.

The time has come to say, *"Let the Games begin!"* You have been let in on some of the most powerful secrets of life and life's games. What are they?

- Life is a game and above and beyond the outer game of our performances is *the inner game* where the real action takes place. Winning the inner game makes the outer game a cinch.
- Behind and above every game is not only a single frame, but layers of embedded frames. And because frames govern games, when we change the frame, the game transforms.
- Life is itself a game played within a frame within a frame, within a frame and all of the embedded frames make up our Matrix. Detecting the Matrix and stepping out begins the adventure for mastering the Matrix.
- Stepping back to detect and quality control our frames enables us to begin to take charge of our inner and outer games.
- Game mastery will come to you through practice and experience. It comes by learning the secrets and applying them in everyday life.
- The force that primarily shapes our lives is *not* the events that we experience. Events do not determine how we think, feel, or respond.

Instead, the determining element lies in how we interpret and evaluate the experiences. It is the *meanings* that we give to things that creates our destiny.

- Our frame of mind controls what we see, how we feel, and predicts how we will behave. Frames govern our lives.
- *Whoever or whatever sets the frame controls the games.* This is what makes frame awareness, detection, and checking so essential skills for sanity, effectiveness, love, passion, and empowerment.
- Running a quality control on frames initiates magic and invites us into the role of a magician. Now we can refuse frames, design new ones, refresh frames, set new frames, and solidify them so that we can keep them with us.

Are you now ready to play? Even if you don't feel like you're ready, just put yourself out there and begin to get a feel for the games that you are already playing, knowing that they are *just games.* Lighten up, enjoy yourself, be playful, and operate from the frame of mind that there are all kinds of ways to transform the games.

Our frames and frames-embedded-in-frames of our entire Matrix are the governing factors of our lives, our emotions, skills, and experiences. Our feelings, personality, identity, and even our destiny results from *the frame games* that we play. Do you know your central frame games now? What new frames will you set in order to play even more fun and enhancing and honoring games in the weeks and months to come?

Now that you know how to *detect* and *flush out* frames, now that you know how to *refuse* a frame and how to *set, install, and solidify* new empowering frames—you truly have at your disposal the key to your identity, emotions, mental health, development of excellence, and destiny!

May you play well with joy as you awaken each morning to an excited passion and hear yourself say,

"Let the Games Begin!"

APPENDIX A

Meta Questions
Diamond of Consciousness

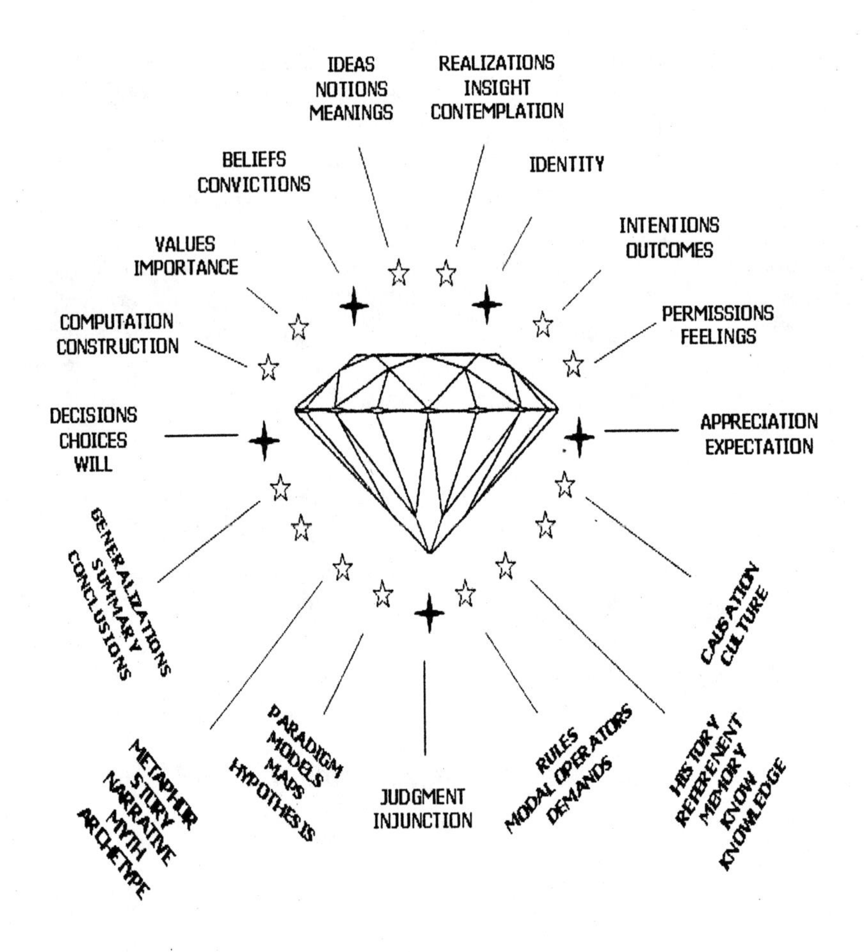

META-QUESTIONS
FOR TEASING OUT META-STRUCTURES

THE META-QUESTIONS

Of all states, *our meta-states are our most important states.* What is the reason for that? Precisely because meta-states, as *higher* states, govern, modify, modulate, control, drive, and organize our everyday primary states, because meta-messages modify lower-level messages (Gregory Bateson, 1972).

The *fluid levels* of meta-states are ever in flux, ever moving, changing, and in process. They are not things, they are not rigid, as mental and emotional energy expressions of representing and framing they arise and vanish according to our thinking. That's why they are so fluid and plastic.

Each of these terms, by which we describe the levels, are included in each level. If you bring a state of confidence to your self, this operates as a *belief*, and because you treat this as important, you *value* it; you *understand* facets of some *knowledge* of that area, this leads to *expectations, decisions*, *identifications, intentions,* etc. Each level is simultaneously multi-layered with all of these levels.

Think of the following as more than 50 ways to move around the *diamond of consciousness* and see, hear, feel and explore the many *facets* of perception and focus. These *facets of focus* give us multiple ways into the Matrix of our mind. So if you use one word or term and it doesn't elicit more information, use another. When we coach to the matrix, we use many questions in each of these categories.

1. Meaning / Significance	What does this mean to you?
Ideas that we hold in mind.	What meanings are you holding in mind?
2. Belief / Believe / Confirm as real	What do you believe about this?
Ideas we affirm, validate, and confirm.	What do you believe about that belief?
3. Frame / Reference	What is your frame of mind about this?
Ideas we set as our frame of reference	What's your frame of reference for this?
and mental contexts.	How are you framing this experience?
4. Generalization / Abstraction	What's your conclusion about this?
Ideas we generalize and draw as	What have you generalized from that?
summary conclusions about things.	What do you abstract from this?
5. Realize / Realization	What are you now realizing about this?
Ideas we develop as new insights,	What realization do you now have about this?
understandings, eureka experiences	Realizing that, how do you feel? (Denis Bridoux)
6. Permission / Allow / Permit / Embrace	Do you have permission to experience this?
Ideas about allowance and permission	Who took permission away from you?
versus ideas about prohibitions, taboos.	Are you ready to allow this for yourself?
7. Prohibition / Taboo / Censor / Dis-allow	Is this experience prohibited in you?
Ideas we do not allow and permit	Does it enhance things to taboo this?
but prohibit and taboo.	Who has tabooed this for you?

8. *Feeling (i.e., love, hate, care, joy, etc.)*	What do you feel about this?
Emotional ideas and feeling	What if you could enjoy this?
judgments we bring to other ideas.	What feeling would enhance this most?
9. *Thought / Notion / Idea*	What do you think about this?
Ideas or thoughts that we bring to	What thoughts come to mind about this?
previous ideas or thoughts.	What's your notion about this?
10. *Appreciate / Appreciation / Celebrate*	What do you appreciate most about this?
Ideas of appreciation or value	What could you appreciate about this?
used to frame other ideas.	Do you appreciate this too much?
11. *Value / Importance / Count / Honor*	What do you value about this?
Ideas we value as important	What's important about this that counts?
or significant, which we esteem.	Do you honor this in yourself or others?
12. *Interest / Fascination*	What do you find of interest in this?
Ideas of fascination, curiosity,	What's fascinating about this?
interest we bring to other ideas.	How curious are you about this?
13. *Decision / Choice / Will / Pros-Cons*	What's your decision about this?
Ideas we "cut off" from other	What choice would you like to make?
ideas as choices we say *Yes*	What pros and cons are you weighing?
and *No* to.	
14. *Intention / Want / Desire*	What's your highest intention about this?
Ideas about motives, intentions,	What do you really desire about this?
desires, and wants.	What intention is driving your response?
15. *Outcome / Goal / Agenda*	What outcome do you have about this?
Ideas we have about goals,	What goal do you have beyond this goal?
outcomes, and desired ends.	What's your higher agenda behind this?
16. *Strategy / Game Plan*	What's your strategy for this happen?
Ideas of our how-to knowledge	What's your game plan for this?
for making something happen.	What strategy could you develop?
17. *Expectation / Anticipation*	What's your expectation about this?
Ideas we have about what we	What do you anticipate will happen?
anticipate will happen	What do you expect about this idea?
18. *Connection / Connect*	What connection do you see about this?
Ideas we have about our	What's the connection between these
connection with other ideas,	ideas?
experiences, and people.	How do you connect this with . . . ?
19. *Cause / Causation*	What causes you to have this experience?
Ideas we have about cause,	What's the causation at the heart of this?
influence, contributing factors,	Who or what do you hold accountable for
what makes things happen, etc.	this? What are other contributing factors?
20. *Culture //Family / School / Religion,*	In what cultural context did you learn this?
Ideas we develop about our	Was this a part of your original culture?
cultural identity, rules, beliefs, etc.	What do you want to pass on as a legacy?
21. *Presupposition /Assumption /Implication*	What for you is the implication of that?
Ideas we use as higher frames	What are you assuming about this?
reflecting our assumptive world	What premise are you assuming about
and understandings.	this?
22. *History / Memory / Referent*	What does this remind you of?
Ideas we bring with us about	What previous examples relate to this?
previous experiences and use as	What memories do you link to this?

our referential indexes	How does your personal history play into this?
23. *Rules /Demand / Should /Must /Shall Authorize / Injunctions / Policy* Ideas we use as rules for the games we play in our lives, modal operators that generate our *modus operandi* (MO).	What *should* you do about this? What do you *have to* do regarding this? What rule governs these thoughts? Who authorizes this policy for you? What injunctions are you acting out?
24. *Judgments / Conscience* Ideas we use for evaluations, judgments, and conscience.	What is your judgment about this? How do you evaluate this? By what criteria? How does this affect your conscience?
25. *Definition /Class /Categorize /Category* Ideas we use to set categories in our mind for understanding	What your definition for this? How do you categorize this? What other definition could you use?
26. *Understand / Understanding / Comprehension* Ideas you have that "stand" "under" you as the mental support for your world.	What do you understanding about this? What background knowledge informs this for you? How do you comprehend this?
27. *Identity / Identify / Self / Self-definition* Ideas we build up about our "self," and use in defining ourselves.	What identity are you using in this? What does this say about you? Are you personalizing this?
28. *Paradigm / Model / Map / Schema* Ideas we have that we use as a complex mappings about things.	What paradigm governs these ideas? How have you mapped your thoughts? What schema would you like to use?
29. *Metaphor / Symbol / Poem / Story* Ideas we form in analogies, stories, and non-linguistic forms.	To use a metaphor, what is this like? What poem or story enriches your ideas? Who storied you? Do you like that story?
30. *Principle / Concept / Abstraction* Ideas we treat as guidelines, laws, and settled conclusions.	What concept governs this? What is the principle that's directing your thoughts? What abstraction would enhance you?
31. *Insight / Contemplation / Scrutinize / Think Through* Reflective ideas as new perceptions.	What insights do you have about this? What's your highest contemplation? What are you now reflecting in this?
32. *Construct / Computation* Ideas we construct for our mental forms and use for reasoning.	What constructs are you making about this? How are you computing this? What computations guide these feelings?
33. *Myth / Archetype* Ideas that grow out of cultural and human stories and metaphors.	What myth is in the background? How aware are you of this archetype? What archetype would you like to use?
34. *Hypothesis / Proposal* Ideas we imagine, conceptualize as models and paradigms.	What's your hypothesis about this? What proposal would you like to make? What's your best guess will happen?
35. *Know / Knowledge / Epistemology* Ideas about information that form knowledge base.	What knowledge informs this thought? What's your epistemology regarding how you know that you know this?

36. Consequences / Implications Ideas about consequences of an action or inaction.	What consequences do you see coming? What will inaction lead to regarding this? What are you implying by saying that?
37. Difference / Comparison / Exception Ideas that enable us to compare and contrast experiences.	What's the difference you want? How are you making your comparisons? When do you not think or feel that way?
38. Inspiration / Inspires / Moves Ideas that move us, inspire us, that arises to bring new insights to us.	What's most inspiring about this? What moves you most in all of this? Is this inspiration in your best interests?
39. Theme / Thematic Ideas that set a pattern or theme in our mind.	What theme is in the back of your mind? How thematic are these ideas? What theme will you like to bring to this?
40. Opens up / Emerges Ideas that open up or emerge as think and reflect.	What's now opening up about this? What emergent thoughts are arising in your mind? What feelings are about to emerge?
41. Reason / Rationale / Rationalization / Excuse Ideas to explain our reasons, the "whys" behind our actions, our background alibis.	What is your rationale for explaining this? Is this just a rationalization for what you want? Will you let this excuse stop you?
42. Reputation Ideas we hold of what others think of us, the public image or reputation we hold.	What reputation is governing this? Who are you in the mind of your loved ones as you say this?
43. Ascribe / Ascription / Affix Ideas we ascribe to an idea, person, or events.	What are you ascribing to this? Are you affixing blame or responsibility? What ascriptions governs your thoughts?
44. Transcend / Transcendence Ideas above and beyond our previous thoughts, ultimate assumptions and beliefs.	What transcends your thoughts about this? If you were to transcend this, what would you feel? What's the highest way to transcend this?
45. Validate / Approve / Sanction Ideas that validate and approve something, that sanction it as valid.	What validation are you bringing to this? As you hear yourself say that, do you approve of it? How have you or others sanctioned this?
46. Dis-validate / Disapprove / Taboo Ideas that dis-validate something as unacceptable.	How are you disapproving this? What dis-validation are you experiencing? Would you like to now dis-validate this?
47. Higher level of consciousness / Meta Ideas that move us to an expanded higher level of awareness.	If you brought a higher level of conscious. to this, what would happen? What's meta to even this?
48. Step back / Witness / Just Observe Ideas that enable us to be as objective about something as possible.	Stepping back, what are you aware of? What happens when you just observe this? As you witness this as a spectator, what happens?
49. Possibility Ideas about possibilities and potentials in our experiences.	What possibilities lie behind and above this? What possibility in this are you aware of? What possibility would you like to explore?

50. *Probability / Degree / Extent / Percentage* Ideas about the degree or extent of an experience, its probability of occurring.	What's the probability this will happen? To what degree are you sure about this? How much are you now experiencing this?
51. *Resist / Resistance / Refusal* Ideas that fight and resist another or experience.	What resistance do you experiencing as you say this? Would you like to resist this partially? How could refusal to this be of value?
52. *See / Insight / Perceive* Ideas that visually represent an idea or experience, or that does so conceptually.	What do you see as you think about this? What insight do you have about this? What's your perception?
53. *Impulse / Urge* Ideas that are experienced as bodily urges, impulses, gut feelings.	What's your first impulse about this? What's your impulse or gut feeling? What urge will you allow about this?
54. *Foreground – Background* Ideas that we can recognize as in the front or back of our mind.	What's in the background of your mind? What do you want to bring to the forefront of your thoughts and feelings about this?

Finite and Infinite Games

James P. Carse

There are at least two kinds of Games,
One could be called finite, the other infinite.

A finite game is played for the purpose of winning,
An infinite game for the purpose of continuing the play.

Finite players play within boundaries,
Infinite players play with boundaries.

Surprise causes finite play to end,
It is the reason for infinite play to continue.

To be prepared against surprise is to be trained.
To be prepared for surprise is to be educated.

The finite play for life is serious.
The infinite play of life is joyous.

The joyfulness of infinite play, its laughter,
lies in learning to start something we cannot finish.

No one can play a game alone.
One cannot be human by oneself.

Our social existence has ... an inescapably fluid character,
we are not the stones
over which the stream of life of the world flows,
we are the stream itself.

Change itself is the very basis of our continuity as persons.
Only that which can change can continue.
This is the principle by which infinite players live.

The Rules of the Inner and Outer Games

#1: **Frames govern everything: it is always a matter of frames.**

#2: **Whoever sets the frame controls the game.**
Whoever changes a frame— alters the game.

#3: **The problem is never the person, it's always the frame.**

#4: **Frames create and direct focus.**

#5: **It takes frame detection skills to master the inner and our games.**

#6: **The name of the game is to name the game.**

#7: **Where there's a frame, there's a game nearby and a mind-body state. Where there's a game— there's a governing frame overhead.**

#8: **Our frame brain frames with the stuff of thoughts.**

#9: **Magic happens when we detect and transform our meaning frames.**

#10: **Brain frames thrive on symbols.**

#11: **The magic of our inner and outer games increases with the intensity of vividness and drama that we put into it.**

#12: **Frame game masters set frames by using repetition, questions, and mind-to-muscle processes.**

#13: **We facilitate the mind-muscle connection by emotionalizing thoughts.**

#14: **Play flows where the game goes—as saith the frame. Energy flows where attention goes—as determined by intention.**

CHOOSING YOUR NEXT BOOK ON FRAMING

If you have enjoyed this fabulous adventure into our frames of mind and discovering your own frames and those of others, if it fascinates and delights you, and if you'd like to continue developing *frame game skills*, the following describes some of the literature in Neuro-Semantics on frames.

Mind-Lines: Lines for Changing Minds

This book about conversational reframing presents a model for *the structure of meaning* and how to intentionally shift and change meaning in more than twenty-six ways. *Mind-Lines* rigorously remodels the original NLP "Sleight of Mouth" patterns and takes the language of influence to new heights. Using Meta-States, *Mind-Lines* offers an excellent study in the language of meaning transformation and persuasion.

Adventures in Time (*Time-Lining*)

This book focuses on our framing of "time" and the results that it creates in our mind-body system. Sixteen new patterns for coding, representing, and playing with "time" are presented so that you can engage in the wonderful adventure of time traveling for fun and profit. The design is that you discover how to truly live in the moment with an eye on a compelling future as informed and resourced by your past successes.

Figuring Out People

As we meta-state ourselves and create frames of mind, this also generates our perceptual filters or *meta-programs*. As solidified meta-states, meta-programs govern what and how we see; they influence our states, skills, and experiences. They influence what and how we learn, our strategies, and so much more. *Figuring Out People* offers this encyclopedia of meta-programs as the key to being able to model a wider range of expertise. Also, there is the *Meta-Detective Game*, a board game for learning and developing expertise with meta-programs.

Meta-States: Mastering the Higher Levels of Your Mind

For a more academic and scholarly approach to the whole domain of *meta-states*, this book describes the workings of our self-reflexive consciousness and how we create state-about-state structures in our mind which become our mental-emotional framing. These higher states do lots of things: they set our frames, they establish our meaning Matrix, they become the attractors in our self-organizing mind-body system, they operate as our highest executive functions, and much more.

Dragon Slaying: Dragons to Princes

Dragon Slaying applies Meta-States to therapy and to therapeutic issues, to our "dragon states." Then, *Dragon Slaying* presents the meta-stating processes for detecting, welcoming, slaying, taming, and transforming our Dragons. The design is to move from dragon states to the more resourceful states possible.

Sub-Modalities Going Meta

Sub-modalities are not *sub* at all, they are actually the editorial frames of our movies. That is, after we have a picture or sound or movie, then we step back (step up a level) and edit that movie using various cinematic features to work with the images, sound track, etc. as meta-frames. *Sub-Modalities Going Meta* completely re-models the old "sub-modality" model so that you can recognize several fabulous insider's secrets about how to use them for transformational magic. Six brand new sub-models are presented in this book regarding Negation, Backgrounding and Foregrounding, Transforming Beliefs, and more.

The Secrets of Personal Mastery

To demonstrate the extensive practicality of *Meta-States*, this book focuses on personal mastery (or genius) and empowers you to set the required meta-levels and frames so that you can step up into higher levels of personal excellence and mastery. An easy to read and understand book, *Secrets of Personal Mastery* covers the basic material in the training, *Accessing Personal Genius* which is the introduction to Meta-States and all Neuro-Semantic trainings.

User's Manual For the Brain, Volumes I and II

For a complete presentation of the materials covered in both NLP Practitioner and Master Practitioner training, *User's Manual* offers a textbook like resource from Bodenhamer and Hall and their years of training. Quickly becoming a classic in the field of NLP, *User's* is now being used as the basic textbook for NLP training around the globe.

The Frame Game Series

Games Business Experts Play

What are the games that we play in business that make for excellence and success? Are you ready for probing into the inner and outer games that will empower you to find and develop your talents and then put on your business cap to take care of business in a way that will allow you to add value in all that you do and succeed in your career?

Games Slim and Fit People Play

Because we all play various games with food, eating, pigging out, and exercise, it's all about the *inner game* of your frames. What are the games that you play? Who taught you to play such games? Do they enhance your life, your health, vitality, energy, self-confidence, etc.? Would you like to play some frame games that will empower you in these areas? The book will not *cause* you to lose weight, but new frames will enable you to play new games.

Games Great Lovers Play

What games do you play with your loved ones? Do they like those games? Do they bring out the best in both of you? Do you have the prerequisite frames which allow you to play with others in ways that honor, support, respect, care, and enjoy them? What are the games that those who fall in love and stay in love play?

Frame Games Hitler Played

How did Adolf Hitler seduce an entire country to play the toxic and morbid games that he offered? How did that "persuasion" occur? What was involved in it? I have a 28 page document on the website about this, a document that seems particularly relevant with others who would "terrorize" us with their rigid and superior world-view. **www.neurosemantics.com**

The Matrix Model

From meta-stating and framing arose the *Matrix Model* as a systemic model for unifying all of the four meta-domains of NLP and all of the patterns and processes in both NLP and Neuro-Semantic. Based upon the cognitive-behavioral sciences and developmental psychology, the Matrix Model is structured with three process matrices and five content matrices. Discover the art of thinking and working systemically with people and how to know what to do when.

Meta-Coaching Series

Coaching Change, Meta-Coaching, Volume I

Coaching is all about change. That makes a coach a change agent, *Coaching Change* therefore presents the *Axes of Change* model based on four meta-programs, the only non-therapy based change model today and the only self-actualization change model. This book presents the Meta-Coaching system for working with the levels of change, kinds of coaching for each kind of change, and the nine coaching roles for facilitating transformation.

Coaching Conversations, Volume II

Coaching is a conversation, and specifically a fierce conversation that gets to the heart of a person's framing and meaning, it is an art of asking the most fabulous *questions* which facilitates the empowering and unleashing of potentials in a client. *Coaching Conversations* offers the Meta-Coaching model of questioning, the meta-questions for exploring a Matrix of frames, and twelve kinds of coaching conversations using transcripts from live coaching sessions.

INDEX

People

BIBLIOGRAPHY

Andreas, Steve; Faulkner, Charles. (1994). *NLP: The new technology of achievement.* NY: William Marrow and Company.

Bandler, Richard and Grinder, John. (1976). *The structure of magic, Volume II.* Palo Alto, CA: Science & Behavior Books.

Bandler, Richard and Grinder, John. (1979). *Frogs into princes: Neuro-linguistic programming.* Moab, UT: Real People Press.

Bandler, Richard and Grinder, John. (1982). *Reframing: Neuro-linguistic programming and the transformation of meaning.* UT: Real People Press.

Bandler, Richard. (1985). *Using your brain for a change.* (Ed. Connirae and Steve Andreas). Moab, UT: Real People Press.

Bateson, Gregory. (1972). *Steps to an ecology of mind.* NY: Ballantine Books.

Berne, Eric, M.D. (1964). *Games people play: The psychology of human relationships.* NY: Ballantine Books.

Bodenhamer, Bobby G.; and Hall, L. Michael. (1997). *Time-Lining: Patterns for adventuring in time.* Wales, United Kingdom: Anglo-American Books.

Bodenhamer, Bobby G.; and Hall, L. Michael. (1999). *The user's manual for the brain: A comprehensive manual for neuro-linguistic programming practitioner certification.* United Kingdom: Crown House Publishers.

Carse, James P. (1986). *Finite and infinite games: A vision of life as play and possibility.* NHY: Free Press: Simon and Schuster Inc.

Ciabattari, Jane. (1999). A Great Reward is Coming, *Parade Magazine.* Dec. 12, 1999.

Cialdini, Robert B. (1993). *Influence: The psychology of persuasion.* NY: Quill.

Callahan, R.J. (1985). *Five minute phobia cure.* Wilmington, DE: Enterprise.

Chomsky, Noam. (1965). *Aspects of the theory of syntax.* Cambridge, MA: MIT Press.

Coyne, James C. (1985). Toward A Theory of Frames and Reframing: The Social Nature of Frames. *Journal of Marital and Family Therapy, Vol. II,* No. 4, pp. 337-344. Washington DC: American Association of Marriage and Family.

Csikszentmihalyi, Mihaly. (1990). *Flow: The psychology of optimal experience.* New York: Harper Perennial.

Dawson, Roger. (1992). *Secrets of power persuasion.* NJ: Prentice Hall.

Dilts, Robert B. (1999). *Sleight of mouth: The magic of conversational belief change.* Capitola, CA: Meta Publications.

Fairhurst, Gail; Sarr, Robert. (1996). *The Art of Framing: Managing the Language of Leadership.* San Francisco, Josey-Bass Publishers.

Furman, Mark E. (1999). Simon Says Trauma Gone. *Anchor Point, Vol. 13,* #11. (Nov. 1999), pp. 37-44.

Gardner, Howard. (1989). *Frames of mind: The theory of multiple intelligences*. NY: BasicBooks.

Gardner, Howard. (1991). *The unschooled mind: How children think and how schools should teach.* NY: HarperCollins.

Gardner, Howard. (1993). *Multiple intelligences: The theory in practice.* NY: BasicBooks.

Gerbode, F. (1989). *Beyond psychology: An introduction to metapsychology.* Palo Alto, CA: IRM Press.

Goffman, Erving (1974). *Frame aalysis: An essay on the organization of experience.* Cambridge, MA: Harvard University Press.

Hall, L. Michael. (2000). *Meta-states: Reflexivity in human states of consciousness.* Clifton, CO: Neuro-Semantic Publications.

Hall, L. Michael. (1996). *The spirit of NLP: The process, meaning, and criteria for mastering NLP.* Carmarthen, Wales: Anglo-American Book Company Ltd.

Hall, L. Michael; and Bodenhamer, Bobby G. (2005, 5th edition). *Mind-lines: Lines for changing minds.* Clifton, CO: Neuro-Semantic Publications.

Hall, L. Michael. (1998). *The secrets of magic: Communicational excellence for the 21st century.* Carmarthen, Wales: Anglo-American Book Company Ltd.

Hall, L. Michael; and Bodenhamer, Bob. (1997). *Figuring out people: Design engineering using meta-programs.* Wales, UK: Anglo-American Books.

Hall, L. Michael; and Belnap, Barbara. (1999). *The sourcebook of magic: A comprehensive guide to the technology of NLP.* UK: Crown House Publishers.

Hill, Napoleon. (1967). *Grow rich with peace of mind.* Greenwich, CN: Fawcett Publications.

Korzybski, Alfred. (1933/ 1994). *Science and sanity: An introduction to non-aristotelian systems and general semantics,* (5th. ed.). Concord, CA: International Society For General Semantics.

Lisnek, Paul M. (1996). *Winning the mind game: Negotiating in business and life.* Capitola, CA: Meta Publications.

Mayer, Robert. (1996). *Power plays: How to negotiate, persuade, and finesse your way to success in any situation.* NY: Random House.

Robbins, Anthony. (1991). *Awaken the giant within.* NY: Simon & Schuster.

Shapiro, Francis. (1995). *Eye movement desensitization and reprocessing: Basic principles, protocols, and procedures.* NY: Guilford.

Walker, Lou Ann. (1999). "The Day I Took My Dad Up the Mountain." Parade Magazine, Oct. 31, 1999.

GLOSSARY OF TERMS

Anchoring: the process of linking or connecting a stimulus to a response, a "user-friendly" version of Pavlovian or classical conditioning.

Association: stepping into an experience to see, hear, and feel as if from inside it.

Beliefs: a thought *confirmed* at a meta-level, a conscious or unconscious generalization about some concept (i.e., causality, meaning, self, others, behaviors, identity, etc.).

Calibration: tuning in to a person's state via reading non-verbal signals previously observed.

Content: the specifics and details of an event; content answers *what?* in contrast with process or structure which answers the *how* question.

Context: the setting, frame or process in which events occur and provide meaning for content.

Dissociation: stepping back from an experience and representing it from an *outside* position, seeing and/or hearing it as if being a spectator or from another very different perspective.

Ecology: examining the overall relationship between idea, skill, response and larger environment or system; the dynamic balance of elements in a system.

Frame: short for frame of reference. We frame things; we frame people, ideas, events, experiences, etc.; a mental, cognitive, or linguistic context for something.

Frame Ambiguity: the fuzzy edges of a frame, the lack of clear bracketing of a frame. It may lead to Frame Failure.

Frame Analysis: the process of analyzing our frames, detecting them, identifying the leverage points for shifting them, the processes for transforming them, the games that they engender, etc. *Frame Analysis* provides a way to clearly articulate the levels of mind and the influence they exert over life's experiences.

Frame Argumentation: the argument that a frame makes in defense of itself, or from out of its perspective. Frames argue for themselves when they feel threatened. This is a function of what cognitive psychology calls state or mood dependency.

Frame By Implication (FBI): This is a frame that we assume or imply. We create it by using various presuppositional language. Behind and above every statement and action there are always implied frames.

Frame Breaks: breaking a frame, interrupting it.

Frame Clearing: when we deframe, dissolve a frame, or bust up a frame—we *clear* out mental and emotional room in a person's model of the world for a new frame.

Frame Confusion and Frame Clearing: the quality of clarity/ confusion within a frame.

Frame Cues: the signals, indicators, clues, linguistic markers of a frame.

Frame-of-Reference: the *reference* that we use to understand something else. The reference can be an actual experience (an event), a person, idea, etc. A referent can be something real and actual or imaginary and vicarious.

Frame of Mind: our attitude or meta-cognition created via repeating and habituating a frame of reference. Over time this leads to making the referent that we represented something always on our mind. The referent then "gets in our eyes" so that we view the world and all of our experiences through the lens of that experience or idea. This turns the referent experience into a perceptual filter.

Frameworks: the embedded system of frames that construct our style and personality, the solidification of our orientation, our characteristic mind-set or attitude.

Frame Wars: in every conflict we have a conflict of frames, two conflicting ways of seeing and experiencing the world.

Future Pacing: process of mentally practicing or rehearsing an event; a key process for installing a program and ensuring the permanency of an outcome.

Games: a set of actions that play out some concept, idea, etc. for some purpose, i.e., to "win" something, another emotion, stroke, transaction, etc. A frame generated realm that describes and creates our virtual reality or matrix.

Game Consciousness: awareness of a game, who it works for, who sets it, how it invites people into it, the states it elicits, etc.

Generalization: process of representing a whole class of experiences based on one or a few specific experiences.

Gestalt: the overall configuration, impression or feel of thoughts and feelings, the whole of an experience that is more than the sum of the part.

Kinesthetic: sensations, feelings, tactile sensations on surface of the skin, proprioceptive sensations inside the body, includes vestibular system or sense of balance.

Inner Game: the game that we play in our minds as we create representations or movies and then frame those movies with layers and layers of meanings. The inner game is comprised of all of our embedded frames which makes up our Matrix.

In Frame: living, feeling, seeing, experiencing, etc. from within a frame of reference or frame of mind. Living in a virtual reality governed and informed by our ideas, ideals, concepts, beliefs, values, etc. See *Matrix.*

Matrix: the total of all of our embedded frames thereby making up the conceptual and semantic world that we live in and operate out of, a metaphorical way of thinking about the universe of discourse that we create perceptually, mentally, and emotionally via our frames. Building meta-levels of frames causes us to become paradigm blind so that we see the world "in terms of our ideas and concepts" rather than what is.

Meta: something "above or beyond" something else and therefore "about" it. A relationship of levels, as when a thought is *about* another thought, a feeling *about* a feeling, a thought *about* a feeling, etc.

Meta-Detective: the ability to *step aside* from our thinking and feeling and to recognize our thoughts and feelings, their layers, etc.

Meta-State: a state-about-a-state, the use of our self-reflexive consciousness as we *reflects back* onto ourselves and our experience, a higher "logical level" (or psycho-logical level) that sets the frame for our thinking-and-feeling that classifies things and generates our meaning structures, a state about a previous state.

Meta-Stating (verb): applying a mind-body state to another state, the skillful process of accessing a state, amplifying it, applying it, appropriating it into a particular context, and then analyzing for ecology and fittingness.

Meta-Model: a linguistic model of distinctions that identifies language patterns of obscure meanings where we have deleted, generalized, and distorted information, a set of questions that clarify imprecision to enrich a person's mental mapping of the world.

Meta-Programs: our perceptual filters which govern our attention and focus, created by habituating a meta-stating process.

Modal Operators: a linguistic distinction in the Meta-Model indicating a person's "mode" for operating (i.e. mode of necessity, impossibility, desire, possibility, etc.).

Model: a pattern, example, or description of how something works. Model with a capital M involves a theory, a set of variables, a set of guidelines for working with the variables, and a set of patterns that result.

Modeling: the process of observing and replicating the actions, skills, knowledge, and states of someone (typically an expert). Modeling discerns the sequence of internal representations and behaviors that comprise the structure of a skill.

Nominalization: a linguistic distinction in the Meta-Model involving a process (or verb) turned into an noun; a process frozen in time.

Outer Game: the external activities, behaviors, gestures, even emotions that result from our inner game of frames. The outer game relates to our performance and achievements.

Out of Frame: activities, thoughts, scripts that do not fit a given frame. An out of frame loosens a frame, and operates as a threat to a frame thereby creating disequilibrium of the frame. When we step out of a frame, we "break frame" or "lose frame" and so become *out of frame.*

Out-framing: going above all frames to create new frame-of-reference, out-framing is another term for meta-stating.

Reframing: altering a frame-of-reference by presenting an event or idea from a different point of view or with a different meaning ascribed to it, creating a new mental context for an event.

References: the idea, person, event, belief, etc. that we have in mind and use in our thinking. *Reference Point:* identifies a singular idea, person, or event. *Reference Frame:* involves understandings of how the points are related.

Representation Systems: representation systems: sights, sounds, sensations, smells and tastes which make up the movies that we play in our mind. There are primary representation systems, called the VAK in NLP for the three key systems of Visual, Auditory, and Kinesthetic and there are the meta-representations of language (auditory digital) or symbols, mathematics, and diagrams (visual digital).

Sensory Acuity: awareness of the outside world via our senses, being completely present in the moment to an experience.

Sensory-Based Description: directly observable and verifiable information; see-hear-feel language one can test empirically.

State: a state of mind- body, which never occurs in isolation, hence *a mind-body state* driven by ideas and meanings (conceptions and the significance we attach to things, a neuro-linguistic or neuro-semantic state). As our states generate an overall *feel* or gestalt, our states are *emotional states.*

Strategy: a sequencing of thinking-behaving to obtain an outcome or create an experience, the structure of subjectivity ordered in a linear model.

"Sub-modality:" the cinematic features of our inner movies of the mind, sensory represents of the qualities and properties of our sights, sounds, and sensations.

Universal Quantifiers: a linguistic term in the Meta-Model for words that code things with "allness" (every, all, never, none, etc.).

Unsanity: term used by Korzybski to describe the stage of poor adjustment between sanity (well adjusted to the territory) and insanity (totally maladjusted to reality); the "lack of consciousness of abstracting, confusion of orders of abstractions resulting from identification practically universally operating in every one of us" (1933: 105).

VAK: a short-hand for the sensory representation systems of **V**isual, **A**uditory, and **K**inesthetic. **K** also including smells (Olfactory) and tastes (Gustatory).

Value/ Valuing: the process of deeming something important; a meta-level phenomena.

L. Michael Hall, Ph.D.

Neuro-Semantics® International
P.O. Box 8
Clifton, Colorado 81520 USA
(970) 523-7877

www.runyourownbrain.com
www.neurosemantics.com
meta@onlinecol.com

L. Michael Hall is a visionary leader in the field of Neuro-Semantics and today works as an entrepreneur, researcher/modeler, and international trainer. His doctorate is in the Cognitive-Behavioral sciences from Union Institute University. He worked as a psychotherapist in Colorado when he found NLP in 1986. He then studied with Richard Bandler and wrote several books for him. When studying and modeling resilience, he developed the Meta-States model (1994). Soon he began traveling nationally and then internationally, co-created the Society of Neuro-Semantics with Dr. Bob Bodenhamer. *The International Society of Neuro-Semantics* (ISNS) was established in 1996. As a prolific writer, Michael has written more than 30 books, many best sellers in the field of NLP. Michael first applied NLP to coaching in 1991, but didn't create the beginnings of Neuro-Semantic Coaching until 2001 when together with Michelle Duval co-created Meta-Coaching trainings. In 2003, the Meta-Coach Foundation was created.

Books:

1) *Meta-States: Mastering the Higher Levels of Mind* (1995/ 2000)
2) *Dragon Slaying: Dragons to Princes* (1996 / 2000)
3) *The Spirit of NLP: The Process, Meaning and Criteria for Mastering NLP* (1996)
4) *Languaging: The Linguistics of Psychotherapy* (1996)
5) *Becoming More Ferocious as a Presenter* (1996)
6) *Patterns For Renewing the Mind* (with Bodenhamer, 1997 /2006)
7) *Time-Lining: Advance Time-Line Processes* (with Bodenhamer, 1997)
8) *NLP: Going Meta — Advance Modeling Using Meta-Levels* (1997/2001)
9) *Figuring Out People: Reading People Using Meta-Programs* (with Bodenhamer, 1997, 2005)
10) *SourceBook of Magic, Volume I* (with Belnap, 1997)

11) *Mind-Lines: Lines For Changing Minds* (with Bodenhamer, 1997/ 2005)
12) *Communication Magic* (2001). Originally, *The Secrets of Magic* (1998).
13) *Meta-State Magic: Meta-State Journal* (1997-1999).
14) *When Sub-Modalities Go Meta* (with Bodenhamer, 1999, 2005). Originally entitled, *The Structure of Excellence.*
15) *Instant Relaxation* (with Lederer, 1999).
16) *User's Manual of the Brain: Volume I* (with Bodenhamer, 1999).
17) *The Structure of Personality:* Modeling Personality Using NLP and Neuro-[illegible]ntics (with Bodenhamer, Bolstad, and Harmblett, 2001).
[illegible]e *Secrets of Personal Mastery* (2000).

19) *Frame Games: Persuasion Elegance* (2000).
20) *Games Fit and Slim People Play* (2001).

21) *Games for Mastering Fear* (with Bodenhamer, 2001).
22) *Games Business Experts Play* (2001).
23) *The Matrix Model: Neuro-Semantics and the Construction of Meaning* (2003).
24) *User's Manual of the Brain: Master Practitioner Course, Volume II* (2002).
25) *MovieMind: Directing Your Mental Cinemas* (2002).
26) *The Bateson Report* (2002).
27) *Make it So! Closing the Knowing-Doing Gap* (2002).
28) *Source Book of Magic, Volume II, Neuro-Semantic Patterns* (2003).
29) *Propulsion Systems* (2003).
30) *Games Great Lovers Play* (2004).

31) *Coaching Conversation, Meta-Coaching, Volume II* (with Duval, 2004).
32) *Coaching Change, Meta-Coaching, Volume I* (with Duval, 2004).
33) *Winning the Inner Game* (2006).
34) *Unleashed: How to Unleash Potentials for Peak Performances* (scheduled for 2007).
35) *Achieving Peak Performance* (scheduled for 2007).